Know it to Shine

HEMESH CHHABRA

Know It To Shine

Know It To Shine

An Insight of Human Behavior, with a view to understand High Social & Moral Standards of conduct. This Tome basically and intrinsically suggests the ways to enhance the Virtues, Refine the Traits & Persona, **to Shine**

By

HEMESH CHHABRA

Know It To Shine

BLUEROSE PUBLISHERS
India | U.K.

Copyright © Hemesh Chhabra 2025

All rights reserved by author. No part of this publication may be reproduced, stored in a retrieval system or transmitted in any form or by any means, electronic, mechanical, photocopying, recording or otherwise, without the prior permission of the author. Although every precaution has been taken to verify the accuracy of the information contained herein, the publisher assumes no responsibility for any errors or omissions. No liability is assumed for damages that may result from the use of information contained within.

BlueRose Publishers takes no responsibility for any damages, losses, or liabilities that may arise from the use or misuse of the information, products, or services provided in this publication.

For permissions requests or inquiries regarding this publication, please contact:

BLUEROSE PUBLISHERS
www.BlueRoseONE.com
info@bluerosepublishers.com
+91 8882 898 898
+4407342408967

ISBN: 978-93-6783-552-4

Cover design: Yash Singhal

First Edition: February 2025

About Author

Hemesh Chhabra born in 1962 in a Digambar Jain Family, in Jaipur, Rajasthan. He did his schooling in the famous Mahavir School of Jaipur and graduation from commerce college, Rajasthan University. His résumé also includes short courses on Journalism, Law, Film Script-writing, and Film Direction. After doing short span services in 5 different Banks and Financial Institutions, ultimately, he joined Mumbai Customs as Preventive Officer in 1986.

Perfection, Self-improvement and to acquire knowledge of any subject have always been his **IKIGAI**. During his service in Mumbai Customs, he did his "Post Graduate Diploma in **Human Rights**" for which he wrote "Jainism and Human Rights" as Master Thesis, which was duly accepted by Indian Institute of Human Rights. He is a strong proponent of Human Rights which was quite noticeable during his entire service career in the Customs and Indirect Taxes.

He published his memoir **"My Encounter with Mini India in Mumbai Customs"** about his insight of experiencing a paradigm shift of Mumbai customs into its mini- India characteristic. Long serving in Mumbai Customs, doing public dealings, especially at Air Port, and having an innate aptitude of learning of human behaviors, helped him to a greater extent to enhance his understanding of human- Virtues, Traits and Persona. His experience and understanding of human behavior and psychology are beautifully depicted in his Books. He retired from the central Government service in 2022 as Assistant Commissioner and now lives in Mumbai.

Know It To Shine

"The heights by great men reached and kept
were not attained by sudden flight
But they, while their companions slept,
were toiling upwards in the night"

----- **Henry Wadsworth Longfellow
(1807-1882)** American Poet

"We know accurately only when we know little,
With Knowledge doubt increases"

- ------ **John Wolfgang Von Goethe
(1749-1832)** German Polymath

"TULSI ASAMAY KE SAKHA DHIRAJ,
DHARAM, VIVEK, SAHIT, SAHAS,
SATYAVRUT, RAM BHAROSA AIK."
*Tulsidas says that Patience, Righteousness,
Wisdom, Equanimity, Courage, Truth and faith in
Ram (God) are the friends in the hard times.)*

----------- **Tulsidas ji**
(1511- 1623) Indian poet, saint &
philosopher, best known for authoring
Ram Charit Manas

Know It To Shine

PREFACE

During my School- College days, I was in the habit of writing, noteworthy quotes, remarkable verses, memorable aphorisms, adages, Catchy Phrases, Famous Sayings, Shlokas, Suktas etc., whatever I could find in the Newspapers, Books, Tabloids, Magazines, Scriptures, Ramayan, Mahabharat, Novels, Text Books, literary work of Kabir, Tulsi etc., on the white painted walls of my Room, with Red Ink. As an example, three of such quotes written by me on the walls of my room, have been shown on the previous page. Subconsciously, I had adopted this habit to make myself a good person, to have good behavioral & moral character, to have good oratory skills and to use these quotes in a conversation or weekly debates in school. And I must say that it acquired me a Persona of **"SADCHIT"**.

When the walls were fully inscribed up to their writable heights, I took a thick note book and copied all the quotes written on the walls, in it. Then I used my Daily Diary to write the valuable quotes, without keeping any specific purpose in mind. I continued this habit till I started my service career in Mumbai Customs. Though, occasionally, I kept on adding insightful & impactful quotes etc. in my daily dairy, whichever fascinated me.

After my Retirement from Central Government Service, one day while going through the old papers, I laid my hands on these old Daily Diaries, Note-books, Note-sheets, and then just as a flash of lightning, it occurred to me to write a book containing this **"Precious Treasure of Wisdom-Words"** along with my 50 years' old acquired knowledge and experience of human character, conduct, psychology and overall behavior.

So, this Book **"Know It To Shine,"** is in your hand. In this book, an attempt has been made to ameliorate the Reader's Savoir-Faire, Acumen and Mettle, and to present as much useful, authentic and substantial material as possible on human comportment, deportment, Psychology, Physiology, Cognition, Health Demeanor, Attitude, Conversational Efficiency, Business Maneuvers, and overall behavior, in a logical and simple language, strengthened and supported by the precious Scriptural Verses, Hymns, Shlokas, of Sanskrit Language, (which are presented in Roman Script in this Tome), and also Hindi & English Citations, Proverbs, Idioms, Sayings, Quotes, etc., which had been garnered in the last 50 years. Their English meanings, have also been provided along with them for the readers who do not know Sanskrit and Hindi Languages.

Readers will find in this Tome, all those things which are necessary for a civilized person to **know and shine** for a purposeful and successful life. In this Tome, there has been no discussion of mere theories, but an indicative account of practical life; a beautiful blend of ancient and modern life sciences will be found. In a way, this is a small encyclopedia on meliorated Human Behavior. I can say with authority that I have written this book with scientific intellect and modern point of view on the basis of classical study of hundreds of books. If the readers get any kind of intelligence enhancement or entertainment through this, then I will consider my effort worthwhile.

There are many learned readers who know Sanskrit Language, and Devanagari Script, along with English Language and Roman Script and also know about Ramayana, Mahabharata, Tulsidas, Kabir and other literary Giants. They may find some obscurity in the translated version of Sanskrit Citations. Roman Alphabets do not have direct equivalents to all Sanskrit sounds. Sanskrit heavily relies on diacritical marks (Like accents and dot) to differentiate sounds. These marks are often difficult to represent consistently in Roman Script. Therefore; while Roman Script can be used to represent Sanskrit, it often falls short in capturing the nuances and precision of the original language. Learned Readers take note of these limitations and also print infeasibilities thereof, while reading the Sanskrit Citations in Roman Script. Erudite Readers are always aware of that potential for inaccuracies and strive to consult original Sanskrit texts whenever possible.

Further, at many places I have also used quotations from well-known Western personalities including writers, thinkers, leaders and intellectuals for the better understanding of Virtues, Traits, Persona and overall Human Behavior.

Here it is also pertinent to state that **"Words have various dimensions"**. Some readers may take, though inadvertently, the unintended meaning of the words and sentences according to their pre conceived notions. Although, necessary precautions have been taken to avoid such misapprehension, yet it is also hoped that readers would carefully consider the intended meaning of the words used in this book.

Know It To Shine

I have made sincere efforts to share my age-old collection of 'precious treasure of wisdom-words', knowledge and experience with the readers to enhance their Virtues, refine their Traits & Character, and amend, wherever necessary, their behavior in personal, social, and public life including financial transactions.

Time changes constantly. Social values change according to the time. New technologies emerge. Diseases get new treatments. The notions of virtues change. New culture, practices, Customs are adopted in the modern society. For instance, gradually Live-in Relationship is replacing the institution of marriage. Nonetheless, this book emphasizes on the age-old concepts of values, virtues and norms of a well - versed and well - behaved person. Apropos, Experts in their field like Physicians, Psychiatrists, Psychologists, Dietitians, lawyers, Social-Reformers etc. may not be in consonance with some of the themes narrated in this Book. I respect their dissension.

I feel it is my foremost duty to express my gratitude to those Scriptures, Parables, Enlighted Souls, Literary Giants, Leaders, whose quoted sentences, citations have amplified the glory of my book. The names of those books or authors have been mentioned at appropriate places.

Due to my haste to publish this **tome** on Human Behavior and demeanors in Life, some errors might have remained unnoticed, albeit inadvertently. That may please be overlooked. Even God's creation is flawed; hence it is not surprising that human creation is flawed.

Kandivali East, Mumbai
14-01-2025   -----HEMESH CHHABRA

Know It To Shine

Key Points -Cum- Index

CHAPTER-1

Need to Shine within self : 01

(1) **Virtues, Traits & Persona** : 03

(2) **Self-Empowerment** : 08

    (a) Self- Confidence : 08
    (b) Self-Knowledge : 09
    (c) Self-Purification : 09
    (d) Fear arises due to these reasons : 10
        (i) Ignorance : 10
        (ii) Doubt : 10
        (iii) Indifference : 11
        (iv) Uncertainty : 11
        (v) Immorality : 11
        (vi) Weakness : 11
        (vii) Incompetence : 12
        (viii) Inactivity : 12
        (ix) Lowliness : 13
        (x) Dependency : 13
        (xi) Intolerance : 13
        (xii) Addiction : 14
        (xiii) Lack of Faith and Trust : 14
        (xiv) Effect of Fear : 14

    (e) Self-Control : 16

		(i)	Resolution	: 19
		(ii)	Efforts	: 20
		(iii)	Perseverance	: 21

(3) **Expansion of knowledge** : 23

- (i) Self-Empathy : 25
- (ii) Curiosity : 26
- (iii) Swadhyay (Self-Study) : 26
- (iv) Education-Experience-Practice : 32

(4) **Improvement of Public life** : 33

- (i) Observance of Public Religion : 34
- (ii) The Value of Good Deeds : 36
- (iii) The Value of Valor and Bravery : 37
- (iv) Importance of Organization : 37
- (v) The Value of Wealth & Position : 38

(5) **Refinement of family life** : 38

(6) **Perfection of personality** : 40

- (i) Temperament : 42
- (ii) Qualities and Character : 44
- (iii) Work Efficiency : 45
- (iv) Voice Strength : 45
- (v) Sincerity : 48
- (vi) Supernaturalism : 49
- (vii) Company : 50
- (viii) Self-Reliance : 51
- (ix) Gradual Development : 51

(7) **Summary** : 52

CHAPTER-2

Brain, Intellect and Soul : 53

(i) The Brain is the main Strength of man	: 53
(ii) General introduction to the brain	: 56
(iii) The Conscious Mind	: 58
(iv) The Inner mind (Subconscious Mind)	: 59
(v) The Inner Self-Conscience	: 60
(vi) Intelligence & Intellect Main matters of Brain	: 64
(vii) Importance of intelligence and Intellect	: 66
(viii) Soul	: 72
(ix) Nature of Soul	: 74
(x) Some characteristics of the soul	: 78
(xi) Rebirth	: 78
(xii) Religion of Soul	: 82
(xiii) Purity of conduct strengthens the soul	: 83

Summary : 84

CHAPTER-3

Health, Exercise, Relaxation: 87

Health : 87

Food is the maker of the Body : 87

- (i) Protein : 90
- (ii) Fat : 90
- (iii) Minerals : 91
- (iv) Carbohydrates : 91
- (v) Water : 91
- (vi) Vitamins : 93
- (vii) What kind of diet should one take : 97
- (viii) How to eat food : 101
- (ix) Importance of water : 106
- (x) Effect of Diet on the Brain : 108
- (xi) Other aids to health : 111
- (xii) Relation of air with the body : 112
- (xiii) Effect of oxygen on the brain : 115
- (xiv) Air intake : 117
- (xv) Swarodaya-Vigyan : 118
- (xvi) Pranayam : 119
- (xvii) Brahmcharya (Celibacy) : 121
- (xviii) Effect of mental condition on Body : 124
- (xix) Psychology : 124
- (xx) Faith : 125
- (xxi) Security: Rest Assured : 126
- (xxii) Mental Disorders : 127
- (xxiii) Company Effect : 128

Health and Exercise : 129

    (i) Brain Exercise : 130
    (ii) Worship is the best exercise for intellect : 131
    (iii) Rest and Sleep : 131

Medicines : 134

Reasons to Health Damage : 139

Consuming Poison : 143

Laziness : 145

Constipation : 145

Anorexia : 146

Health Examination : 147

CHAPTER-4

Rich have all the Virtues : 148

Means of Earning Money : 150

Keep these points in mind : 151

1. Do not sell your self-respect & Morality : 151
2. Do not depend on the mercy of others : 151
3. Do not be content even by mistake : 152
4. Look into the future : 152
5. Catch the time : 152
6. Recognize the time : 154
7. Keep the powers of the mind alert : 155
8. Be tolerant and hardworking : 157
9. Be well behaved : 157
10. Become a master : 158
11. Do the work diligently according to your interest and ability : 158
12. Collect virtues and become extraordinary : 159
13. Adopt the spirit of service : 159
14. Consider financial purity as religion : 160
15. Hold your position, seat firmly : 161
16. Churn the ocean of life : 161
17. Give importance to success of the task : 162
18. Think about your daily income and expenditure- : 163
19. Be cautious in Money transactions. : 163
20. Donation increases wealth : 164
21. Do not disguise yourself as a rich person : 164

22. Be like a Bania (businessman) : 164
23. Five principles to be kept in mind : 165

(1) If you are a businessman : 167

1. Capital, hard work and ability : 167
2. Be prepared for competition : 167
3. Business grows with popularity : 168
4. Utility in all things : 168
5. Management : 169
6. Meditate like a sage : 170
7. Increase National Wealth : 171

(2) If you are an officer or an Employer : 171

1. Lead : 171
2. Be fair and trustworthy : 172
3. Be serious, calm and mysterious : 172
4. Be simple in nature and speech : 173
5. Be above others : 173
6. Above all, be courageous : 174
7. Know how to work and how to get the work done. : 175

(3) If you are an employee : 177

1. Keep your ambition strong : 177
2. Do not work only for food : 178
3. Do more work than what you are Paid : 178
4. Do not think yourself to be Irreplaceable : 178
5. Just be like a seed in the soil : 179
6. Follow the rules of the place : 179
7. Do not be action-hating : 179
8. Show your talent in your work : 180

9. Be careful in your conduct	: 180
10. Do not be overly hardworking	: 180
11. Spread your roots like a tree	: 180
12. Engage yourself in some interesting activities	: 181
13. Do not become a servant of two Masters	: 181
14. keep looking for suitable Opportunity	: 182

(4) If you are an Unemployed : 182

1. Eliminate fear and despair	: 182
2. Resolve to become self-reliant	: 183
3. Make a plan for the future	: 183
4. Increase your acquaintances	: 184
5. Do not sit idle. Get out to work	: 184
6. Keep bouncing like a ball	: 185
7. Spread your wins and keep flying	: 185

CHAPTER-5

Conversational Skills : 186

The power of speech : 186

    (a) Mental restraint and ability : 192
    (b) Authority over Voice : 196
    (c) Words and Grammar : 197
    (d) Knowledge of Human Nature : 199
    (e) Don't talk big with a small mouth : 199
    (f) Don't say "I"- "I" all the time : 199
    (g) Do not be a pain in the ass : 200
    (h) Do not try to show off by starting a fire : 200
    (i) Do not pluck stars from the sky : 200
    (j) Do not praise or criticize yourself : 201
    (k) Don't be a theoretician : 201
    (l) Do not rush to slur : 201
    (m) Do not become a judge or critic : 202
    (n) Keep knowledge by heart : 202
    (o) Keep originality and topicality in mind : 202
    (p) Speak with Purpose and Impact : 203
    (q) Speak Fluently : 204
    (r) Speak Chitravaani : 204
    (s) Be an admirer of virtues : 205
    (t) Speak Beneficial Words : 206
    (u) Do not show inexperience : 207
    (v) Meet elders and Seniors : 208
    (w) Impress with your Personality : 208
    (x) Listen carefully : 209

Summary : 210

CHAPTER-6

Behavioral Efficiency : 211

Home Policy : 213

    (1) Family does Not belong to just one person : 213
    (2) There must be a Mukhiya in a home : 214
    (3) There are three types of behavior : 215
    (4) Special attention has to be paid for Hospitality : 215

Friend-policy : 216

    (1) There should be mutual Trust and Rapport : 216
    (2) Do not become friends abruptly : 216
    (3) Qualities of Good Friends : 217
    (4) Help friends in their days of Troubles : 217
    (5) Do not take unfair advantage from a friend : 217
    (6) There is no consideration of high or low : 218
    (7) Always be cautious in dealing with Friends : 219

Public Policy : 219

(1) Politeness is the soul of public Behavior : 219
(2) Do not become, selfish, arrogant etc. : 220
(3) Strive for the peace in the Society : 220
(4) self-respect and the respect of others. : 221
(5) Protect the dignity of the women : 221
(6) In anger, show strength not unruliness : 221
(7) Do not always find faults of others : 222
(8) Read the situation and circumstances : 222
(9) Avoid false promises, deceit etc. : 222
(10) Be careful in remaining silent and while talking : 223

Business Policy : 224

(1) Do not do work hastily : 224
(2) Work should be ready before the scheduled time : 224
(3) Show your prowess in meetings : 224
(4) Do some research of the person before you meet : 224
(5) Put your strong arguments in soft language : 225
(6) Do not show flattery and stubbornness : 225
(7) Goal must be to accomplish the desired Task : 225
(8) Avoid conflicts in business. : 226
(9) Special care in communications : 226

Fool-Policy : 227

- (1) Be aware that there is No medicine for fools : 227
- (2) Do not tease fools : 227
- (3) Nourish the Ego of fools to get the work done : 228

Exceptional Policy : 228

- (1) Do not be too good for all the people : 228
- (2) Collaborate with other illusionists : 229
- (3) Adopt the ways as per circumstances : 230
- (4) Do not stick to ethics : 230
- (5) Be diplomatic in dealing with enemies : 230
- (6) Have bigger virtues than your enemy : 230
- (7) Find flaws of enemies : 231
- (8) Do not worry about weaker enemies : 231
- (9) Know the shelter of enemies : 231
- (10) Do not be carried away by flattery : 231
- (11) Do not dance before blinds : 231
- (12) Stand firm in your place : 232
- (13) Control your inner conflicts : 232
- (14) Do not run away from difficult situation : 233
- (15) Fight for the Rights : 233

Policy- Brief : 234

CHAPTER-7

How Is Your Appearance : 235

Main Characteristics of a Perfect Body	: 238
1.... Head	: 241
2.... Countenance	: 243
(i) Forehead	: 243
(ii) Eyes	: 244
(iii) Ears	: 246
(iv) Temples	: 247
(v) Nose	: 247
(vi) Face	: 248
(vii) Beard	: 249
(viii) Cheeks	: 249
(ix) Teeth	: 250
(x) Chin	: 250
3.... Face-Reading	: 250
4.... Torso	: 254
(a) Neck	: 254
(b) Chest	: 254
(c) Shoulder	: 255
(d) Stomach and Waist	: 255
(e) Hands	: 255

(f)	Palms and Fingers	: 255
(g)	Thumb	: 257
(h)	Fingers	: 258
(i)	Palms	: 259
(j)	Lines on the Hands	: 261
(k)	Wrists	: 266

5.... From the buttocks to the soles of the feet, and other things : 266

(a)	Buttocks	: 266
(b)	Thighs	: 266
(c)	Soles	: 267
(d)	Height	: 267
(e)	Life-Span	: 268
(f)	Voice and Gait	: 268
(g)	Testing of Husband wife Relations by weight	: 269
(h)	Some other ways of Body Examination	: 269

6.... Look at the whole Body : 269

Summary : 272

CHAPTER-8

<u>Neither Accept nor Reject</u> : 273
<u>Anything Without knowing</u>

(1) Mind is the cause of the functioning : 273
    of all senses
(2) Symptoms of emotions are immediately : 273
    visible on the body
(3) Disposition sits on the head : 275
(4) Do not fall in the trap of beauty : 276
(5) Keep the country, time and situation in mind.: 277
(6) Think with a free mind : 279
(7) There is natural affection or hatred between : 282
    human beings
(8) Do not test the personality of any great man : 287
    immediately

The methods of human testing : 289

Test yourself with these things : 294
    (1) Speech : 295
    (2) Behavior : 301
    (3) Facial expressions and body gestures : 301

These things should also be kept in mind : 309
    (1) Home Conditions : 309
    (2) Economic condition : 312
    (3) Company, profession : 313
    (4) Dress : 313
    (5) The power of knowledge : 314

(6) Etiquettes	: 315
(7) Food and drink	: 315
(8) Laughing	: 315

Know something more : 316

(1) An arrogant person's gaze is above everyone's head	: 316
(2) A gentleman praises someone's qualities openly	: 317
(3) A person who wastes words is also a waste of time.	: 317
(4) A civilized person shows simplicity by showing respect and affection on his face	: 317
(5) A good man never says that this is his principle	: 317
(6) When two people have mutual trust,	: 317
(7) By knowing what is someone's favorite subject	: 317
(8) Do not get confused	: 318
(9) Look at your faults too	: 319

SUMMARY : 321

Some personal questions : 323

Weigh your answers : 332

CHAPTER-9

Some Relevant Excerpts, Quotes : 333
And
Self- Evaluations

Denouement	: 333
Few Verses, Hymns etc. written in Our Scriptures in **Ancient Era**	: 333
Few wisdom-Words written by Sages, Literary Giants in **Medieval Era**	: 334
Few quotes, Citations etc. from the World-leaders, Saviors, Legends of **Recent Era**	: 336

Self-Evaluation	: 338
Questions	: 338
Explanatory Answers	: 345
Summary	: 369
Epilogue	: 370
Afterword	: 372

Chapter-1

Need to Shine within Self

In the world of struggle and competition, man cannot stand without self-upliftment, without making a definite place for himself. Everyone is ambitious, everyone is worried about livelihood, prestige and happiness, so everyone strives for them. In such a situation, it is difficult to achieve success in life without gaining strength by way of enhancement of virtues.

It is the natural law of the world that immovable things are consumed by mobile creatures and among creatures, the cowardly creatures are the food of the brave. Refinement and Improvisation of Body, Soul and Virtues, given by the God, need to achieve the success in life and prove more valuable in the society. In the words of Mahatma Gandhi, **'If every person improves himself, then the whole country can be saved**.' It is the ultimate aim of a man to develop himself in all the dimensions - moral, physical, personal, social and public conduct and become a "Paragon of Virtues" and reveal these in his Traits and Persona to achieve success in Social and public life.

Every person is his own ancestor. Man develops himself not with the help of external means but mainly with his own self-power. Every person is his own creator. In other words, we do not remain as God makes us. We are what we make ourselves with our own means.

Society does not give as much respect to our God-made form as to our self-made form. All are "Dwij" (Born Twice), in one form they are born as humans, in the other form they are born and considered as God-like men (Nar-Dev), or wicked Men (Nar-Pishaach), or a Jaanvar, an Animal like-man (Nar-Pashu or Gardabh).

It is clear from this that man is counted according to the form he projects through his persona. There is no special respect for the human form, rather humanity. Demonism or animality is identified on the basis of virtues and Traits shown in social and public life. The kind of exhibition of Virtues, Traits and Persona before the larger section of the society brings him any of the above titles.

"KARMAYATAM PHALAM PUNSAAM BUDDHIH KARMANUSAARINI". Believing in reincarnation of the Soul will also have to be accepted as truth that every person is his own ancestor and gets 'the results according to his actions (Karmas)- Development of wisdom, construction or destruction.'

"MAHAJANO YEN GATHH: SA PANTHA"
That is the right Path on which great man walked

One should ponder over how spiritual progress is achieved or can be achieved. The field of life is very wide. People are seen moving ahead in many directions by many means and methods. Talented people create means according to the opportunity. People with extraordinary talent usually make their own path, they do not follow the path of others. It is also said that **LEIK CHHANDI TINO CHALE, SAIR, SINGH SAPOOT** (Kabir) 'Leaving the ordinary path, the three, Sick, Lion, & Worthy-Son Walk on their own path".

In such a situation, it cannot be said by pointing towards any one path that this is the path of success. Only some such basic Virtues can be pointed out which are found in the basic character of successful people. On the basis of them, man can make or find his path of life by doing sadhana himself. The right way is that until the strength comes in his legs and the power of thinking independently in his mind, till then ambitious people should consider the work of great men as their path

Human behavior is a complex fabric interwoven from a multitude of threads, including virtues, traits, and persona. The interplay between these elements is dynamic and ever-evolving. Our virtues guide our actions, our traits color our perceptions, and our persona shapes our interactions. These elements are not static; they can change and develop over time, influenced by our experiences, relationships, and personal growth.

So, let us have a clear understanding of Virtues, Traits and Persona:

(1) .... Virtues Traits & Persona

Every Person takes birth with certain instinctive divine Virtues, Traits and a Physique, and these also make him an enterprising creature by nature. He is never satisfied with these three celestial boons and constantly thrives to upgrade.

The level of human perfection is determined by the discipline and his efforts to use his virtues to the fullest, acquire flawless Traits and thus adopt a Persona which can make his life commendable and successful.

Man stands between two extremes, the lowest is below the beasts and the highest surpasses even the angels. 'Human Behavioral Science' is the study of the movement between these two extremes. Mastery over other sciences, devoid of ethics and value, would obstruct insight. That is why it has been said that, **"knowledge without morality and ethics is the thickest of veils'**, which prevents man from seeing the reality." By improving their morality people can improve their Social and public Conduct. Moral virtues bring eternal happiness, while moral corruption leads to everlasting unhappiness.

Man must purge blameworthy traits before he can integrate ethical and moral virtues. "It is the purification of the soul from inclination towards evils and sins, and then development of its innate virtues towards goodness, which leads to its uprightness and its reaching excellence. Attempts to obey God's commands are successful when one is purified; only then the soul can receive God's grace.

In view of the above general Moral discourse now we advance to our Major Premise.

"Virtues": - (in Hindi "SADGUN") comes from Latin root 'Virtus'. Virtue is the quality of being morally good. **Virtues are moral excellences, deeply ingrained habits that drive us to do what is right and good. Think of them as the compass guiding our actions** Virtues are moral qualities or standards considered praiseworthy or admirable by a civilized society or other individuals. Virtues are essentially mental characteristics. They are generally associated with good ethical behavior and character.

Virtues like honesty, compassion, and courage shape our responses to the world around us, influencing our choices and interactions.

Virtues are often a reflection of a person's moral excellence. His Behavior shows high moral standards, good qualities or habits. Virtues are attitudes, dispositions or character traits that enable one to act with generosity, fidelity, Integrity, Honesty, Charity, Chastity, Diligence, Prudence, Purity, Rectitude, Humility Righteousness, Kindness, Patience, Courage, Compassion, Temperance, Fairness, Self-Control, Justice etc. In a way, cultivation, development and refinement of these vital and potential Virtues **need to Shine within self**.

"Traits": - (In Hindi **"VYAVHARGAT KHASIYATEN"**) Traits are essentially behavioral attitude and acts involving, mainly, but not necessarily, physical characteristics and personality along with the intuitive virtues. These include things such as body shape, color, muscles, the Five senses, Eye, Ear, Nose, Tongue, and Touch. Traits are the characteristics about human that can be described or measured. **Traits are the distinctive qualities that make us who we are. They can be both positive and negative, ranging from optimism and kindness to pessimism and cynicism. Traits are often more ingrained than persona, forming the bedrock of our personality** Traits are also relatively enduring patterns of thoughts, feelings and behaviors that reflect the tendency to respond in certain ways under certain conditions and circumstances. Traits are distinctive characteristics or attributes of a person generally considered innate or naturally occurring. Lust, Gluttony, Greed, Sloth, Envy, Wrath, Being Extroverted or Introverted or Open-minded, Boastful, Agreeable,

Conscientious, Industrious, are some of the behavioral characteristics qualities or tendencies that someone has, that forms a person's particular traits. Aggrandizement of high intelligence, cognition and the capacity of reasoning, (which significantly influence behavior, conduct and reactions and are the essential parts of a person's Traits), **need to shine within self.**

Virtues have all the positive features whereas Traits may have or may not have negative attributes. Historically Philosophers like Aristotle have combined both as a midpoint between two extremes- A balance that is often challenging to achieve but crucial for self-improvement and societal wellbeing. Virtues are qualities that are universally or generally considered to be good and desirable. Whereas some flaws may find a place in traits.

"Persona": - (In Hindi **VYAKTITVA**) Persona is the particular type of personality that people project to the world. Persona means public image. Persona is the mechanism that conceals a person's true personality, thoughts and feelings, especially in his adaptation to the outside world. The word "persona" comes from the Latin term *"persona,"* which means "mask" or "character." In ancient Rome, actors used to wear masks to portray different characters in theatrical performances. *The word "persona" was later adopted in psychology "to describe the aspect of an individual's character that they present to others".* Persona is one of the most influential formulations by a person in his public life and social behavior.

One of the notions of persona was put forward by the Swiss psychiatrist **Carl Jung**. In Jung's personality theory, the persona is one among several "selves". **People can have multiple personas that they use in various** situations; this can include work, being with friends, at home, etc. Depending on the individual's circumstance, a persona which they consider stronger within their specific social situation can be created because they put a higher emphasis on social interactions. Jung warned about using personas too much, fearing that people might lose their own individuality to their persona. There are many types of Personas, but for the purpose of our Book, we will discuss Authenticate Persona viz. is Genuine Personality, Idealized Persona viz. Aspirational Personality, Socialistic Persona viz. public Image and Professional Persona viz. personality projected in relation to Work and profession. To demonstrate their persona in a reliable manner, persons **need to Shine within self.**

      In essence, our behavior is a reflection of our inner compass (virtues), our inherent qualities (traits), and the image we choose to portray (persona). Knowing their intricacies can help us to better understand ourselves and others, fostering empathy, compassion, and more meaningful connections. All the three Motifs namely Virtues, Traits and Persona, are reflected in the intricate interplay of all the human activities. Being aware of our Virtues, Traits and studying the Persona projected by successful men, we can focus on our talents and abilities and thus, **Shine** in different areas of life. Now we will discuss these motifs with a focus on the combination of each other for the purpose of better understanding of human comportments and deportments, in the forthcoming pages and Chapters to enable ourselves to **Shine within self.**

(2)....Self-Empowerment

(a) Self-confidence

The firmness and strength of self-power brings success everywhere. Without self-confidence, the tendency of self-reliance does not arise in a person and without self-reliance, he is unable to lift himself. An ambitious person should have the utmost faith in self-power. He should have the belief that his life is not futile; he has some special powers, that is why God has given him a human body, if he was insignificant then he would have got the body of a bedbug or a grasshopper instead of a human body. If one's body looks like a human body when seen with the eyes, then one should definitely believe that one can be the same as any other human being, and along with that one should believe not in one's own transience, but in one's divinity. This belief gives self-realization, awakens the sleeping power of man.

The famous Russian writer Gorky once said while giving a speech to the farmers of his country, **'Remember that you are the most important creature on earth.'** There is no reason why a person should consider himself unnecessary. Unless he himself considers himself important, how will others consider him important. Therefore, one should not betray oneself; one should recognize one's humanity. The great poet Shakespeare has written that **the most important thing is to be true to oneself**. The best way to be true to oneself is that a man should not deceive himself, should have faith in his virtues, humanity and the powers available to a man; should believe that he has not been thrown like a dead body to float in this ocean of the world. He is a living being, so it is his duty to swim across the ocean of the world by becoming alive and powerful.

(b) Self-knowledge

The second major requirement is self-knowledge. Self-knowledge means to know yourself completely, to know your strengths, to understand your supportive and hindering mental attitudes. Weighing your desires, imaginations, ideologies and physical strength is self-knowledge. Ancient ethicist Appaya Dixit has written that there are many scholars of ethics, scriptures, astrologers, Chaturvedis, Shastris and Brahmagyanis, but very few people are found who understand their ignorance.

NITIGYA NIYATIGYA VEDGYA API BHAVANTI SHAASTRAHGYA: BRAHAMGYA API LABHYAH: SWAGYANGYANINO VIRLAH:

Only by understanding one's ignorance, one's incompleteness and one's inability, one can become cultured, enriched with knowledge and virtues and rich in self-power.

(c) Self-Purification

Only a person who sees the Self honestly can be self-aware. A doctor who is an anatomist will not be considered a self-aware person. Any person who can analyze his strengths and weaknesses can be a self-aware person. After self-awareness, self-purification is of utmost importance; because the divine qualities of the soul are surrounded by many demonic qualities or tendencies, just as the ancient sages were surrounded by night-demon even during the day. Only by getting rid of his mental ailments can a man develop himself with a healthy mind. Therefore, self-purification is absolutely necessary. This self-purification is not done by drinking castor oil, but by driving away the false disorders of the mind. The army of mental ailments is very large. **Most of them are born out of fear** and become fear-causing themselves - like a mother's daughter becomes a mother herself in a few days. Mental fear stops progress in life, so it is important to know something about it. For Self-Purification, we must get rid of the causes which beget Fear.

(d) Fear arises mainly due to these reasons:

(i) **Ignorance-**When a person does not understand a subject, he fears it. Just as one is afraid before entering a dark room, similarly, if one is ignorant about a task, one is afraid of doing it. Fear is naturally destroyed by light - whether it is sunlight or the light of the soul or the light of knowledge.

(ii) **Doubt-** the doubt that arises from not understanding something or even after understanding, fear arises immediately due to the feeling of confusion that arises naturally. When there is doubt in the mind, even a small object seems big, a ghost can be seen even in a bush. Doubt gives rise to delusion and delusion gives rise to despair.

(iii)Indifference - Due to dullness or indifference, the two main horses of the chariot of life - passion and enthusiasm - die and man finds the world dark, illusory and fearful. Indifference does not lead to courage but to despair and fear.

(iv)Uncertainty The restlessness of mind or the anxiety that arises due to uncertainty or restlessness is also ultimately a cause of fear. When a man moves with determination and purpose in a definite direction, then his fear is overpowered in a critical situation and he does not fear.

(v) Immorality- is the mother of fear. It is caused by weakness of character. Man is afraid at every step. The seeds of fear are sown not only by physical crime but also by mental crime. The soul trembles from within due to lust, anger, greed, attachment, arrogance, selfishness, hatred, feeling of revenge and unfair partiality. Fear definitely increases due to false speech, false behavior or false belief or superstition. Fear spreads terribly due to violence or cruelty. A great French author (Balzac) has written that **cruelty and fear shake Hands together**. In a fearful state, the morale of the people falls. A man commits cruelty and after committing the crime, he feels afraid. Man is afraid of immoral behavior and when he is afraid, he commits immoral acts. But when the moral aspect is strong, a person has the strength of many people.

(vi) Weakness- Weakness and fear are like father and son. When the body is weak, the fear of disease comes in the mind, when the mind is weak, the fear of circumstances comes in the mind and when the personality is weak, the fear of the enemy comes in the mind.

Similarly, when one is afraid, one becomes weak in all matters. Nervousness and weakness caused by disease - both increase the pulse rate, the heart beats. From this it should be understood that the effect of fear and weakness is the same. When a person finds himself weak, then only he gets frightened by the thought of pain or pain. Small children are weak, that is why they scream in fear at every small thing. When one is weak, one is afraid not only of others but also of oneself. A weak person is always afraid that the beat of his heart may stop. Children who are physically and mentally weak sometimes get startled by the sound of their own screaming.

(vii) Incompetence- Due to incompetence, a person always fears that he might commit a mistake and due to fear, in the mind, he actually commits a mistake. Even the remaining ability does not come to the fore; even the speech of the person stops; he becomes bewildered.

(viii) Inactivity- Sitting with folded hands makes fear stand in front with open mouth. Due to laziness, man's efforts are weakened and dreadful circumstances overwhelm a man. He sees only ghosts of fear all around. Fear definitely ends with work. When a man starts walking in a direction, fear comes under his feet. It has been seen in the battlefields that before the start of the war, many soldiers are afraid of imagining the future destruction, but when the war starts, even the frightened soldier runs fearlessly in the shower of bullets. The only reason for this is that fear ends when one is active in work; then the man is not afraid of even his death. Physical labor definitely drives away the fear of the mind. The feeling of helplessness due to imaginary fear in laziness is very soul-destroying. Due to physical and mental laxity, often there is failure in life.

(ix) Lowliness- whether it is the poverty of family or of nature or of courage-enthusiasm or of wealth, it generates fear. Financial poverty shows helplessness. Due to family poverty, a person fears others considering himself inferior. Due to the poverty of nature, a person fears even from his servants despite being a master. A poor person is always anxious and downtrodden.

(x) Dependency- In helplessness, one has to face fear everywhere. We call helplessness that situation in which a person loses his independent personality. In that condition, instead of being self-reliant, he becomes completely dependent. By developing an independent personality with full self-confidence, a person becomes self-dependent. By making oneself dependent on someone or by becoming a part of the crowd, self-power gets weakened. Superstition and fear arise in the crowd. If fear spreads while being in a crowd, a stampede occurs, people do not have the ability to understand the situation or face it. The tendency of the crowd to become sheep arises. Patience becomes stronger when one is alone. Even a dog, when alone, faces a difficult situation. Napoleon said that **They Walk with speed who walk alone.** And this was also the saying of the fearless Hitler that **the strong man is stronger if he remains alone.** This means that fear is eliminated by becoming an independent person.

(xi) Intolerance- Intolerance leads to fear. When a person is intolerant, he naturally considers even small things as fearful, gets angry and in the end, he feels sadness, remorse and regret. He suffers from fear.

Intolerance is caused by hysteria. Feeling of fear is also intensified by extreme hysteria or sentimentality.

(xii) Addiction- Every addiction is fearful. Because it binds and makes a living being fearful. When one gets acquainted with some pleasure, one gets attached to it and as a result, one develops hatred for pain and fear arises from the imagination of future pain. An addict or a luxurious person is never seen to be free from fear.

(xiii) Lack of faith and trust- Lack of faith and trust leads to the feeling of self-helplessness and there is a fear that the whole world is ready to attack us. The famous George Eliot has written that **"What loneliness is lonelier than distrust?"** It gives rise to the imagination of one's helplessness. Gandhiji has also said that **"To trust is a virtue.** It is weakness that begets distrust". And we know that Gandhiji always remained free from fear by trusting even his enemy. Distrust gives birth to hopelessness and from the womb of hopelessness, a child called fear is born.

(xiv) Effect of Fear-Taking fear as the basis, we have already mentioned many mental diseases. In short, it should be known that until the mind is not pure and well-organized, man cannot decide his duty judiciously. When the mind is in disarray due to natural cowardice, despair, instability, anxiety or ignorance or inexperience, the whole life becomes in disarray. In that condition, dual or ambivalent feelings arise in the mind and man becomes confused about what to do. When he is confused about what to do, terrible situations arise. Many tasks of life are spoiled due to the disorder of mind and fear. Hitler knew this psychological secret. When he became the head of the state in 1933, he had said: **"Our strategy is to destroy the enemy from within, to conquer him through himself. Mental confusion, contradiction of feelings, indecision, panic are our weapons"**.

Well, we know that Hitler had on many occasions destroyed the enemy's army by making them shaky and fearful. There is a mythological story about this. Once Yamraj called his messengers and said that he needed four hundred dead people, go and get them. The messengers reached the world with weapons to kill four hundred Vyasnis (addicted) people. They returned to Yamraj with eight hundred dead people on the horses instead of four hundred. Yamraj got angry and asked the reason for bringing unnecessary people. The messengers said that what could we do; we were killing four hundred people, while leaving, we came to know that four hundred people died on their own due to fear of that massacre. So, we had to bring their bodies too.

Understand the essence of this story. It is that most people die without dying. The ghost of fear remains in their mind. That ghost comes to the mind due to impurity, because even the ghosts of ghost believers are heard to live in dirty places, ruins and crematoriums only - not in temples and houses of gentlemen. When fear makes one's own feet start to falter, then man cannot stand in the struggle of life.

Therefore, to uplift the soul, the mind must be made free of Fear, doubts and clean; its bad habits must be removed. Only after their removal will the liberated soul be as conscious as one's independent motherland. It must be remembered that self-purification cannot be achieved in one day or in one go. It does not happen. For this, daily practice is required so that the brain does not corrupts. While doing my duty, I should not be afraid that my mind is disturbed. There should be equanimity in doing some work. If there is no enthusiasm to do my duty then I should accept that there is cowardice in my mind, and I am afraid.

(e) Self-Control

The work of Self-Purification can only go on when the programme of Self-Control is also carried out simultaneously. The brain is the root of thoughts. If someone wants to avoid being nourished by bad thoughts, then good thoughts will have to be arranged in their place. Good thoughts mean awakening and organizing one's basic instincts. Truth and non-violence are the main ones among the basic instincts. Nothing can be more complex and simpler than truth. The work of nature is carried out on the basis of truth and non-violence; therefore, these are the basic religions of man, the main symbols of nature. Cruelty and cunningness etc. are the evil religions. In the visible world, we see that truth wins in the end. Wealth and pride etc. remain safe and permanent only when they are defended by justice. The unjust lose in the end.

Patanjali has written that when truth is established, the result of action becomes independent: **'SATYAPRATISHTHAAYAM KRIYAPHALA SHRAYATVAM.'** The ultimate religion of non-violence is also established by truth. According to Vyas: **'AHIMSA PARAMO DHARMAH: SA CH SATYE PRATISHTITHA'**. Non-violence means kindness. It should be taken in the sense of protection of any 'Jeev.

(Creature) and even refrain from the thoughts of violence. Truth and non-violence are promoted by simplicity of nature and character and generosity. These qualities increase the trust and it should be remembered that trustworthiness is the carrier of your Persona in public life. It is essential to be reliable for the advancement, being bound in the thread of the world.

Apart from these, other important emotions of self-development are hope, courage and patience. Hope is a special quality of the human soul. We see that as long as there is life in the body, hope remains attached to it. Therefore, it should not be suppressed and it should not be made dark. By thinking about a bright future, the spiritual nature remains alert. There is no greater power in the world than enthusiasm.

Vyas has said, **'NAASTYUTSAAHAT PARAM BALAM.'** According to the poet, nothing is difficult to obtain in the world through enthusiasm. **'SOTSAHASYA HI LOKESHU NA KICHIDAPI DURLABHAM'**. And in the same words, according to Hanuman, enthusiasm is always the reason for the success of all tasks: **'ANIBANDHO HI SATATAM SARVARTHERSHU PRAVARTAKAH:'** Courage gathers manliness and morale. Patience has a very high place in this category of virtues. Patience is the bearer of mental strength generated by hope, faith, enthusiasm and courage etc. Without patience, all mental powers are short-lived. No matter how enthusiastic or courageous a person is, if he loses patience, he will sit down in despair, if he faces any obstacle, he will end his work before the completion of his work and if getting heated up once, he will cool down again.

Patience gives success in all areas of life. Look at the inventors in the field of science and knowledge they do not give up even after failing repeatedly. While inventing electricity, Edison had failed in 900 experiments, but he did not lose hope and patience. Ultimately, he invented electricity. Look at Gandhiji's efforts in the field of politics. Even after losing repeatedly, he was found standing patiently in the field. Ultimately, he was victorious. England's famous former Prime Minister William Pitt once asked many scholars what should be the most important quality for a Prime Minister. Some said hard work, some said enthusiasm, some said eloquence. Pitt said that there cannot be any better quality for a ruler than patience. The statement of that experienced Prime Minister was true. We have witnessed it in Indian politics that with patience and intelligence Sardar Vallabhbhai Patel gradually removed the crowns of about 560 such Maharajas, (Raje-Rajwade) each of whom was pretending to be Mahipal, Dharmavtar, Naresh, Annadaata and what not. This is the effect of patience. The same patience with which Krishna established peace. The same patience with which Chanakya laid the foundation of the Maurya Empire by diplomacy and eliminating the enemies slowly with patience.

These are some virtues and mental qualities whose accumulation strengthens manliness and acquires valor. Maryada Purushottam Ram had these special virtues. Sita had recalled these qualities of his in Lanka and told Hanuman that enthusiasm, manliness, strength, non-cruelty, gratitude, valor, influence - all these qualities belong to Ram:

UTSAH: PURUSHAM SATTVAMANRISHASYAM KRITAGYATA VIKRAMASHCHA PRABHAVASHCHA SANTI VANAR RAGHAVE.
(Ramayana)

At this point we will again say that **'MAHAJANO YEN GATAH SA PATHA'**. Only by organizing and intensifying one's strength through mind-control can a man hope for, finding the way on which great men walked, for victory in life. One should cultivate one's health, character, nature and knowledge through self-control. By controlling these, will-power naturally becomes strong.

(i) Resolution

One should awaken one's desires and see which is the strongest among them. All people have one or the other desire in their mind and their mind naturally inclines towards it. One's interest can be known by simple concentration. Ordinary desires should be discarded and one specific desire should be held on to. Literature, business, politics, science or art-skill, whatever seems to suit one's nature, that should be considered as one's main subject and one should run one's mind after that.

After catching the strong wave, one should then think with a determined mind about what one should become and how one should become. Make a firm resolve about that I shall fulfill my desire and become prosperous. By making a vision of life and resolving to fulfill it, the path of life becomes visible in front of us, there is inner inspiration to work hard. After deciding the goal, we should let our imagination run. The imagination element of the brain is its main artist or painter. It can make a beautiful map of the future of life. Accordingly, the intellect thinks of ways, tries to make the ideas come true and whatever is lacking is fulfilled by external knowledge or power. Therefore, we should let our imagination run far and wide, we should become farsighted.

(ii) Efforts

Success is achieved only by making a definite program and working accordingly. Desires never succeed without hard work; this should be remembered. Hard work is the real effort. Hard work is the key to self-development. Napoleon once said that he **multiplied himself through hard work.**

In this regard, we should adopt the opinion of learned Carlyle: "Have **a purpose in life and having it throw into your work such strength of mind and muscle as God has given you"**. So set a goal in life and then use all the physical strength and mental power that God has given you for the purpose of accomplishing the task and achieve your goal.

While celebrating his 90th birthday, the great genius and entrepreneur George Bernard Shaw had once described a simple formula for success. According to Shaw, **the only way to lead a happy life is to be engrossed in the work of one's liking and not spend any time worrying about happiness and sorrow.**

The advice given by Vidula to her own Son Sanjay is worth to remember by heart that "Get -Up! Leave

Lethargy. Engross yourself in the work of public welfare. If you work with care, you will surely succeed: - **UTTHATAVYAM JAGRATAVYAM YOKTAVYAM BHUTIKARMASU BHAVISHYATITEV MANAH: KRITVA SATATMAVYATHA:** - (Mahabharata)

The statement of extreme experienced scholar Vyas is also worth keeping in mind - Intelligence, influence, sharpness, strength, desire to rise, industry - a person who has all these, how can he fear for his livelihood:

BUDDHIH PRABHAVASTEJASCHA SAVATHMUTTHANAMEV CHA. VYAVASAYASCH YESYA SYATTASAYVRITTIBHAYAM KUTAH: - (Mahabharata)

(iii) Perseverance

Success in work is achieved only by starting a business and continuing it with dedication till the end. Continuous hard work as per the work plan is called Perseverance. According to Kautilya, this is the exercise: **'KARMAARAMBHAANAAM YOGAARADHANO VYAAYAMAH'**. Thinking carefully in one direction with concentration, practicing the work with full effort and pursuing the goal is **ADHYAVASAAYA or exercise**. This is Karma-Sadhana. This sadhana has to be done every day and every moment.

In the course of doing work (Karma), one faces many daily obstacles, compulsions and failures at every step. Only by overcoming them can the wish be fulfilled. Therefore, one should be prepared to face difficulties in the path of Karma. One should not forget the main work by falling into ordinary temptation. There is a Russian proverb that **when you go to plough, do not waste time in catching a mouse on the side.** One should keep one's memory sharp too because if the memory is lost, the past experiences do not help in the future and the planning does not go smoothly. One should also avoid self-forgetfulness. By getting some success through hard work and slackening the pace of work, the God of goal runs away. By self-forgetfulness, man gets away from the knowledge of time.

When after suffering, and suddenly getting a chance of comfort, even the sage Kalgya-Muni forgets himself and his duty and does not value time. The ten years spent with Menaka seemed like one day to the ascetic Vishwamitra. Similarly, there was a sage in the Vishnu Purana, **Kundu Rhishi** who forgot his Penance and Jaap after being lured by an Apsara named Pramlocha. As per the belief, he stayed with her on the banks of Gomti for 907 years, 6 months and 3 days and forgot himself and remained in oblivious state. When she was leaving, the sage took a kamandala and went to do Sandhya-worship. On this, the Apsara asked how did you remember to do Sandhya-worship after so many days? Then the sage said, what are you saying, I have already done the worship yesterday evening, today I am going again, all these days of happiness seemed like one day to him.

What we mean to say is that one should work tirelessly while being alert and keeping in mind the pace of time and one's main purpose. One should not lose one's way and get misled. This disrupts one's perseverance. Also, one should not get distracted by unexpected events and calamities. One should remember this statement of a well-known former Prime Minister of England that **no person ever becomes great or good without making many and big mistakes-** W.E. Gladstone.

It is wise to learn from your mistakes and work hard continuously to improve yourself. The one who is doing spiritual development should understand that giving up karma is no less dreadful than giving up life. This world is called the world of karma: **'KARMABHOOMIRIYAM BRAHMAN'** (Mahabharata). In this world, karma is the most important: **'KARMA-PRADHAN VISHWA KARI RAKHA'** (Tulsi). Therefore, it is natural self-destruction to happen due to the wastage of karma.

These are the main points regarding spiritual development. In the field of life, success is achieved everywhere through these spiritual means. Apart from these, there are many other means which have to be used for self-upliftment. We will give a brief introduction of them as well, in the forthcoming pages.

3.... Expansion of Knowledge

Knowledge is of utmost help in the progress of the soul. It is through it that the intellect is refined. By marrying knowledge, intellect becomes the mother of ability, eloquence and success. By acquiring knowledge, an intelligent person becomes Sahasradhi and Sahasraksha. One reason for the supreme supremacy of God is that He is the Omnipresent. Man may not be omniscient in a short life, but he can certainly be very knowledgeable. The more one knows, the more independent and extra-ordinary he becomes; his field of action becomes much wider.

There is no limit to knowledge. The ocean of natural knowledge is so unfathomable that even after thousands of years of hard work, man has not been able to measure its depth. He did not even know the power of an ordinary atom. Who knew that they are also messengers of Yamraj. Looking at the infinity of knowledge, no one can say that we have nothing to learn now. To make life progressive, it is always necessary to acquire some knowledge. Here 'Some' does not mean that whatever is found in front of us should be taken to heart.

In this regard, Chanakya's opinion is that there are innumerable scriptures, there are many kinds of knowledge, time is short, there are many obstacles, therefore, just like a swan separates the milk from the water and consumes it, in the same way, only that which is in its essence should be consumed:

ANANTASHASTRAM BAHULASHCHA VIDYA, ALPASYA KALO BAHU VIDHNTA CH. YATSAARABHUTAAM TADUPASANIYAM, HANSO YATHA KSHIRAMIVAMBUMADHYAT.
(Chanakya)

Only that knowledge should be accumulated which is useful, illusion-free, i.e. accurate, which not only fill the mind but also mainly nourish the soul, which not only increases knowledge but also builds the soul. There is enough space inside the brain, it should be made an office instead of a museum so that people-friendly work can be done and one can also make a living out of it.

After properly understanding the subject of knowledge, one should see the means by which it can be accumulated. There are two types of knowledges (1) knowledge and (2) science. Classical knowledge is called 'knowledge'. Experimental, creative or professional knowledge, proven by experience and achieved through practice, is called 'science'. According to Shukracharya, speech-related activities are called 'vidya' and such activities which can be done without the help of speech are called 'kala'. We can call 'vidya' and 'kala' as 'Gyan' and 'Vigyan' respectively. In short, this is the introduction of knowledge-science, 'vidya-kala'. The main means of their attainment are self-experience, curiosity, self-study, education and experience and practice.

(i) Self-Empathy

Much knowledge springs out of the consciousness, concentration and awareness of the intellect. The essence of the soul and humanity is known only through empathy. By opening the windows of the mind, not only does **self-knowledge shine**, but the rays of the light of knowledge from outside also enter the temple of the mind automatically. When the mind is clean, the impression of the character of others is silently imprinted on it, and according to that, man experiences the knowledge of duty. By keeping the intellect active, much knowledge becomes accessible through the soul itself because it (the soul) itself has drunk water from many ghats.

(ii) Curiosity

If a person keeps his intellect alert and does not let his natural thirst for knowledge be satiated and tries to understand every mystery that he does not understand with a sense of curiosity, then the mind becomes rich in knowledge. Famous English poet Rudyard Kipling has written that "**whatever I know is told to me by my six obedient servants; their names are 'Where, What, When, Why, How and Who**"

(iii) Swadhyaya (Self-Study)

Swadhyaya does not mean reading Vedas and scriptures. It means self-study. This study can be of a book, of a situation, of time and place or even of human nature. In Sanskrit, apart from a Veda reader, a city trader is also called a Swadhyayi because he studies the market, understands the fluctuations in prices, reads and weighs them.

If an uneducated person studies on his own, he can become a scholar of practical knowledge. For self-improvement, practical knowledge is far more useful than classical knowledge. The famous journalist Louis Fisher had published a series of articles on Stalin. In one of the articles, he had written that **Stalin's knowledge capital was his ability to understand people and situations; he was not very educated, but he had learnt what was necessary for a ruler, how to keep power safe after taking it.**

Self-study is definitely done by standing and lying in the struggle of life, by seeing and hearing, by meeting and interacting, by travelling around the country and by participating in social activities. At least knowledge of the progress of time and public ideology becomes available through it. Sometimes man learns or becomes aware after facing the shock of circumstances and sometimes after losing something. Gandhiji had written at one place that **"Deep tragedy is the school of great men"** Most of the intelligent people learn from their defeats also. All these are considered as self-study.

In comparison to all these means of self-study, self-study through Books, Print Media, Electronic Media and social media is better. It is certainly easier to do so. The knowledge experienced through these means is accumulated in mind, therefore they should be made the main means of self-study. Both general knowledge and specialized knowledge are attained through books and various Media. For general knowledge and current affairs, News Papers, Books, Magazines should be read and TV Channels should be watched which provide life-education, character-education and public-education and information.

Maharishi Patanjali has considered knowledge of three subjects useful for all human beings- knowledge related to mind, knowledge related to speech and knowledge related to body. Therefore, for the improvement of mind, speech and body, he has written one book on each of the three subjects- Yoga-Darshan, Grammar Maha-Bhashya and Vaidya-Shastra. Every person should at least acquire practical knowledge of general psychology, language-behavior and physiology. Apart from these, literature, history, economics, sociology and politics should also be made the subject of one's study. It is not necessary to be proficient in all the subjects, but one should have knowledge in many subjects. We have already said that multiplicity makes personality broader.

There is an art of reading a book. Experts say that one should read fast and not slowly, because speed and knowledge have a deep relationship. By reading fast, the flow of thoughts is not interrupted and the complete idea of each sentence gets fixed in the mind. A person who memorizes each word does not grasp the idea of the sentence together; hence he is not able to remember it properly. It should be remembered that the complete idea is not given by two or four words but it is found in the entire sentence.

One should not pay much attention to the meaning of the words. Full attention should be given to the meaning of the entire sentence, because true reading is done only to understand the meaning of the sentences in totality. One should understand the essence of the sentences without getting entangled in the story, sequence of events and the web of words. While reading, both imagination and memory should be kept alert. The subject described by imagination should be seen in reality. Then it becomes clearer. By keeping the memory alert, knowledge is absorbed correctly. If the memory is not good, then there is no benefit in reading a book; it only provides momentary entertainment. The condition of a person without memory becomes like that of Germany's Nazi Secretary ' **W.R. Hess'**. During the days of the famous Nuremberg trial, 'Hess' had lost his memory. He used to read the same book seven to eight times and every time he felt that he was reading it for the first time.

When reading and thinking go hand in hand, only then does the reading have an effect. Reading to become "Tota Ram" (Poor Reader) is futile. if we are satisfied only by knowing that our ancestors have flown in airplanes, then the hard work of reading does not become successful. It becomes successful only when this information gives us self-motivation and self-inspiration. We should understand the essence and think to what extent the opinion of the author is acceptable. We should weigh it, test it on the touchstone of practicality with logic and intellect and form our independent opinion on the basis of reality; only that which is worth accepting and useful should be adopted. Knowledge memorized becomes our own, bookish knowledge is of no use. A woman becomes a wife only when she is married, otherwise she remains her father's daughter.

If a subject is not memorized easily, it should be read aloud and concentrated. Pronunciation awakens the intellect, that is why the teacher's roar restores the intellect of the student. By pronouncing and reading yourself Knowledge also reaches to the mind through the ears. The ancient teachers believe that knowledge is passed- on more through hearing. Earlier, students were taught not only through the Granthas but also through the ears. An intelligent person is naturally fond of hearing. Therefore, it is easy to reach the mind through the tunnel of the ears.

This can happen only when knowledge is in the form of sound. As per general belief, even God wakes up in the morning with the recitation of **Mangal Stotras**, so one should also wake up one's agility with sound. Knowledge should be imbibed in the heart in whatever way possible. Yes, one should keep in mind that along with it, meaningless things should not also remain like fog in the memory. Very sharp memory is also harmful because it keeps collecting unnecessary things due to which the mind becomes heavy.

For general knowledge, one should take one's favorite subjects and choose one's favorite authors. Authors have different styles, so books written by many authors on the same subject cannot have the same effect. It is beneficial to read such books written by authors who can stimulate one's thoughts and intensify one's emotions. Therefore, only such books should be taken for self-study which can increase one's knowledge along with entertainment. One should not always read only for knowledge. One of the purposes of reading books is to remove mental fatigue. Entertaining novels, stories and poems nourish the imagination part of the brain and provide rest. Therefore, reading entertaining literature at night for one's own pleasure induces sleep. To make the brain interesting, reading interesting literature is as important as life literature. Along with useful books, entertaining books should also be taken for self-study.

Nowadays the best means of self-study is the, newspaper, electronic & social media. Current knowledge of public progress is obtained from, social media like WhatsApp, Facebook, Twitter (Now X), Instagram etc., TV, newspapers and magazines. Not only public opinion is advertised, a lot is also created through newspapers & tv News Channels. Earlier an American scholar, Wendell

Philips had written that "**we live under a government of men and morning newspapers**".

In modern times, Reading Newspapers, watching TV News Channels, keeping an eye on social media like X, Facebook, Instagram etc. are very necessary to keep oneself in tune with the nation and society. By not doing so man does not keep up with the modern age; his knowledge availed through books becomes stale and he himself becomes a creature or a ghost of many generations back.

For specific knowledge, one should identify one's basic inclination and decide on one's future career, then one should study one subject and become proficient in it. Being an expert in one or the other subject increases a person's importance, helps him in earning his livelihood and fame; therefore, one should carefully study a useful subject and make his knowledge original on the basis of it by understanding its basic principle. In this way, a person can become an expert in that subject. For freedom of thought, one may use the ideas of others because that is the purpose of knowledge.

Whatever he reads and how he reads or learns it, the reader should always keep in mind that the knowledge should not be a matter of indigestion. The knowledge which is not put into practice becomes poison: **'ANAABHYASE VISHAM SHASTRAM.'** In the eyes of the people, A person is considered, knowledgeable only when he is a hard worker **'YAH KRIYAVANS PANDITAH'**. Famous thinker Herbert Spencer had written that **the main aim of education is not knowledge but action.** Therefore, first of all, practical and constructive knowledge should be collected and along with collecting it, one should also use it and wait to see to what extent it is useful. Education and the purpose of Swadhyaya is achieved only then. The usefulness or uselessness of the principles is known only when practiced. Knowledge becomes meaningful only through action, otherwise it is useless.

Knowledge related to arts is acquired by self-learning and working. Books do not give complete information about them. By working, one gets habitual knowledge and that is considered mature knowledge. Therefore, to acquire at least professional knowledge, one should practice a subject daily. **One should learn while working and work while learning**. When learning and thinking go hand in hand, only then knowledge increases.

(iv) Education-Experience-Practice

Much has been written above about education, experience and practice. One should know that man cannot learn everything himself. He is such a being who becomes educated by being educated by others; therefore, one should fearlessly take education from people more capable than oneself. The knowledge that can be obtained in an hour by qualified teachers and by the education of good men cannot be obtained even by reading a hundred books. The same thing happens with experience. One important thing that happens while experiencing is that it reveals the necessity and necessity is the mother of inventions. We have already said that knowledge remains active with practice.

In this regard, we will again say in the end that one does not become knowledgeable merely by getting education or by reading a lot of books without any purpose. It should be remembered that Arjun did not win the battle by listening to the recitation of Gita; he got success by behaving according to the discourses of Gita. Shiva is not pleased by merely uttering 'Bam-Bam' five to ten times a day. No one seems to get the grace of the divine. Acquiring knowledge with a purpose and then performing actions gives success. Donating Knowledge increases knowledge greatly—whether it is given to a person or as a service.

Along with the Knowledge, one should enhance one's character, worthiness, wealth and happiness through education in all ways. Education leads to worthiness and worthiness leads to humility, humility gives wealth, wealth leads to Religion and religion leads to happiness.

VIDYA DADATI VINAYAM, VINAYADYATI PATRATAAM PATRATVADHVNA MAPNOTI DHANADHARMA TATAH SUKHAM. (Hitopadesh)

4.... Improvement of Public Life

Man is purely a social being. Society is his field of work, field of means and field of life. Therefore, he has to take full care of his public life, has to take care of the customs and dignity of the society and has to make himself suitable for the society. Understand how strong the society is from these things - public religion is the most accepted religion; public power is the most important power; public prestige is considered to be the biggest treasure of man; work approved by the public is duty; public service is the most important means; public opinion is the divine opinion and divine power for man. Public custom is the biggest bond; public shame is the 'police' that prevents indiscipline; public view is the examiner of human action and the accomplishment of public welfare is humanity. Who will deny the power of Panch-Parameshwar (Public)? Who is so intelligent that he does not aspire to become popular even by displeasing himself!

To become successful in public life, man sacrifices his selfishness. In fact, society is based on sacrifice and sympathy. Everyone sacrifices his selfishness a little and lives in society by creating an artificial form (Persona) to some extent. If this does not happen, everyone's needs cannot be fulfilled. Therefore, everyone has to suppress unfettered tendencies. They have to suppress their free-spirited attitudes, look after the interests of others along with their own, cooperate with others to get their cooperation and bow before the moral values of society. Public life has now become a part of human nature.

For the development of public life, the following points should be kept in mind:

(i) Observance of Public Religion

By Dharma we do not mean any sectarian religion. In the words of Mimamsa, that which is auspicious, which gives happiness, is Dharma: **'YA AEV SHREYASKARAH SA AEVA DHARMASH ABDENOCHYATE.'** Bliss is the ultimate aim of life. Dharma is moral conduct in accordance with the country, time and society. Society is run by it. Therefore, according to Shukracharya, in society, the one who is engaged in self-religion is the one who shines: **'YO HI SVADHARMNIRATAH SA TEJASVI BHAVEDIH.'**

Truth, non-violence, justice, faith, modesty, courtesy and good character are the main public religion. These form the character of a person, form the framework of duty and ensure public welfare. In short, morality should be considered public religion. Public dignity is established by it. Immorality, shamelessness or sexuality etc. break the public order, hence they are not respected in society.

Public service helps one attain prominence in society. One who selflessly serves the public, especially the suffering, gradually becomes the **'Jana-Gana-Man-Adhinayak'**. Jesus has said that **the one who is the greatest among you shall be your servant**. There is no doubt that a great man is a servant of the people and that a servant of the people is a great man. The nature of people is such that if you serve everyone, everyone is ready to serve you.

If the person sacrifices his life for the public, then the whole society also wants to make the place of the person permanent in the world. Public service fulfills the most important desire of a person: that is to earn fame. True fame is achieved through this and according to the scholars, only the one who is famous is alive: **'KITIRYASYA SA JIVATI.'**

There are many forms of public service, such as country service, social service, literature service etc. Any creative work which is of public interest is public service. For the development of soul, one should do such work which ultimately brings fame and happiness:

TATKARMAPURUSHA: KURYAD YENANTE SUKHMEDHATE

(ii) The Value of good deeds

Respect in society is achieved only by virtue and action and thus, self-upliftment vitally important. The reason is that everything in the world is full of qualities and actions. All things are engaged in one or the other action while advertising their qualities. Man's usefulness is proved by qualities and actions. It is written in Vishnu Purana that a man without qualities lacks strength, courage etc. and a weak and disabled man is insulted by everyone:

BAL-SHAURYAARDYABHAVASHCH PURUSHANAM GUNAIYARVINA LAGHNIYAAH SAMASTASYA BAL-SHAURYA-VIVAJITAH.

Vyasa has written that a man becomes a leader in this world by his good deeds. Not from Dhan or Vidya: **'VRITTEN HI BHAVATYARYO NA DHANEN NA VIDYA.'**

Good deeds have a ripple effect. Seeing someone act with kindness can inspire others to do the same, creating a chain of reaction of positive change

(iii) The Value of Valor and Bravery

The braves have always been respected in the world. **'VEERBHOGYA VASUNDHARA'**. Shukracharya has written that the respect a man gets from his valor and bravery and not from Ancestry (Clan) **'NA KULAM PUJYATE YADRAG BAL-SHAURYA-PARAKRAMAH'**. People naturally make the brave their hero and do not care about the submissive person. Even the sages of the Vedic period, while making Indra the lord, used to say that you should not be submissive by anyone, become our leader: **'ADABDHA: SUPUR ETA BHAVA NAH'** (Rigveda)

(iv) Importance of Organization

The one who has the power to form public opinion or to organize public opinion is considered strong in the society. It is written in Durgasaptashati that power lies in unity: **'SANGHE SHAKTIH'**. With the ability to unite, a person can combine the collective powers of many in one task. With cooperation or unity, even the impossible becomes possible. To strengthen unity, ability, cleverness, trustworthiness, self-valor are required.

The power of union does not mean that a person should raise an army or establish a union. The biggest union in national life is the government, by strengthening it, the people's power becomes strong. The biggest union in personal life is the circle of friends. It should be remembered that the power of friends is a great strength of a person, which makes his life progressive.

(v) The value of Wealth and Position

Pride in society also increases with wealth and position. Money not only fulfill desires, but it fulfills the entire life also. Emptiness leads to smallness everywhere whereas fullness leads to glory, this is what the great poet Kalidas has written in Meghdoot. **'RIKTAH SARVOBHAVATI HI LAGHU: PURNATA GAURAVAYA.'** Man without; wealth, work and home is nothing. In the absence of money, man's good Deeds and Pride are ruined.

A person's status is elevated by his position and he makes his name as an authority meaningful.

5.... Refinement of Family Life

Refining of family life is also a part of self-shinning. Society is the battle-field of man's life, home or family is the camp. It is the night-shelter of the soldier tired of the battle of life. Home is the place where man's selfishness is fulfilled. It is where he is completely free and fulfills his natural desires. In society, many tendencies of man remain suppressed because there he has to live according to others. In the family, those tendencies get an opportunity to be fulfilled.

There is no doubt that for the general public, it is important to develop a family life. Happiness and prosperity of the home leads to self-prosperity, and strengthens our foundation. Therefore, becoming a successful householder is beneficial for everyone. Married life begins with marriage. Marriage is the sweetest event in human life. Two strangers become acquaintances. There is unity in public life. Man has a heartfelt desire to have something that he can call his own, something that he, and only he, can use freely. The husband gets that thing in the form of his wife and the wife gets that thing in the form of her husband. The wife is influenced by the manliness of the husband and the husband is influenced by the charm of the wife, which is natural in women. In this way, a stream of sweetness flows in the field of struggle. It affects the character and the development of the entire life.

There are many such examples which show that many men have become great men or enterprising successful businessmen with the inspiration of women. A man naturally has to prove his manliness in front of a woman. But there are instances also where many people have done great deeds for mankind after being fed up with the misbehavior of women. Kalidas became a great poet from a fool not only because of the inspiration of women but also because of their kicking. Same thing happened with Tulsi who was insulted by his wife.

It cannot be said that life develops only through marriage. The famous Indian-devotee French writer Romain Rolland was of the opinion that a married man is half-man or a fragmented man. In English, the wife is called one's better half. In this way, Poor Man becomes handicapped.

It happens. Anyway, we are not writing all this to confirm the opinion of Romain Rolland. What we mean is that an intelligent person can rise even while being independent. The opinion of foreign scholars that wives only make husbands stand in the field of work is not universally accepted. In our country, what inspiration did Ram get from Sita, Krishna from Radha and Buddha from Yashodhara, I do not know. Chanakya and Patel certainly did not get any inspiration from women. There are thousands of examples of sages and saints like this.

The truth is, married life is essential for leading a restrained and happy worldly life. For one who wants to devote his life to public service, it is not so essential. But a good family life certainly helps him. If one gets a bad-tempered wife, then self-development is a far cry, and self-destruction begins. A Sanskrit poet has said that a prostitute wife is better than a bad-mannered woman: **'VARAN VAISHYA NA PUNARVINITA KULVADHUH:'**. Family life can be either joyful or full of great disasters. One should try to make it happy, because it organizes a society which otherwise is completely devoid of self-happiness. One should keep in mind this English proverb that **a happy family is an earlier heaven.**

6.... Perfection of Personality

Developing your Virtues, Traits, Persona and complete personality is true self-shinning. Despite being a part of society or family, every person has his own independent form, an independent position, that is called his personality or belongingness. The general meaning of personality is the natural form, his appearance, health, and vibrations oozing out from a particular person. But its practical meaning is more comprehensive. Physical and natural differences are present in everyone from birth. Everyone's personality cannot be decided on this basis. Despite having differences in body and nature, those who do not have any specialty are counted among the common people. Those who increase only the number of the crowd are considered as mere parts of the society, caste or any clan. Those who are known by the name of society, caste or clan are not considered as independent personalities.

Personality is that which reveals one's independent power, self-ability, influence, superiority and extraordinariness. When there is originality and uniqueness in the personality of a particular person, then only his nature is considered different from the common people. In other words, in worldly life, the expression or uniqueness or specialty of someone's extraordinariness gives him an independent personality. In this regard, this principle of philosophy is worth keeping in mind that the greatness of a person is the reason for its being visible or expressed. Atoms and molecules remain invisible because they are minute. The same thing applies to humans as well. Someone's extraordinary greatness gives him an independent personality. By remaining insignificant, man becomes unexpressed, unknown and devoid of power and importance. The personality of the person which radiates influence, attraction, brilliance, self-confidence, virtue and positive traits, is registered in the society.

Therefore, we should know that the form in which a person is recognized by his own name, and not by the name of a particular society, caste or class, is his personality. This form is acquired by birth to some extent and is created by oneself to a great extent. Many people are endowed with special characteristics from birth itself, their appearance reflects brilliance, their behavior and thinking exude the aura of their talent and innate virtues and they appear more liberated and superior than the ordinary people.

The innate personality has a great impact on the development of the personality. Many people, despite not being exceptional by birth, make themselves great in the eyes of others by self-study, accumulation of virtues, demonstrating good Traits and refinement through good work. On the other side there are many people who despite being born sharp and influential, spoil their virtues and traits. Therefore, understand that real persona is the one which is made by you and only then it becomes permanent.

Now we discuss those things which make or break the personality.

(i) Temperament

Nature (Swabhav) is the true advertisement of the intrinsic nature of a person. It is by nature that a person becomes liked or disliked, respected or despised. Nature affects not only other people but also one's own body. It leaves its mark on, behavior, speech, body parts, gestures and surroundings. Scholars have believed this since ancient times. Apart from Indian scholars, Greek scholars also believed that the nature is reflected in the physical structure and a person's personality is formed according to it. The famous poet **Homer** was its supporter and expert. Philosopher Pandit **Socrates** also believed and gave importance to this secret. The unique western philosopher **Aristotle** has described the examination of human nature on the basis of shape, color, body parts, speech etc. in six chapters in one of his famous books. Among the later non-Aryan Brahmins, Herbert Spencer, Darwin etc. have proved its truth by scientifically analyzing this subject. Everyone is of the opinion that every emotion has a special characteristic, which is manifested on the body. And the body movements are in accordance with it. When a mood becomes permanent in the form of a nature, then its permanent symptoms are found on the body and in bodily movements.

In every situation, nature is reflected by the appearance. In this context, an incident is mentioned in ancient Greek texts. Once, a psychologist, looking at Socrates, said that he appears sensual, stupid and lazy from his appearance and characteristics. Those who listened did not believe the psychologist, but Socrates said, "What he said is true - these things were inborn in my nature. But I have cultured myself by studying Philosophy of it." The summary is that by the simplicity, cunningness or complexity of one's nature, differences can be seen in the shape and size of a person, his mutual behavior and his overall personality. Therefore, one should make his nature simple and advanced. It increases the natural attraction of the personality. Intelligence ignites his efforts. A simple nature will reveal his personality, otherwise a person may look like a racketeer. Unless his personality is simple, how will it be clear? No one cares about devious people. **Birds do not go to the salty sea to quench their thirst.**

(ii) Qualities and Character

A person gets special prominence due to his qualities and character. He becomes virtuous and respected due to his qualities. A person with good virtues and good character is influential and respected even if he is ugly, poor and of low caste. The importance of caste and lineage diminishes in front of these. Caste and lineage are certainly helpful in shaping a personality, but not to that extent. One's greatness or smallness is not proved due to caste and lineage alone. Sugar is not respected because it is the daughter of jaggery. Even if it is born from fire, Ash (Rakh) remains ash. Due to the influence of qualities and character, the low caste Vyas is respected in the society even though he was the sinful child of unmarried Matsyagandha. Sage Parashar made her a Yojanagandha (i.e. one whose body fragrance reaches up to a Yojana - Eight Miles) and gave birth to Vyas through her. Vyas raised his personality by washing away the stain of his family with his scholarship, penance and good conduct.

If you look in the ordinary public life, you will find that only the virtuous and the people with good character have respect in the society. Just as in a painting we give importance to its art and not to the combination of its colors; just as in a poem we give importance to its sentiments and not to the words; and in a flower we give importance to its natural form and fragrance and not to its shape and external beauty; similarly, in relation to a human being, we do not give importance to his physical shape but special importance is given to his Virtues, Traits, qualities and character in his persona. A prostitute may be physically beautiful, but society does not accept her personality; although she may have some qualities, she does not have character. Respect increases only when morality is present along with qualities. It is because of them that a person becomes attractive to the people. Due to the loss of morality, one becomes degenerated. Napoleon said that **even great people go astray and lose their dignity due to their character weakness.** Many people destroy themselves for women.

(iii) Work Efficiency

Being adept, skilled, expert, specialist in any subject a person's self-confidence and usefulness is expressed and his authority is acknowledged in his field of work. There is no doubt that by doing any creative work properly, a person elevates himself.

(iv) Voice-Strength

The development of the power of speech leads to great development of personality. With the mastery of speech, a man becomes a popular leader. Man's inner strength and his power of influence are manifested in it.

For self-upliftment, one should take recourse to this great means. The sign of being alive is to speak. If the voice stops, the creature is considered dead or like a dead person. The sign of being alive as a human being is to speak meaningful words; because among living beings, man is the only living being who can make his feelings meaningful by making them linguistic. Therefore, with the development of this extraordinary power of his, one must achieve excellence.

There are many forms of Voice-Strength. The most effective form is speech. Leaders control the public through their speeches. A good speech is the one that is thought-provoking, touching and serves the public interest. The purpose of a speech is not to shout loudly for a long time. Only a speech given on a plan, with patience, confidence, with evidence, even in a short form, is effective.

To become a good speaker, one should have a broad viewpoint, one should have a goal, one should express a principle and a moral opinion. In short, a speech as pithy as a photograph, told with effect, is far more heart-moving than a long lecture. There is a strange custom in some tribes of Africa. There, the speaker has to deliver the lecture standing on one leg. As soon as the raised leg falls, he has to finish his speech.

The purpose of the inventors of this custom seems to be that more pithy things should be said in the least time; the listener's time should not be wasted. The second thing is that 'if you get distracted, then you are gone.' Therefore, one should deliver the speech firmly, one should speak with a decisive mind, becoming an angel of hope, wealth and faith. If the public is foolish, then it should be driven; if it is timid, then it should be pulled by holding its hand; if it is wise, then it should be shown the way forward - it should be led; it should be warned before the crisis and pointed towards a bright future. By speaking logic and justice, public opinion is in one's favor and thus the personality of a skilled speaker rises in the eyes of the people.

Speech encompasses written forms of communication as well. So, the second use of the power of speech is in writing. With the power of writing, man becomes all powerful. With it, he can bring about revolution or peace in the country or society. People who present life literature and ideal literature in a beautiful and concise style, make a special place for themselves in the public through their creations. Their economical, familial, physical and character constraints get hidden behind their literary fame.

Bernard Shaw was ugly, but appears very handsome in his writings; his talent covers up his ugliness. There is an incident in his life that once, after the performance of one of his plays, its main character, an incomparably beautiful woman, became fascinated towards Shaw due to his literary grandeur. She said that if we get married, then the child that will be born as a result of it will be unprecedented because it will have the same unique characteristics as the father and a beautiful look just like mine. Bernard Shaw said, "Okay, but what if by chance the opposite happens, that is, if the child is ugly like me and having insufficient intellect like you, then how that child will be....? The meaning is that the power of writing increases the charm of a personality. Not only attraction, but strength also increases.

Nowadays, one big advantage of being a journalist or a TV Anchor is that public opinion is in one's hands. Everyone is afraid of a good journalist and a Reporter. Great Hero like Napoleon was also afraid of newspapers. He once said that **I am more afraid of three newspapers than one lakh bayonets.**

One can certainly reveal one's mettle by becoming a writer or a journalist or a critic. Everyone considers even a critic to be great man. Who considers a critic to be small? Even the government is suspicious of him.

One should always keep in mind in speech and conduct that truth should not be killed. Suppressing the truth reduces the effect of speech. With fearlessness, freedom of thought and alertness, the soul, intellect and mind are established in his body and speech becomes alive.

(v) Sincerity

The value of a person increases with the seriousness of thoughts, words and deeds. Lightness is shown by restlessness. It is true that a person does not mingle with everyone by being serious, but he appears more solid than others. People respect him; they think that who knows how many gems and crocodiles can be there in this deep sea!

As long as a public leader or a high-ranking official remains serious, only then his subordinates respect him. As soon as he becomes accessible to everyone, his personality melts like sugar in water. Being serious and calm is considered an extraordinary quality of rulers and public leaders. Cardinal Richelieu, a very famous politician of France, said that **for a person who rules the nation properly, it is absolutely necessary to listen more and speak less.** A famous writer has written that the most essential quality for a ruler is calmness. **Coolness is the most important quality for man destined to rule.**

Instability, intolerance and anger destroy the peace and seriousness of the mind. And the least result of anger is that the authority loses its dignity and becomes subservient to his dependents. That is why scholars are of the opinion that one should become serious when angry, because delay in expressing anger is the only sure cure for its destruction.

(vi) Supernaturalism

We have already said that a person's personality becomes extraordinary by appearing supernatural in the mundane world. That supernaturalness does not mean that one should do unnatural things. It means that a person should remain beyond the reach of the ordinary. Ordinary people are selfish; therefore, selflessness is a supernatural quality. Ordinary people are trapped in desires, therefore, to be free from desires is supernatural. To be free from temptation and attachment is supernatural. When there is no trace of ordinary human weaknesses in someone's character, only then we consider him a supernatural being and respect his personality.

There are many such incidents which show that as long as a person remains extraordinary, people worship him like a god. If he becomes corrupt by falling in love with a woman or shows any other character weakness, then people think that he is as ordinary and weak as us and belong to our category. Respect and devotion towards him end there.

Therefore, one should not make the mistake of ordinary people. While occupying a high position, one should not give anyone the opportunity to think that one is only a normal worldly being - that is, one is the same as others. For this, one has to make one's personality mysterious to some extent. One should keep a form which appears the same even after seeing it again and again, which is as impressive from a distance as it is from close. The saying 'name is big but appearance is small' **"Naam Bade Aur Darshan Chhote"** should not prove to be true. Even by keeping the personality simple, it can be made serious, clever, and mysterious. The sky is mysterious even when it is clear.

(vii) Company

Company also has an effect on personality development. In the words of Tulsi, **'SATSANG MAHIMA NAHIN GOI.'** That is, the glory of good company is not hidden. And in his words, **'KO NA KUSANGTI PAAI NASAI.'** Who is not destroyed by bad company! This effect is not only on our character, but it has an even greater effect on the development of our personality. Understand this from these lines, **'GAGAN CHADHAI RAJ PAVAN PRASANGHU.'** (Tulsi) and" **GARDE RAAH HAIN MAGAR AANDHI KE SAATH HAIN.'** (Akbar). By associating with elders, even small people become big or look like elders. There is great success in the name of elders. By merely seeing them, good inspirations arise in the heart. Man sees an ideal of life directly. Staying in contact with good men from all aspects is self-developing. Mahatma Vyas has written that the sight of great men never goes in vain, even if it happens due to hatred, ignorance, negligence or even by chance, it is beneficial like If iron touches the Philosopher's Stone (Paras Patthar) it becomes gold:

**MAHATAN DARSHANAM BRAHMAN JAYATE
NAHI NISHPHALM DVISHADJNANATO VAPI
PRASANGADDHI PRAMADTAH: AAYAS:
SPARSHSUNSPARSH RUKMTWAYAIV JAYATE**
(Mahabharata)

(viii) Self-Reliance

For the development of personality, one should always take recourse to self-reliance. Sitting around waiting for helpers stops one's progress. In this regard, Tagore's advice **'EKALA CHALO RE'** is valid. One should decide on one's duty and balance one's spiritual power and move on to a path. One should make the subject of one's interest original and devote oneself to its practice. Wherever difficulties are encountered, one should not shout 'Help, Help' but should give the test with full morale and effort. Gold becomes pure only after passing through the fire test. A diamond becomes valuable only after being cut and polished. Thinking this, one should jump into difficulties with courage. The one who overcomes the crisis is respected by the people.

(ix) Gradual Development

Personality remains permanent only when it develops gradually. Development takes place when there is a chain of success after success, when fame remains unbroken. An English thinker said that it is a punishment for being famous that a person has to keep on progressing continuously. If the sequence is broken, it is difficult to reconnect it.

Credibility, once uprooted, does not settle down again. Therefore, one should keep increasing one's influence every day. This is possible only when one does more than one says. Speech or merely saying or acting greatness does not get reliability. The great character who plays Ram in the cinema can never have the same reputation as Maryada Purushottam Ram. Only reality has value. The aim of the person who is doing self-upliftment should always be that he will show himself as authoritative, unique, exclusive and the leader of all. He should do self-advertisement by being united in his thoughts, words and actions **MANASA VACHA KARMA** and according to his ability, he should continuously endeavor to increase and accumulate Fame, wealth and health.

Summary

Man is like a clock whose operating mechanism is hidden and the working hands are outside. When both are in good condition, man progresses with time like a clock. Therefore, one should combine his Virtues, Traits, Persona, mental strength and efforts and move ahead at a constant pace.

Chapter-2

Brain, Intellect and Soul

The Brain is the main Strength of man

In the words of Atharvaveda, the brain of man is a **"HIRANYMAYA KOSH"**. That is, it is a treasure filled with gold. One clear proof of this is that a Laborer who does pure physical labor earns at most few hundred rupees in a day, but an intellectual businessman can earn lakhs and crores of rupees in the same time. Those who earn money, do earn money. The second proof is that the value of the body's bones, flesh and chemical elements can be up to tens of thousands of rupees, but a single element coming out of the human brain sometimes becomes worth crores of rupees.

The meaning of 'Hiranyamaya-kosh' is not that the brain is a tool to make a rupee. Its wider meaning is that the brain is the main asset of human life. It is the producer of all the assets and specialties of man. It is the basic foundation of his prominence. It is also said that **'SARVESHU GAATRESHU SHIRAH PRADHANAM'** - the head is the most important among all the organs. The development of brain power is considered to be the first sign of humanity.

Physically, man is a very ordinary creature. There is no such strength and action related to the body in which some animal or the other is not superior to him. How can man have the strength and sound of a lion, the size and shape of an elephant, the sight of a vulture, the power of movement of a bird, the load-bearing power of a horse or a donkey! He comes to earth physically disabled from birth, bound, crying and screaming, half-mad; without being taught, he can neither stand on his feet nor do any work. The children of animals and birds are capable from birth and self-reliant in physical activities.

Despite his disabilities, man becomes the most powerful and the most important creature only by the superiority of his mental power. After God, he is considered the most powerful. By inventing means with his brain power, he conquers the animals, takes extra power from nature and creates a new world of his own within the world. Sitting on airplanes, he travels in the sky at the combined speed of hundreds and thousands of birds. With loudspeakers, he makes such celestial voices heard that they echo from one corner of the earth to the other. Man-made machines contain the power of thousands of horses. The load of lakhs of donkeys is carried on a freight train. With telescopes, he even peers into distant planets. Those which are not visible even with them, he sees with astrology and mathematics. With his vision of knowledge, he has the ability to see everything- past, future and present. With that, he sees not only the visible, but also the invisible. Experiences and captures the infinite energy waves pervading the world.

There is a limit to physical strength, but no limit has been observed till date for mental strength. A man can run only up to a certain limit with his feet, and he can run with his body till death, but the limit to which the thoughts of the mind can run has not been determined till date. Even after the death of the body, the mind remains immersed in the centuries of the future and its thoughts remain alive for many ages.

The height to which a man can rise with the power of the mind cannot be measured. Poets, thinkers, inventors, politicians and strategists, one after the other, keep being born. Their vastness cannot even be estimated. Even a small creature keeps a vast world in a corner of its mind. Not only this, it keeps inviting the God in the form of a giant to sit in its heart. Its stomach gets filled with a kilo or two of food, its pockets and safes get filled with a few lakh rupees; but the mind cannot be filled even with all the wealth of the world and sometimes it is filled with just a few things.

In reality, brain power is limitless. Due to its limitlessness, human power is also limitless. People, in their delusion, create an imaginary limit of their capability in their minds. That is their personal limit. No limit can be set to the development of the brain, this is known from numerous evidences. It is clear from all these things that the brain of a human being is his Kalpataru (wishful tree), the shield that gives all success, the essence of importance and everything.

Just as if 'one' is taken out of a thousand, then the remaining zeros become only zero - that is, valueless. In the same way, if the brain is separated from human life, its 'unity' or importance and all humanity is destroyed. This thing can be understood properly by looking at the condition of a mad person. Despite being alive and being physically strong, such a person becomes more weak, helpless and useless than an animal. Consider the importance of mental power from one more perspective. Even if physically weak, an intelligent person is seen establishing his supremacy over millions of strong men.

The power of the brain has always won over the strength of the body. It is the brain that gives a man wealth, that is, divinity in the world. It is the symbol of man's glory not only from within, but also from outside. By raising the head, man's humanity is raised, by bowing it, his humility is diminished. Things indicating grandeur are kept on the head only - like turban, cap. Men wear the victory mark and women wear the fortune mark on the forehead. Greatness is revered everywhere.!

General introduction to the brain

Even after understanding the power of human brain, it is difficult to understand the nature of the brain itself. The truth is that no one can tell exactly what it (brain) is and how it is. In its gross form, it **is a small consciousness device secured inside the skull, which, being connected to the consciousness-chakra (Nervous System)** of the entire body, gives consciousness to the senses and obtains knowledge of subjects through them.

This is its physical form (Ang-Form). It also has an Abstract-form (Anang Form), which is more powerful and independent. Both "Ang and Anang" are synonymous with the brain. The Ang-form of the brain is the one which all anatomists know and through which all the consciousness-work of the body is done. Anang-form is full of emotions, is full of elements and is experienced, but not directly. It is bodiless but can carry emotions. How it is in that form, how big it is, no one can tell this. Therefore, only this much is known about the brain that what it does and how it does it and how it is expressed. The powers or tendencies through which its consciousness-feelings are operated, are only experienced. One more thing is experienced that the physical form of the brain itself is the bearer of its action-elements. If it gets distorted then the consciousness-power itself cannot influence the body.

Psychologists have studied the functioning of the brain and divided it into two parts. The advanced part in front is called the big brain or conscious mind and the back part is called the small brain or inner mind. Emotions, thoughts or physical functions related to cognition take place from these two. These are the centers of the nerves. In other words, these are the conscious places of the mental tendencies and sensations. These two organs are operated by the element called mind (Mun). 'Mun' is also used in the sense of mind, conscience, heart and brain. The ancient philosophers have described the emotional qualities of the heart, by which they usually mean the brain. This fact has been proved with logic by the late scholar Mahamahopadhyaya Dr. Gananath Sen in his famous book **'PRATYAKSHA SHARIR'**. Therefore, we should consider the mind as the functioning element of the brain. We should know something about both its parts.

The conscious mind

It is the source of knowledge and thought. This is the part that imagines, contemplates, thinks, analyses and discerns. Man has complete control over this part. It can be made especially active, sharp and enlightened with education, practice, knowledge, exercise and nutritious elements. It can be focused and controlled as per the wish. Knowledge and complete humanity develop with the development of this part. It is the creator of man's future or destiny. That is why people say that man's fate is written on the forehead. Apart from being experienced, it is also a thinker and inventor.

The conscious mind is naturally free, restless and swift. No other thing in the world is so willful and swift. It runs to heaven and in a moment, even if the body is lying on the bed, the mind can reach someone's closed bedroom at a distance of a thousand or two thousand miles. There is no obstruction to its coming and going; it moves on its own chariot, which is called Manorath. This quote of Tulsi, said about Brahma, is also true in this case –

**PAG BINU CHALE, SUNE BINU KANA,
KAR BINU KARM KARE VIDHI NANA -** (Manas)
He walks without feet and hears without ears. Without hands, he does many types of work.

This mind sometimes gets lost, sometimes gets stolen, sometimes gets burnt to ashes, sometimes swells up, sometimes becomes small and sometimes drowns by getting engrossed in some pleasure. Sometimes it gets hurt by mere sarcasm, sometimes by mere words, and sometimes it listens to abuses with love- like in marriage. Whatever it gets involved in, becomes charming for man, no matter how ugly it is. Wherever it breaks away, the connection of life breaks there. This description of the conscious mind is not poetic but real. When this mind eats the Modak (Laddoo, sweet) saliva drips from the mouth involuntarily. In this state of mental misconduct, the senses become restless without any reason. The body becomes heated due to imagined anger. Imagination born in conscious mind affects not only the body but the entire life.

In short, it should be understood that the field of conscious mind is very fertile. Ideas are created in it every moment. It does not only acquire objects with the help of senses, but also works independently. When it is engaged in some work, it thinks about that only, but when it is not working, it naturally starts running outside and it should be understood that the involvement of conscious mind in some work means the involvement of the entire physical strength in that work, because it is the consciousness of the body.

The Inner mind (Subconscious Mind)

The inner mind or Subconscious mind, is the storehouse of knowledge of the conscious mind. In physical Form, it is spherical in shape and when cut, small pieces like the pages of a book are found in it. This part does not have the fibers of knowledge and thought. Like the conscious mind, it is neither independent nor connected to the external world. Whatever is experienced by the conscious mind from outside, it remains stored here in the form of memory. Everything seen, heard or thought sits here and is combined with the thoughts as per their requirement. By seeing, hearing or thinking the same thing again and again, its deep impression is left on this mind and when the time comes, the conscious mind immediately recognizes the person according to those shapes, sounds etc. It usually happens that on seeing someone, you recognize him, but his name, place of previous acquaintance do not come to mind. Many things remain in the mind, but they are not remembered properly or do not come to the tongue. The reason for this is that their impression is not deep on the inner mind, but it is definitely there. What happens is that many things settle in the inner mind and then get lost. Sometimes they appear spontaneously and sometimes they are entangled with many other things.

The main reason for the strange scenes sometimes seen in dreams is that the sequence of events imagined, read or witnessed in a person's inner mind get entangled and appear in a strange form. These dreams reveal the inner state of the person. It is known from dreams what kind of thoughts the conscious mind is filling its house with. And what is the inner state of the person.

The Inner Self-Conscience

The inner self is not only the protector or holder of thoughts, it is also their director and producer. The desires and tendencies of life arise here and they silently influence the thinking of the conscious mind. Innumerable tendencies of the mind, feelings, lusts, which are in the form of nature, keep sleeping in this section. Feelings and bad feelings such as hope, faith, pride, faith-devotion, love, fear, greed, anger and attachment etc. arise here. Inner self is the father of all perceptions. These desires or feelings have a strong influence on thoughts. If there is a ghost in the mind, a ghost is seen even in a bush, if there is lust in the nature, any Sita-Like woman can be taken as hooker and if there is good will, the shadow of a sister is seen even in a prostitute.

If there is a feeling of deceit in the inner mind, then the imaginative mind makes the person sit with a garland in his hand and wishes for donations. If there is remorse in it, then the thinking mind thinks of suicide. If there is detachment in him, then the person considers wealth worth lakhs and crores as worthless. Actually, our external viewpoint is formed according to the feeling in our inner heart.

One person sees the reflection of God in the idol of a temple, another person considers the same to be a lifeless piece of stone. Why? - Because the first person has the feeling of God in his heart, according to which he sees his reflection in the stone idol. Gods do not live in stones; they live in the heart. The other person does not have that feeling in his heart, so how will he see God outside! One person looks at someone with utmost respect and reverence. Whereas the other person looks at him with hatred and contempt, the reason for this is also the same- the feeling of hatred or excessive respect arises according to the resolutions of the mind: **'PRADVAESHHO BAHUMANO VA SANKALPAADU- PAJAYATE.'** - (Swapnavasavadatta). In the words of Tulsi: As is the feeling of the person, so is the image of the Lord seen by him. **Jaki Rahi Bhavna Jaisi, Prabhui Murat Dekhi Tinha Taisi** (Manas)

A western thinker has also written that we see an object not in its true form but in the form in which we ourselves are (**We see things not as they are but as we are**) It has also been said in English that "**Beauty lies in the eye of the beholder**". It is a universally experienced truth that it is our inner self which makes our thoughts interesting or dull, hopeful or hopeless, in which our natural and acquired qualities get accumulated and form our perspective. It is the basis of our entire character and personality. It is our resource area.

In this context, it should be remembered that the inner conscience is not in contact with the external world. It contains some innate tendencies of man, which inspire the conscious mind. Both good and bad feelings reside in it. In every person, one of these is dominant.

Man cannot nurture or eliminate them voluntarily. If there are bad feelings, they cannot be easily cleansed from the heart. There is only one way to eradicate them. If we think good thoughts through the conscious mind for a long time, then good thoughts of the inner conscience will be nurtured. When they become strong, the bad tendencies are suppressed. The inner conscience is cultured by thinking about welfare, by practicing good qualities and by education. By any other means, good qualities cannot be created in the inner self.

If the opposite is done, then gradually bad feelings develop inside; man becomes addicted, lustful and prone to bad habits. In essence, it should be understood that our habits, our nature, our state of mind, mood are formed by good thoughts and bad thoughts, by good deeds and bad deeds respectively, and then our entire life is formed accordingly. When our nature or state of mind is evil, our thoughts become weak and our senses become immoral. If a man is tainted by his mind, then all his efforts become futile.

The writers of Upanishads have rightly written that the mind is the reason for the bondage and liberation of man: **'MUN EVA MANUSHYAANAAM KARANAM BANDHAMOKSHYOH'**. By concentrating on their mind, some become more capable and independent by accumulating morale and some become bound by the slavery of their habits. Once something becomes a nature, it changes with difficulty, so it is important to remember. The saying: - **"SVABHAAVO DURATIKRAMAAH"**.

There are a few other things worth knowing about the inner self-Conscience:

1. The natural actions of the body parts are directed by the inner mind. As soon as any thought comes to the mind, this mind immediately controls the body parts. Whatever bad thoughts arise or awake in it, their effect is seen in the physical actions and facial expressions.

2. The emotional part of everyone's brain is stronger than the consciousness part. All may not be thinkers but they are definitely emotional to some extent. Everyone has some natural emotions, so heart-touching or poignant things have a greater impact. By stirring the emotions, one's ideology moves in their favor, but in the field of pure knowledge, the display of emotions is like the moon at sunrise. Both have different occasions. Where the use of knowledge is fruitless, there the awareness of emotions works.

3.   Two inner tendencies are dominant in all - one is economic and the other is psychological. The first includes hunger or livelihood related instincts; the second includes love, prestige, feelings of achievement etc. These cannot be uprooted by the force of thoughts. Therefore, thoughts have to be molded in such a way that hunger and pride etc. can be satisfied.

4.   The first blow of excessive excitement of thoughts or feelings falls on the inner mind. It becomes weak. When this memory organ becomes weak, the intellect is destroyed; because if the supporting organ itself is weak, where will the thoughts stay, how will the chain of thoughts be formed! The memory of mad people is destroyed first. In anger also, memory is destroyed first, due to which a person cannot recognize good and bad and does senseless things. The main reason for the difference seen in the personality of many people is their weak memory. Due to the slackness or inactivity of thoughts or feelings, the brain becomes inert. Therefore, the program of the small and big mind can remain correct only when there is mutual exchange between the two. Man progresses when his thoughts rule over his emotions. Therefore, success is achieved by considering the conscious mind as the husband of the house and the inner mind as the mistress of the house and keeping them within their limits.

Intelligence & Intellect-Main matters of Brain

On the basis of the functioning of the brain, its general introduction has been given above and it has also been indicated that its operator is the element called mind.

Apart from this, there are other parts of the brain, which are called Intelligence and intellect. Intelligence is the ability to understand, reason, and solve problems, while intellect is the ability to think and reason logically and rationally. Both are the elements that illuminate the mind. They remain connected with the mind. The functions related to knowledge, discretion and memory, mentioned above, are done only with the help of Intelligence & intellect. Or you can say that with the help of the mental parts, the intellect and Intelligence do imagination, contemplation etc. We are describing the Intelligence and intellect together and interchangeable to express some of their characteristics.

Intelligence is the main power of the brain, most of which is available to everyone from birth. It also has one special form, which is available to very few: Talent. Talent is considered to be that intelligence which has the ability to create original ideas. Such extraordinary intellectual power is given to extraordinary people by birth, and is not created by making them. By using the intellect, any person can become intelligent and by studying and practicing; but not everyone can become talented.

According to the Nyaya Shastra, there are two types of ordinary intelligence – Anubhuti (experience) and Memory(smriti). Their description has already been given under consciousness and inner mind. According to its use, the writers of scriptures have made some more types of it. It is necessary to know their brief introduction also. This type of intelligence is called Attached Intelligence. It gets attached to a subject and then thinks about it with selfishness. Therefore, it forgets its main virtue – justice or discretion and is unable to describe the true form of the subject. The best intelligence is detached, which describes a thing in a just manner. The difference between the knowledgeable and the ignorant is made on the basis of attached intelligence and detached intelligence.

The intelligence, which is full of illusions, is dirty and is riddled with dilemmas is always doubtful. The intelligence of the people with less knowledge, criminals and fickle nature is doubtful and therefore unstable. The other type of intelligence which is decisive, is stable, serious, clean and illuminated by knowledge.

Similarly, many types of intelligence are made on the basis of its proper use, misuse and non-use. Insightfulness, sharpness, foresight, meticulousness, quick wit etc. are considered its special qualities whereas procrastination, inertia, fascination etc. are self-destructive defects. Simplicity, clarity of thoughts, expression of feelings in a systematic manner, eloquence, activity, concentration and result-orientedness - these are the qualities of a good intelligence. The intelligence which is active, thinks with a purpose which inspires a person to put his thoughts into action is called special intelligence. The worst intelligence is that which is slow and timid like a jackal. Such people with low intelligence or lack of intelligence are called slow-witted and jackal-witted respectively.

Importance of intelligence & Intellect

For fear of going into unnecessary expansion, we have given a general description of intelligence above. Regarding its proper use, we should first say that humanity is established only by the usefulness of intelligence.

Whatever we have written about the importance of brain power in the beginning of this chapter is actually a description of the superiority of brain power. Being an intellect-dominated creature, man is the most important creature. It is rightly said in Hitopadesha that the one who has intelligence is powerful: **'BUDDHIRYASYA BALAM TASYA'**. In the human world, we see clearly that only those who are intelligent are independent, prosperous and powerful. Due to intellectual freedom, a man remains free even in a prison. Gandhiji was completely independent even at that time when the whole country was under foreign rule, because he was independent in intelligence. Gandhiji was extremely powerful even though he was unarmed and who does not know that that feeble man stood alone and with only his intelligence, drove away the conquering British across the seven seas! See in your ordinary life – there is no difference in the physical actions of an intelligent person and a fool in the execution of any task, there is only a difference of intelligence, due to which the task of an intelligent person is successful and that of a fool is unsuccessful:

PRAGYASYA MURKHSYA CH KARYYA YOGE SAMATVAMBHYETI TANURNA BUDDHIH. Despite working harder than the intelligent person, the fool does not succeed just because he is not efficient but due to his lack of intelligence and slavery to his thoughts, he remains dependent on the intelligent people. It is written in Hitopadesha that the intelligent people make a living from the unintelligent ones: **'VIDUSHAAM JEEVANAM MURKAHA:'**

Consider the usefulness of intelligence from one more angle- Time. which is same for everyone, but the intelligent person makes it his Kamadhenu and uses it as his milk. Whereas a fool wastes it. When time passes away from a person's hands and his intelligence slips away like an arrow, then he becomes conscious and runs after the lost opportunity in a confused state. That condition is hell. An English thinker has written that the **"Hell is the opportunity missed and truth seen too late."**

To escape from this hell, it is necessary to use the intellect at the right time. Vyas's Saraswati, sitting on Vidur's tongue, has rightly said that the grace of the gods is manifested through good intellect. Gods do not protect anyone with a stick like a shepherd; they equip the person they want to protect with the power of intellect.
NA DEVA DANDAMADAYA RAKSHANTI PASHUPALVAT, YENTU RAKSHITUMICHHANTI BUDHHYA SAVIBHAJANTI TAM- (Mahabharat)

On the contrary, misuse of intellect leads to the destruction of man's humanity: **'VINASHAKALE VIPRITBUDDHIH'**. The direct natural proof of this is that when the time of death approaches, man's intellect suddenly changes or becomes opposite and he becomes incapable of recognizing his good and bad. This quote of Tulsi is worth mentioning:
JA KAHAN PRABHU DAROON DUKH DEHI, TAKAI MATI PAHLEHI HAR LEHI. (Manas)

From whichever angle we look at it, it appears true that the reason for the rise and fall of man is his intelligence. Intellectual development leads to the development of human power and its decline leads to the destruction of power. Not only this, misuse of intelligence leads to misuse of humanity. Intelligence is such an influential power that when it becomes crooked, it ruins not only itself but many others. They cause total destruction. Therefore, their use requires as much caution as the use of a gun or pistol.

What is the right use of the intellect? - According to Valmiki, these are its qualities, from which its use can be ascertained: desire to listen, listening, receiving, grasping, deciding the principle by reasoning, science and philosophy.
'SUSHRUSHRVANCHAIV GRUHNAM DHARANAM TATHA UHOAPOHOARTHVIGYANAM TATWA GYANAM CH SHRIGUNA: (Ramayana)

Everything has been covered in essence in above, but it should be discussed in detail. The main function of the intellect is to find the truth and to reveal it. It is its special duty to know the secrets of life and the secrets of nature. It is a lamp with which the mind sees its way in the deep darkness. The intellect can lead life, only when it is adept at seeing the truth.

With the eye of intellect, an intelligent being first sees the truth of life, which is called self-knowledge. He recognizes himself, sees his inner powers, understands his natural tendencies and grasps his most important basic tendencies. He sees where his brain is naturally inclined. He sees how strong his animal instincts are and thinks of a way to get rid of them through self-control. He achieves self-knowledge, through intellect, and self-knowledge is the ultimate knowledge, this is the opinion of ancient scholars: **'ATMAGYANAM PARAM GYANAM'**. Western philosophers also consider self-knowledge as the basic principle of philosophy and say that one should recognize oneself. **Know thyself.** This knowledge is easily available through the use of intellect. Apart from self-knowledge, it is the duty of intellect to recognize others. Only after recognizing oneself and others, man can decide his duty. Thus, the function of intelligence is to know what is right and wrong, what is just and unjust and to understand the truth and purpose of life and then develop it.

The second main use of intelligence is to understand the truth of Nature or Creation (Srishti) and make human life in accordance with it. What is the truth of Srishti? It is written in 'Shatapath Brahman' that this whole universe is a Verse (Chhand): **'CHHANDAANSI VAI VISHWA ROOPAANI'**. Chhand is that movement of sound which dances in rhythm. Just as in a rhythmic composition, many words combine at their places to express a feeling. Similarly, all the means of this creation of the universe, despite being separate and fighting with each other, seem to be striving for the fulfillment of a single purpose.

Just as a poet combines words at their places and gives them the form of poetry, similarly all the natural forces have been combined in a sequence by a **'poet'**, only then the work of Creation runs according to cosmic rules. Just as the talent of the poet is behind the poem and the art of the painter is behind a painting, behind the creation of the universe, the creative intelligence and existence of a skilled Creator is felt. According to his sentiments or plans, all sentient beings purposefully move within their limits, according to their own fixed Dharma and due to this system, the entire universe keeps moving at a regular pace.

Its emotional artist or regulator is called by names like Ishwar, Parmatma, God, Allah, Waheguru etc. This is the biggest truth of worldly life, which can be understood only by the intellect. On the basis of this truth, the entire outline of human life is made, the character of man is formed and a limit of humanity is set. Man understands that he is not alone in the world, he also has a companion who inspires him. He considers him the guide of life and the evening of life and moves forward patiently. And the most important thing is that on the basis of this truth-belief, the morality of human life has prestige, through which success is achieved in life. The unity in diversity that is seen in society is due to the prevalence of this moral aspect of life.

There is a very important essence of public life, Wisdom is required to understand it. In the words of the Upanishads, it is this: **'Anand (divine bliss) is the only flow'**, knowing this, all beings are born from Anand. When born, they live for Anand (bliss) and on death they merge in Anand.' **ANANDO BRAHMATE, VYAJAANAT, ANANDADHVYEVA KHALV- IMANI, BHOOTANI JAYANTE, ANANDEN JATANI JIVANTI, ANANDAM PRAYANTYA BHISAMVISHANTITI**

It is necessary to know this because every living being desires the happiness and comforts, The world can be blissful only when everyone behaves according to the rules of creation. This fact can be understood only by intelligence.

In short, it should be understood that the wandering tendencies of the mind are stopped by the intellect, i.e. the mind is concentrated, that is called yoga. (1) By suppressing the bad tendencies, (2) mental powers are stimulated, (3) the essence of life is understood and by (4) accumulating knowledge from outside as per the need, all four are created. According to Socrates, **knowledge is Virtue.**, According to western philosophy, **knowledge is power**. According to Indian philosophy, the work done with knowledge is the main power. Practical knowledge is the real wealth of the intellect.

In the words of the great poet Goethe, "**To put one's thoughts into action is the most difficult thing in the world**". converting thoughts into action is the most difficult task in the world. Therefore, the work of the intellect is not only to acquire knowledge, but also to use it; and to use it in such a way that it brings dignity to human character. Gandhiji has written that **knowledge without good character is a destructive force,** as is evident from the example of the majority of the world's accomplished thieves and cunning bad-hearted people. For character, the intellect has to take refuge in its soul rather than outside.

Soul

Before ending this description of the mental elements, it is necessary to write something about the soul as it is the life-giving element and according to philosophers, it is from it that the 'mahat' (intelligence and intellect) of one's nature is generated, which leads to the development of humanity. Many people do not believe in the existence of the soul and consider the material aspect of life to be everything. They do not give as much importance to the spiritual power as to the 'power of the atom'. Although in this very age Gandhiji has proved that the spiritual power is the main power in the world. Those who do not believe in the existence of the soul, they believe more in their inertia than in their consciousness.

What better proof can there be of the existence of the soul than the fact that it is the element with whose association the earthly body acquires consciousness and with whose separation the earthly body again merges into the earth. Even after death the body remains the same, but there it lacks some **unknown element** in it due to which it becomes lifeless. The second direct proof is that every person, whether he is in trouble, seriously ill or an innocent child, is afraid of death and tries to save himself. Even frail old people want to avoid the agony of death till the last moment of their life, although everyone believes that death ends the physical suffering. The reason for this natural fear is that although no man experiences the pain of the death, but there is some element in the body which is familiar with that terrible pain and is afraid of experiencing it again. That element or thing is the **soul.**

The object cannot be the intellect because the difference between the intellect and the soul is not only felt but also directly proved. In madness, the intellect is completely destroyed, yet the body remains alive. In the Yoga state of Manolaya, unconsciousness in yoga, all mental activities are suspended, but the person remains alive. This gives an idea of that extra power.

Sometimes a person feels remorseful for committing an immoral act and sometimes, when he is alone and does something wrong, he feels afraid of himself. These things prove the existence of the soul. These cannot be intellectual activities because the act is done with the cooperation of the intellect and the criminal cannot become the judge himself. There is someone else whom both the mind and the intellect fear. And when the mind starts becoming unruly, the cautious intellect warns it that there is an outside observer peeping inside. Man feels that there is a watcher inside, a witness. A spy of God is with everyone. Even the biggest tyrant becomes weak from within while torturing an innocent person; because that ambassador of God does not cooperate in immoral acts. In moral acts, the soul power naturally increases because the radiance of the great power that keeps the whole-body sharp throughout life is manifested. This is the same light that Mahatma Gandhi used to search for within himself. We get a glimpse of that radiant element through our own experience. Like a tree without a seed, a life without a soul cannot be imagined.

Nature of Soul

Even if we accept the existence of the soul, it is difficult to decide its nature correctly. Whatever its nature, it is certain that it is supremely conscious, blissful, radiant, knowledgeable, unchangeable and indestructible. These variations are experienced by the strength of the soul. The ideals and objectives of human life appear to be based on these Virtues. If these things were not present in the soul, then how would they be present in nature and thoughts! Seeing the divine activities in nature, man imagines the same qualities in God.

With self-control, he experiences special consciousness, joy, intelligence, knowledge, wisdom and immortality within himself. Certainly, this is the form of the soul which is the soul of all beings**, Brahma**. That is why the scripture writers decided that the soul itself is Brahma or the soul is the form of the Supreme Being, or in the words of the great poet Tulsidas, **'God's part, the**

indestructible soul' "Ishwar Ansh Jeev Avinashi". It is the doer, who gives birth to character, nature, duty and curiosity. He is the knower of the field, who sows emotions in the fields of different individuals.

The soul is Brahmamayi, this should be understood from a couple of other proofs as well. It is written in the Vedas that in the beginning there was only Brahma, he resolved that I should become many from one. After the resolve, he started the creation of the universe and merged himself in it. Instead of arguing whether God really made such a resolve or not, its truth should be seen in this form that one soul is present in all beings, only then all the powers are working in unison. Without resolve or plan, God would have fallen and shattered like this. He would have done self-development by strengthening the feeling of **'EKOHAM BAHU SYAM'**.

If we look carefully, this feeling of becoming many from one is also visible in human nature. Through work, sympathy, and by gaining prestige, man wants to expand himself and we see clearly that the more a person expands himself, the more prosperous he becomes. World poet **Rabindra has rightly written that 'the more people in the country and time a man is able to see and manifest himself in, the greater is he.'** -The divine spirit of Self-Development resides in the heart of every human being.

The second thing is that even the most ordinary creature is ambitious. He wants to be the lord, wants to be authoritative and prosperous. By earning money and fame, man wants to achieve godliness over others; the one who is not successful outside, wants to remain the lord of his wife and children at home; the one who is unable to gain control over anyone, finds self-satisfaction by showing his dominance over the animals of the house. This public aspiration of becoming the lord comes in the heart of the person from some part of the God. Along with this, it should also be understood that everyone is a lover of rights by nature, that is why no one can gain sympathy by snatching someone's right.

Another strange quality of God is embedded in the human psyche. It is that prosperity is achieved not by accumulating power or wealth but by distributing them. God has spread his glory in nature, this is how we get a sense of his divinity. If you look at human society, you will find the same thing. The one who can give to others - whether it is power or wealth or position - and the one who can sacrifice for others, people by nature, (not by intelligence) consider him great or powerful. It is seen that wealth or power is attained only through service, sacrifice and charity. In view of this, this statement of God in Skanda Purana can be understood correctly: **'DADAAMI CHA SADAISHWARYAAMISWARASTEN KIRTITAH'**. That is, I always give wealth, that is why I am considered God.

Kubera is called the lord of wealth, but no one worships him in the world. "Lakshmi" is worshipped everywhere; there are festivals for her worship, there are idols of her and devotion is found towards her among the devotees. The reason is that Lakshmi is famous for making others prosperous; she does not hoard like Kubera. The power that holds this tendency is the soul itself, which is the form of Brahma. The human soul rebels against the one who does not give wealth. This very tendency of the people brought down those Indian kings who, instead of giving wealth to others, snatched their wealth, they themselves wanted to remain wealthy. Their godliness was artificial and hence intolerable. They had taken the title of God but never tried to become many from one, that is, establish democracy and make themselves omnipresent among the people.

Brahma and the soul are of the same nature. There is another strong proof of this. From a worldly point of view, man does not love anyone more than himself; he is selfish and most of his works are done with the motivation of selfishness, but his entire world is not built on selfishness. There is another strong feeling within man, which suppresses selfishness. If this feeling is strong, then man gladly sacrifices even that life for which he accumulates selfishness and for the protection of which he is ready to sacrifice everything. That is a moral feeling.

Man does not have any attachment to life for the protection of his ideals. He is seen happily sacrificing himself for the love of country, caste, religion and his soul gets inspired only when the question of protecting moral life and the honor of humanity arises. In that condition, he forgets himself for the service of the people. Only then it becomes apparent that man lives not only for himself but also for others. He wants to leave his name and status in the society - whether the body remains or not, this feeling of following the ideals and the desire for immortality itself shows that the soul has the burning fire of God. And it seems true that God has made man like himself, has given him a creative and ambitious mind like himself. It is through the soul that these divine elements come into the body.

Some characteristics of the soul

There is no doubt that man gets access to divine element in the form of soul. It is the soul that sows the seeds of knowledge, consciousness and all the basic instincts in the physical body, there can be no doubt about this also. Soul is very powerful. It is very beautiful, who will not accept it! It is foolish to not accept the power and authority of the one who has the capacity to give life and take life. Whatever be its form, it is certain that it is Brahmamayi. Keeping these things in mind, we should also understand some other things related to the soul.

Rebirth

Reincarnation is the fundamental principle of Hindu philosophy. It not only proves the existence of the soul, but also solves many puzzles of life. Many of the peculiarities of life are not understood by the great western psychologists of today; where the intellect is unable to understand cause and effect, they take refuge in nature and get rid of them. The principle of reincarnation answers all questions.

Briefly, this is the explanation of reincarnation. The soul present in the body does not get destroyed with the destruction of the Body. It leaves one body and enters another body. While living in one body, it remains detached. After the destruction of the body, it enters another body carrying the acquired deeds of that life. Those deeds are called Karmas and Sanskar. This action is like the wind going to another Garden or place carrying the fragrance of one Garden.

To understand this mystery, pay attention to the birth and death of a human being. Sexual arousal occurs due to the stimulation of Nervous System in the brain of a man, the fire of lust is lit. With the force of the life-air inspired by the fire of lust, the energy of the body in the form of sperm grows and moves and is combined with the female menstrual fluid. In that life-air, due to whose inspiration the energy of the body moves, the soul is absorbed from outside and goes with the sperm. It is absorbed in the same way as smell in the air. In this way, the foundation of a new body is laid by the union of the soul with the semen-sperm.

There is evidence that the soul of a child is not the soul of his father. If there was only one soul, then the behavior, thoughts, looks and appearance of both would have been similar. But this is not the case. Two sons of the same parents have different natures - some are intelligent and pleasure-loving; some are stupid or fools. Many have such interests which their ancestors do not have even a trace. Some are born with an interest in literature and some in creating stories. All this shows the difference between the soul of the child and the soul of the father and also shows that every soul brings different birth-related Sanskars. That is why there is difference in interests and difference in intelligence among people. There are many examples of this that many children tell stories of their previous births when they become adults and after investigation what they tell is found to be true. Therefore, it has to be believed that the soul of a son is a completely independent soul, not a borrowed one.

Yes, it must be accepted that the soul enters the new life carrying not only the Sanskars of its previous life but also the Sanskars of parents. As it passes through the life path of the father, it must be influenced by his environment. Apart from this, sperms also carry the Kulaj (Clan's) tendency, which affects the soul. Due to the body staying in the womb of the mother for nine months, the soul is mainly influenced by the Sanskars and thoughts of the mother. The effect of those Sanskars is so much that the parents naturally feel pain due to the son's pain. That pain is not felt by the body, but by the soul. The physical pain of one does not cause physical pain to the other. It is because of this affinity that it is said **'AATMA VAI JAYTE PUTRA:'**. This affinity does not arise due to Sanskars or due to the soul being of the same religion. The soul is bound to behave according to the nature of the body in which it goes. The nature of the body of the child is influenced by the nature of father and Mother.

The body structure is influenced by their organs. According to **Sushrut**, (An ancient Surgeon from Kashi. 700 BCE) the fixed elements of the body, i.e. hair, moustache, hair, bone, nails, teeth, head, artery, nerves and skull are paternal and the soft elements, i.e. flesh, blood, fat-marrow, heart, navel, liver, spleen and intestines are maternal. (He considered nourishment, strength, complexion, health, ill health as being generated by menstruation and senses, knowledge, science, longevity, happiness and sorrow as being generated by the sperms.) This structure affects the soul and mainly the blood has a strong attraction. The body is formed from the blood essence of menstruation and semen; hence there is a natural unity in blood having similar qualities. Many traditional diseases prove the truth of blood relation. The effect of the strength of blood relation on the soul is often visible in other births also. This is the reason why some people have natural love for someone: **'PREETI PURTANA LAKHAI NA KOI'** (Tulsi).

How do the Sanskars of life affect the soul? The answer is this – the symptoms of any thought or action are immediately visible on our body parts. Daily character has the same effect on the soul. The way virtues and vices affect the body, the same way they affect the soul. Just as the result of today's actions is seen tomorrow or after ten years, or the result of mistakes of youth has to be borne in old age, similarly the result of the qualities or actions attached to the soul has to be borne in one life or after that. This tradition of qualities continues even after the death of the body. When we get the good result of the previous life or this birth in the future, then we call it the rise of virtue or Karma or luck.

An intelligent person develops those qualities further after getting a glimpse of them. The disorders of the previous or this life keep the fire of the soul covered with smoke. Then the light of the soul does not spread and those disorders burst out like boils in time. We call that condition sin or misfortune. A foolish person breathes in the same smoke.

The clever person recognizes those bad Sanskars and frees his soul from them. A thief becomes a pure soul through penance and self-restraint. The secret of accidental events, grave sins and virtues is revealed through the principles of the soul's rebirth. And it is also known why many people seem talented, extraordinary, lucky or simple by nature and why others are slow, irritable or thieves.

This is the effect of Sanskars. Just as the air of a bower comes spreading the fragrance of flowers and the air of a crematorium comes with the smell of dead bodies, similarly the soul keeps expanding the qualities of the previous life. If there was no effect of Sanskars, all children would have been equally intelligent. One Guru teaches fifty disciples, but the development of all is not the same, because the effect of Sanskars is different.

We have given this introduction of Sanskars so that the reader knows that luck and bad luck are not divine events. Sanskars are not permanent qualities of the soul, they can be changed, or if they are not strong, they can be made stronger. Consider the soul to be an object like mercury. Mercury also remains pure, but many defects are attached to it. A capable Vaidya (Aurvedic Doctor) makes that mercury pure and beneficial by purifying and modifying it. A capable person can also purify the soul in the same way and make it useful and take benefit from it as per his wish.

Religion of Soul

The soul does not operate the senses on its own while living in the body. Most of its instincts remain in a state of unconsciousness. They are awakened through the intellect. When the intellect is united with the soul, only then does it get the energy or inspiration of the soul. When the soul is aroused in great adversity or by Sadhna (Meditation), it takes additional power from its Mahatattva

(Divine Energy) and becomes more powerful. It easily runs towards its homogeneous element for sympathy. The clear proof of this is that at the time of birth of a child, when a woman suffers unbearable pain and her mind and intellect become restless, then the soul of the woman calls out to her parents or to Ram (God). She does not pray to her husband or doctor for relief from her troubles. That is why the call of the pure soul is heard in times of sin and pain.

The second main duty of the soul is that it awakens the feeling of brotherhood, truth and non-violence in living beings. It inspires that all are fruits of the same tree. It awakens unity. It creates the feeling of **'VASUDHAIVA KUTUMBAKAM'** (Whole world is like a family) and **'ATMAVAT SARVABHUTESHU'** (All creatures are like our soul). By understanding this essence, people make even strangers their own, and tame even violent animals. Those who do not recognize this essence, they make even their family members strangers by false behavior and cruelty.

Purity of conduct strengthens the soul

The third characteristic of the soul is that it is certainly becomes more radiant by celibacy, physical purity and good thoughts. The secret of the natural simplicity, purity and sincerity found in children is that till that age their conduct remains pure, the soul is aglow and the mind and intellect are not so strong that they can stop its natural aura. The innocence of children shows their pure Soul.

These are some important points about the soul. There is no doubt that it has great power, but it does not move like a lorry, spreading dust of blessings. It gives blessings only when asked for and that too only when the one asking to its Atmajaa (daughter) wisdom. Just as gems are not found on mountains but in the depths of the ocean, similarly the gem of the life is found in the depth of inner self i.e. Soul.

Summary

1...... Man is not as ordinary as he mistakenly thinks himself to be. Innumerable supernatural powers surround us all the time. By combining those powers, man can become very powerful, this is proved by the extraordinary characters of many great men. There is a very famous proverb in English, which means that man is more powerful than he thinks. **Man is stronger than he knows.** The limitlessness of his mental power proves its truth.

2. ...... Where there is a gathering of so many powers, if there is no proper administration, unity and order, then there can be a 'Hindu-Muslim riot'. For that, self-control is required. This is possible only when the intellect, guided in the light of the soul, works with cleverness. The intellect-power with the soul is called Dev-power (Divine Energy) and success can be achieved only when Dev-Bal and Man-efforts (**purusharth**) remain together. In the absence of Purusharth, Dev-power is wasted and the mind becomes frightened due to uselessness. Similarly, Purusharth is fruitless without Dev-power.

3....... Being an intellect-oriented creature, it is the first duty of man to develop his brain. That development takes place by acquiring knowledge. It should be remembered that knowledge has no limit or age. One's age does not measure his mental age. Sometimes a man becomes thirty-forty years old physically, but his brain remains in the same state as it would have been at the age of ten-twelve years. That is called 'immature brain' **Undeveloped mind**. Often, at a young age, the brain of some people grows more than the proportion of their physical age. Due to the increase or decrease in the brain, people behave accordingly. Anyway, these are natural differences. Here, what we mean to say is that even at a young age, a man can be knowledgeable, as according to Rama, Bharat was: **'GYAN VRIDDHA VAYO BAALH:'**. Kalidas has also written that the Age of a Vibrant person is not considered: **'TEJASAN HI NA VAYAH: SAMIKSHYATE'**

There is a small story in Buddhist scriptures in this regard: There was a poor boy named **Jeevak**, who had to suffer a lot in his childhood. Once he fell ill, he could not even get himself treated due to lack of money. He thought that there would be lakhs of poor people suffering like this. Therefore, with the resolve to free people, he went to Takshila and studied medicine for four years and after passing from there, he started travelling around the world. In Ayodhya, he met a widow who had been suffering from a terrible disorder of the head (Migraine) for years. When Jeevak went to treat her, the old woman said that you are still a child, what will you do; even the elders and experienced Vaidyas (Aayurvedic Doctors) could not treat my disease. To this the young man replied that **'science is neither a child nor an old man.'** He cured her disease. Once when Buddha fell ill and other doctors could not treat him, his most loved disciple Anand called him after hearing about the fame of this young man. The son of a poor man,

Jeevak, achieved the honour of being the destroyer of the diseases of **Bhava-Desteroyer.** From this story and hundreds of examples of our own time, we can understand that knowledge has no age.

KARAT-KARAT ABHYAS KE JADMAT HOTH SUJAN
By practicing continuously, even the stupid becomes intelligent

The gist of it is this- like the ocean in a pitcher, the brain is the universe filled in a small skull. In a way, the temple of the great boon-giver Shiva is built on our body right from birth. Dedicated effort (Sadhana) is the only means to acquire a boon. By practicing with determination, the Brain and Intellect can be made sharp and knowledgeable and **Shine the Soul** even in a short time.

Chapter-3

Health, Exercise, Relaxation

Health

Food is the maker of the Body

The scriptures have called food the creator of the world. **'ANNAM KE PRAJAPATI'** (Prashnopanishad). Juice is formed from food, blood from juice, semen from blood and life from semen. Thus, the body is sustained, nourished and reconstructed from the outside only. Charak has also written that the body is formed from food only: **'DEHO HYA-AHAAR SAMBHAVAH:'**. It is a matter of simple understanding that the origin, condition and growth of the body depends on the food. The most important support of the human being for the life and health of the body is outside in the Form of Food. In philosophical language, the gross body is called **ANNAMAYA KOSHA.** Storage of Food.

No one will deny the fact that the strength, brightness and invigoration that develop in the body is produced by the food only. The Food gives health and longevity, which is called health. According to the physicians, food gives instant consciousness, nourishes the senses, and enhances intellect, memory and vitality.

Considering the importance of diet, we should briefly consider what kind of diet develops physical health. It is well known that the purpose of food is not only to fill the stomach, but mainly to nourish the body. The purpose of diet is not achieved by just filling the stomach. Only that food is healthy which is suitable for the body. If it is unfavorable, it is not Prajapati but Pranpati (Yamraj) for the body, that is, it is a burden and destructive. To understand which diet is suitable for the body, we should first understand carefully the following things related to the structure of the body:

1. Like a house made of bricks, the body is made of innumerable microscopic atoms. (Cells) These are of different shapes and sizes and are organized into different groups and are called 'dhatus' (Tissues). Flesh, blood, vital energy and nerves etc. are formed and operated from these Tissues of different types.

2. The entire body including the Tissues, is constituted by five basic elements, i.e. there are five main elements on the basis of which the body is formed. They are considered to be the base of the atoms or Tissues bases or the body assembled by them. According to Ayurveda, these are **earth, water, fire, sky and air**. In the scientific language of modern chemists, those five basic substances are: (a) protein i.e. meat type (nutritious) substances, (b) fat, (c) minerals or earthy substances, (d) carbohydrates i.e. sugar type substances, (e) water.

Under these, a total of twenty-three elements are found in the entire body, out of which oxygen, hydrogen, nitrogen, carbon, phosphorus, lime, Sulphur, chlorine, sodium, iron and potassium are the main ones. Apart from oxygen, all others are found in compounds form and all are divided into the above five categories. Scientific examination shows that the proportion of water in the body is fifty-seven percent, the proportion of minerals is twenty percent, the proportion of fat, protein and carbohydrates is twenty-three percent. This means that when these basic elements are present in the body in these quantities, then only the Tissues are active and the body remains in its natural state i.e. healthy. When the combination of the five great elements mentioned in Ayurveda is also present in their proper quantity, then only the bodily functions are carried out properly. Whichever opinion you may believe, it is certain that body is made up of five elements. To explain this topic from a contemporary perspective, we will consider it according to the modern view at this point.

3. These chemical substances do not always remain in the required quantities because millions of atoms are destroyed every moment due to bodily activities. Healthy red atoms of blood alone are destroyed in the multiple numbers of 10,00,000 every day. The body cannot compensate for this loss on its own, and when it cannot do so, it is not possible for the elements to remain in the required proportion. For this, it is necessary to take some substances from outside, which can produce new atoms in place of the destroyed atoms and thus keep the elements balanced and keep the bodily activities stable and running. These substances can be taken only in the form of food.

One thing is clear from the above description; that the composition of the diet should be the same as the composition of the body itself. In other words, while choosing edible items, it should be kept in mind that they provide the essential elements of the body in appropriate quantities. Only Panchtatva diet can be suitable for a Panchtatva body. The composition of the dhatus gets destroyed due to their abundance or deficiency. We will also briefly discuss what functions they perform in the body and from which substances they are available.

(i) Protein

Protein is the main element of life of the atoms of the body. It is the source of Tissues growth and the compensation of natural loss of Tissues. Tissue- fibres cannot be produced from any other substance except protein. It is available in sufficient quantity from nitrogen-rich substances - meat, pulses, eggs and fruits and vegetable compounds. If these substances are taken in more than the required quantity, then the excess protein that comes out in the form of essence **gets accumulated in the body in the form of FAT.**

(ii) FAT

In the form of fat, permanent energy is stored in large quantities for the body, warmth and power are generated from it. It is found in abundance in animal fat, vegetable oil, butter, peanuts, almonds and other dry fruits. The energy of fat is one and a half times more than that of carbohydrates.

Know It To Shine

(iii) Minerals

Minerals help in the formation of Tissues. Bones are also made from them. They have little or no effect on physical strength but they have a special effect on the body's nutrition, digestion and Tissue-Carriers. 5/6 part of bones are built from Minerals. Minerals are also found in abundance in red blood cells, teeth, hair, digestive juices and brain and these organs are specially nourished by them. They are available in sufficient quantity through milk, eggs, green vegetables and cereals etc.

(iv) Carbohydrates

Carbohydrate is the substance that produces and provides strength to physical power, energy and heat. The capacity for physical exertion is obtained from it. If present in appropriate quantity, it keeps the functional power of the body active; if present in excess, it gets stored in the form of fat. Carbohydrate is found in abundance in rice. Carbohydrate is the main nutrient of fruits, honey, jaggery, sugar, wheat, potatoes etc. It should be remembered that this great element is obtained only through plants. Protein and fat elements are certainly obtained in large quantities from meat diet, but carbohydrate is obtained only from grains, cereals and fruits.

(v) Water

Water is an important element of the body. All the elements are formed with its help. They flow in the body and their equilibrium is also based on it. It helps in taking food into the body and removing useless substances from the body. It does not generate any power in the body, but without it the atoms can neither live nor spread in the body and do their work.

The substances which enter the stomach in the form of food are digested in the Metabolic system with the help of digestive juices. The metabolism transforms food in a natural way. They take in the essence of the protein, fat, minerals, water and carbohydrate parts of the eaten substances and convert them into blood and other elements. The tissues destroyed by them are again received by the body and the permanent energy of the body is not harmed. The natural heat of the body is generated by the transformation of food.

Apart from taking in the essential elements of food i.e. the essence of food, the internal system also performs another function. They separate the food and excreta. The unnecessary parts of the unsuitable substances of the body and those which are produced inside in the process of transformation of food, they expel them through stool, urine, perspiration and breath. During the transformation of food, the constructive and destructive functions of food happen simultaneously. It is important to know that when the body system gets the essence-rich substances in sufficient quantity, then their energy is not wasted. They extract as much essential elements from them as possible. When useless substances are found, their much energy and efforts are spent in separating the discarded substances.

In this context it is necessary to mention other types of substances. Modern scientists have proved that although these five elements are essential for the body, yet complete health cannot be protected and growth cannot be achieved only through them. The five elements may keep the body stable but they cannot protect it from the attack of disease. For physical growth and health, another element is also required, which is called 'vitamin' in foreign scientific language and '**Jeeva Dravya**' in source language.

(vi) Vitamins

It is necessary to know this much about Vitamins that they are the living parts of food and make the five elements more active. They are extremely useful for the life force of the body; hence their introduction is given here.

There are 13 essential vitamins, which are categorized as either fat-soluble or water-soluble: There are Four Fat-soluble vitamins: Vitamins A, D, E, & K and Water-soluble vitamins are: Vitamins B-6 (thiamine, riboflavin, niacin, pantothenic acid, biotin), B12, folate and vitamin C

Vitamins are essential for the body to function properly, and they help with many things, including: Wound healing, Boosting the immune system, Energy production, Supporting cardiovascular health, and Aiding eye health

Vitamin A- This element is essential for physical growth and protection from infectious diseases. Due to its deficiency, the body becomes diseased, weak and feeble and the lungs, digestive system etc. become weak. The growth of children stops due to its absence. Night blindness (night blindness) occurs due to its deficiency. Vitamin A is found in abundance in green vegetables. Apart from milk, curd, butter, it is also found in eggs, animal liver, fish oil (cod liver oil).

Vitamin B- There are seven subtypes of Vitamin B... Vitamin B-6 (as mentioned above) and **Vitamin B-12**. Their usefulness is different. This substance is essential for the nourishment of the skin and nervous system. It is obtained from black gram, peas, wheat, the inner part of rice, peanuts and eggs etc. It is found in abundance in the bran of wheat and barley and the upper layer of grains.

Vitamin C- Vitamin C is essential for increasing the life force of the body, for nourishing and protecting the teeth and for increasing the complexion of the body. Milk, mango, lemon, orange, green vegetables, cabbage, potato, carrot, onion, tomato, turnip and sprouted grains are its producers.

Vitamin D: Vitamin D nourishes the bones and makes the blood thick. Due to this, teeth get strength. In its absence, children suffer from rickets because their bones do not grow. This substance is mainly obtained from the rays of the sun. The amount of this substance is more in buffalo milk than in cow milk. It is also obtained from the Butter, Egg, and oil of fish.

Vitamin E: It is considered to be the bearers of male power. Its consumption strengthens the reproductive power. Parents who do not have this vital substance in their bodies, their reproductive power is weakened and their children are either not born at all or are very weak. It is found in grass, butter, seeds or their oil, wheat and green vegetables.

The most important thing that should be kept in mind regarding vital substances is that they are usually safe in raw substances and in fresh fruits and green vegetables only. Their potency is reduced or completely destroyed by boiling or becoming stale. This is the secret of the improvement in health due to fruits, grains and vegetables. Fruits, grains and vegetables etc. get their vital energy from sunlight. Therefore, such substances which are in contact with the rays of the sun contain more vitamins than the tubers. These elements are found especially in the upper leaves of grains. Therefore, polished rice is useless. Regarding grains, it should be remembered that when they are sprouted, apart from their nutritious elements, vitamins are produced in large quantities.

Vitamin K…It is an essential nutrient that plays a critical role in blood clotting, wound healing, and bone health. People who don't have enough vitamin K in their system are at **greater risk of increased bleeding and bone fractures.**

Vitamin-B-9 - Folate……It is natural form of vitamin B-9 that helps the body make red cells, DNA and RNA and metabolize amino acids. It is found in many foods and supplements, and is important for pregnancy, blood health, and stroke. Folate is naturally present in many foods, notably dark green vegetables, beans, and legume

After the discovery of vitamins, the viewpoint of scientists has changed in relation to physiology and at least pathology. Till now, people were in favor of boiling each and every substance with various means to free it from germs, washing it with chemical substances and making it clean and then eating it. They believed that this is the only way to prevent diseases. But now scientists have proved that by unnatural methods of treating vegetables etc., the natural essence of the substances gets destroyed.

This is the reason that children who take natural diet due to poverty are healthier and live longer than those children who are brought up on externally extracted food. Compared to earlier, now children suffer from more digestive disorders, more dental problems, more diseases like gout, etc. are also common, although now people consider themselves more civilized than before in terms of food habits. The reason for this was that now natural food is not taken in a natural way. Often, we also see that in chronic constipation, when green vegetables and barley are taken in a natural way, then they also become disease-free because then vitamins reach the body in a live form.

After thinking about these things, we reach at a conclusion, that is, the world is reaching the same place where the ancient Ayurvedic people had reached, at least in the matter of food. The method of drinking lukewarm milk directly from udder as prescribed by ancient scientists was considered unhealthy till now and people used to recommend boiling milk three times so that the germs in it die. Now vitaminologists prove that boiling milk destroys its life element.

The summary is that due to fear of germs, people destroy the essence of food items, which if not destroyed can protect the body from the attack of even more powerful germs. In a way, they behave like the monkey who threw a stone at his master's nose to shoo away a fly sitting on it.

(vii) What kind of diet should one take

Keeping in mind the usefulness of the nutritious elements and life-giving substances of food, it would be appropriate to say that we should consume such foods that are nutritious and **sattvic**. In this regard, the following points should be kept in mind:

1. Nature has prepared natural food for all living beings. By taking food according to one's nature, the natural health of that living being develops. Whatever the non-vegetarians may say, but we will have to accept that at least in this country, the natural food is food grains, milk, fruits and vegetables. Meat contains sufficient quantity of nutrients and it provides nourishment as well as stimulation, there is no doubt about it, but it does not have the capacity to increase life force and longevity. Not only humans, but even herbivores animals and birds live longer than non-vegetarian animals and birds. Among animals, elephants and among birds, parrots are found to be the longest-lived and both are Herbivores. Both are also more intelligent than other living beings. Among humans also, vegetarian persons are not weaker than non-vegetarians in intelligence and physical strength, as is evident from the lives of Gandhiji and Bernard Shaw. Vegetarianism is also more beneficial from the point of view of cleanliness.

2. One should take such food which contains the essence of nutritious elements in sufficient quantity and which the digestive system can easily absorb. Take milk for example. Milk is considered the best food for man according to both ancient and modern views. All the nutritious elements useful for life- protein, fat, carbohydrate (milk sugar), water, iron, sulphur,

phosphorus, lime, potassium, minerals and all the essential vitamins are found in it. Therefore, it is considered a complete diet. Apart from these qualities, milk is easily digested. The senses do not have to waste energy in digesting it. Along with all these qualities, milk is also a strong destroyer of intestinal poisons and insects. From all points of view, it is the natural diet and life-saver of man. Being nutritious, life-saving and easily digestible, it is suitable. Soybean was much talked about in the past few years and it was proved by scientific tests that it contains the same nutrients as milk.

But now it has been found out that despite having all the qualities, the digestive system does not absorb its essence because it does not suit its nature. Therefore, the glory of soybean has diminished now. In reality, the essence of substances is available only according to the receptive power of the senses. No matter how nutritious food you eat, if it does not suit the inner nature, the body will not accept it.

Apart from milk, take banana. Along with Vitamin B and C, it contains fat, protein, carbohydrate, water and minerals like iron, phosphorus, lime etc. and it is also insecticide. It is also considered a complete diet. Ayurvedacharya Dr. Bhaskar Govind Tanekar has written in his commentary on Sushruta Samhita that **'three well-ripe bananas and one and a half litre of milk is the best diet for a person at one time.** All the vitamins can be available when banana is mixed with milk because Vitamin B and C are found in banana and A, D and E are found in milk.

3. Without getting into the details of nutrients and vitamins, we should broadly accept that the natural food material produced in a particular place and season is the most nutritious and life-giving food of that place, that time and that people. This is the arrangement of nature. Those foods should be taken in appropriate quantities and in a natural manner. They should be cooked for hygiene and taste; but keeping in mind that their useful parts should not burn or go waste. Take rice for example. Many people throw away the starch of rice. All the elements of rice go out with it. Many people eat polished rice, the upper layer of which is peeled. All the nutritious elements of rice remain in that cover. If it comes out, it becomes useless and causes serious diseases.

Therefore, food should be taken in its natural form as far as possible. Along with this, seasonal vegetables and fruits should be taken. It is important to keep in mind that their qualities become different when they are cooked properly or not. When they are cooked properly, then along with eating them with taste, the digestive juices of the mouth also get mixed with them in the right amount and they are easily digested.

4. Food should be taken according to personal interest, suitability, need and digestive power. The same diet cannot be suitable for everyone, because everyone's nature and physical structure is different. Therefore, keeping in mind the interest, one should take such food which suits the body and which the intestines can digest without any fuss and take its essence as per the need. That food should be such and in such quantity that there is no wastage of physical energy in digesting it.

Along with interest etc., the needs of the body should also be kept in mind. It is good to eat food as per the requirement of nutrients in the body. A hardworking person needs protein and carbohydrates in particular. Therefore, it will be beneficial for him to eat such things which provide these elements. A person who does mental work while sitting may be harmed by consuming these in large quantities because they will increase fat. Therefore, there is a saying in English that the thing which may be meat (nectar) for one person, may be poison for another.

5.   The quality of a food item should not be judged by its market price. The price of a commodity is not determined by its nutritional value. Market value is determined by how difficult or easy it is to get it, how much is it is in supply, how it is consumed and how it tastes. Therefore, do not be under the illusion that only an expensive product will be healthy. Also, a healthy product should not be considered more valuable than health. The product which is beneficial for health, even if it is expensive, becomes cheap later because the cost of medicines is saved. A cheap but unhealthy product becomes expensive later. One should take those products which are cheap along with being healthy. Nutrition is more important than filling the stomach, this should not be forgotten.

6.   While choosing food, it should be kept in mind that their consumption should not cause any kind of blood disorder. All the functions of the body are carried out by blood and blood is formed from food. Health remains good only when it is pure and flows properly in the body. If it is contaminated or loose, the body becomes weak. Taking stimulants causes dryness in it. If the blood flow slows

down, the body becomes loose. If the blood flow to the brain is reduced, dizziness occurs and the vision of the eyes becomes weak. If it is too much, it causes headache and if it is blocked at some place, it causes paralysis.

Along with blood purification, the nervous system should also be kept in mind, because the body depends on the strength of the nervous system. It becomes weak later on due to stimulating food. If there is no proper organization of phosphorus and calcium etc. along with vitamins in the blood of the brain system, then various types of disorders occur in the nerves and the body becomes useless due to nervous weakness. Therefore, only blood-enhancing and blood-purifying substances should be considered as diet.

(viii) How to eat food

It is also very important to know how to eat along with what to eat. The following points should be kept in mind in this regard:

1. Food should be taken with taste. Even ordinary food taken with taste becomes good chemical for the body. The digestive juices of the body naturally mix with it and digest it. Even the best food eaten without taste is not digested properly and becomes a burden or manure for the body, in which only worms or stinging insects of diseases are produced. It should be remembered that natural taste is produced only by hunger. The attachment for food that arises in the mind of a person who is glutton (Bhukhad, who has no other thing in his mind except food) is not a sign of taste but greed. This advice given by Vidur to King Dhritarashtra is noteworthy in this context:

SAMPANNTARMEVANNUM DARIDRA BHUJJATEY SADA, KSHUTSVADUTAN JANYATI SA CHADHYESHU SUDURLABHA -(Mahabharata)

That is, whatever a poor person eats, it is always good food, because he eats with hunger. The hunger that produces taste is rare for the rich. Those who wish to be rich always suffer from poverty.

2. One should always eat with a healthy mind. The state of mind affects food and digestion. Food eaten without unhappy mind is not digested by the body. Even ordinary food is satisfying when eaten with happy mind. When the mind is happy, digestive juices are secreted regularly by the digestive glands. When the mind is restless, there is aversion to food; food remains in the stomach like an uninvited guest, no one cares about it.

Disorders like worry, fear, mental anxiety, jealousy, hatred and anger have an immediate effect on the digestive system. Food becomes ineffective in worry; you can understand this by looking at the condition of a lonely person. You can experience it yourself that worrying about any subject for a long time makes one have to urinate repeatedly. Excessive mental exertion and worries are the main causes of diabetes.

It has been heard that excessive worry or extreme fear can cause hair to turn white within 24 hours. When it has such an effect on the overall physical health, why would it not have an effect on the eaten food and digestive systems? The effect of fear is even more evident. You must have heard that many people urinate and defecate when they are afraid. When they are frightened, the internal organs become weak. Therefore, they do not have the power to hold back the food brought in. Students often ask for permission to leave to urinate if they have not memorized the lesson or fearing the teacher's cruelty. This cannot be called their excuse; in reality, they need to urinate. Digestion is definitely affected by anger etc. because anger agitates the blood, its pressure increases and it moves away from the digestive system and gets stored in the brain. Due to this, food is not digested because the senses become weak and the appetite power is weakened. This statement of Maharshi **Sushrut** is worth accepting:

IRSHYABHAYKRODHPARIKSHITEN LUBDHEN RUGNDAIN YAPIDITEN, PRADVESHAYUKTEN CH SEVYAMAN MANNAN NA SAMYAK PARINAMMETI (Sushruta)
Food eaten by people suffering from jealousy, fear, anger, greed, worry, poverty and hatred, tested by lust and pain is not digested properly.

The ancient rule of eating in the dining hall after taking a bath and washing hands and feet, aims not only at external purity but also internal peace. When a person eats with a peaceful mind in an environment where there are no other attractions, then the mind remains engaged in food. Eating with some friends and co-workers is more satisfying than eating alone, because then the mind remains free from worries and people eat with fun and enjoyment.

Internal satisfaction and contentment are the special purpose of food. That satisfaction is not obtained only from delicious food. No matter how sweet the food is, but if the housewife is quarrelsome, then it will not taste good. If the wife, who gives food, is well behaved and soft spoken, even Rough & Dry food is satisfying. Mental peace and unrest have the same effect. The husband of a shrewd woman is always in a state of doubt as soon as he enters the house whether he will get food or abuses. He chews food less and his pain more. The husband of a soft-natured woman is sure that whatever he gets or will get will be the best, because it will be given with love. There is no digestive juice better than love. Man is not only hungry for food but also for respect and prestige. Even if he gets good food without respect and hospitality at the house of a miser, he is not satisfied.

The dry food of an ordinary but generous person seems very tasty to the guest. Krishna had eaten Vidur's saag with great relish. A man's food should be such that it satisfies not only his stomach but also his mind.

For self-satisfaction, it is also necessary to eat food earned by hard work. Even though it may be ordinary, it increases strength and energy. Stolen money cannot be digested because mental remorse melts it and makes it worthless even before it is digested. Self-satisfaction is destroyed by greed, hence there is never satisfaction and food without satisfaction becomes useless. One more thing is worth remembering in this regard. It is that the cleanliness of food, its color, smell, form etc. also have a considerable effect on the mood of eating food. These characteristics of food should be kept in mind to arouse interest. The mind gets irritated by dirt etc.

3.   While eating food, it should be chewed slowly and thoroughly before it is handed over to the intestines. Eating quickly is never good. As far as possible, simple and bland

food should be eaten regularly at fixed times. Excessive use of spices and chilies certainly gives pleasure to the tongue, but it causes harm to the intestines. They increase the dryness of the blood; digestive juices are wasted and destroys virility. It should also be remembered that excess salt is scientifically destructive. Excessive use of chilies, spices and salty things leads to drinking more water. Drinking excess water during and after meals makes the digestive material thin and the digestive juices themselves become so thin that the food is not digested properly. Therefore, one should drink water little by little and take such food which does not demand more water: **'MUHURMUHURVARIPIVEDABHURI'** (Bhavaprakash).

4. Physical and mental exertion should be avoided after eating. When the food starts getting digested, the blood circulation of the body mainly takes place in the intestines. There is a lack of blood in other organs, mainly in the brain, due to which one feels lethargic, cold and drowsy etc. In that condition, by doing physical or mental exertion, the blood stops supporting the digestive system and runs towards other muscles, due to which proper digestion does not take place. Therefore, Sushrut has said that after eating, as long as the heaviness of the food remains, one should rest like a king (without any worries), after that one should walk a hundred steps and lie down on the left side.

BHUKTVA RAJVADASIT YAVDANNAKLAMO GATAH: TATAH PADSHATAM GATVA VAMPARSHVARYEN SAMVISHET.
(Sushrutasamhita)

Nowadays, one of the main reasons for poor health is that people often start working after eating. Clerks, students, businessmen etc. rush after eating and then do mental work. Due to this, food is not digested properly and the result is indigestion, constipation and loss of energy. There is an ancient Sanskrit proverb that death runs after the one who runs after eating: **'MRITYURDHAVATI DHAVAT'**.

5. Phlegm increases in the body after eating. That is why Sushrut has written that to suppress it, it is appropriate for an intelligent person to consume paan, smoke, camphor, clove or astringent, bitter and pungent substances. Sushruta has also written that after eating, one should avoid words, form, taste, smell and touch that disturb the mind.

(ix) Importance of water

It is necessary to mention some special things about water because it is the main basis of life. Its Sanskrit name is also Jeevan and Jeevika. Food and water keep the body alive. Its importance has been accepted since ancient times. Vedas have praised "Jal" (Water):

AAP: IDWA U BHESHJIRAPO AMIVACHATNI AAP: SARVASYA BHESHJIASTE KRINVANTU BHESHJAM. (Atharvaveda)
Water is the only medicine; That is the cause of disease and destruction; That is the medicine for all diseases. Water! You become people's medicine.

Water itself does not contain any nutritious element, yet it is the carrier of the nutritious elements of the body.

When it becomes impure, other elements become impure. Its absence causes dryness and restlessness in the body, because chemical substances start drying up and the blood circulation slows down. Water has a special effect on the functioning of the brain. One proof of this is that in summer, due to lack of water, one feels restless and the mind is not in place. After working hard, when a part of the water comes out of the body through sweat, then one feels tired. By drinking water, both the mind and the body become healthy.

A famous Russian doctor (Dr. E. Podolsky) has written some useful things in this regard. He has written that proper amount of water is required for smooth functioning of mental activities. If it is too less or more than required, it is extremely harmful for the brain. This leads to loss of mental functioning power.

When the quantity of water becomes more or less, it often causes confusion, drowsiness and loss of consciousness. Water keeps the essential elements mixed and combined. When the quantity of water in the body becomes less or more, the thinking power of a person becomes disturbed. The efficiently functioning brain also requires proper amount of water too little or too much is disastrous, not only resulting in decrease mental efficiency, but when this balance is profoundly upset it leads to delirium, stupor and coma. Water holds the essential chemicals in solution and in the required amount of concentration. A shift in the either direction may result in distorted thinking.

Water should always be taken in pure form and as per thirst. Thirst tells us when the body and mind need it.

Sometimes, we feel artificial thirst as well; like when we eat spicy and stimulant foods. When we eat meat, we need more water because more water is needed to flush out the polluted substance called uric acid produced by it. In such a situation, we have to drink more water than required, otherwise blood disorder occurs. We have already written about the ill effects of drinking too much water above. Therefore, it is best not to eat such food that causes unnatural thirst.

After brushing teeth in the morning and drinking water to the stomach is as beneficial as nectar. It is called Usha-paan. It cleanses the stomach, purifies and soothes the blood and is beneficial for the eyes. Some experienced people claim that by drinking Usha-paan regularly, one does not suffer from headache and the hair remains black till old age. Ghagh has also written:

PRATAHKAL KHATIYA TE UTHIKE, PIYEAY TURANT PAANI, TA GHAR KABHU VAIDYA NA AAWE, BAAT GHAG KI JAANI
Drinking water immediately after getting up in the morning, the doctor would never come home, Remember this advice of Ghagh....

(x) Effect of Diet on the Brain

How diet affects the brain, it should be understood precisely. You should know this because all the activities of the body are controlled by the brain. Food has a momentary and permanent effect on the brain immediately, as can be understood from the effect of alcohol consumption.

The above-mentioned Russian doctor (Dr. E. Padolski) has published some important facts after studying this subject in detail. He says that the mineral elements which are extracted from the food items have a special effect on the brain. Their mixture is found in the right quantity in the blood of a healthy brain. But in an unhealthy brain, they are found in more or less quantity. As these chemical elements are more or less than their natural quantity, the mental attitude and intelligence of the person changes and almost the entire personality of the person changes.

On scientific examination, the sugar content in the brain of many types of mad people has been found to be more than required. After examining many mad people, it was found that there was calcium and phosphorus in their brain in excessive quantity. Many such patients were examined whose thinking power had vanished and it was found that the sugar content in their blood was very less. Many mental functions have been seen to become paralyzed due to the deficiency of sulphur and iron elements. Many types of mental diseases have been found to arise due to their excess, because the excess of sulphur and iron elements makes the brain excited and deranged.

The brain is very quickly affected by excessive acid or alkali-specific substances. In the brain of a diabetic, there is abundance of acid fluid. Disorders like epilepsy, mental restlessness and unconsciousness are usually caused by abundance of alkali substances. Both calcium and phosphorus in appropriate quantities provide strength, sharpness and energy to the nerve fibers. If these decrease, then symptoms of laziness and inertia appear. And due to their increase, thoughts become restless, one gets irritated and feels restless. Iron element gives firmness to thoughts and strengthens the brain. The iron content in the nerves of children is less as per their age as compared to adults, hence they are restless and irrational. As they get iron through their diet, their brain gets nourished.

Why eating green vegetables and fruits clears the mind can be understood from the above description. They contain abundant amount of minerals which are good for the brain. It should also be remembered that minerals do not get converted into juices through digestion and then get mixed in the blood like other substances. They get mixed directly in the blood and hence their effect is seen quickly.

In this context, we will mention a couple of other things worth knowing because there is some confusion among people about them. The first thing is that which compound is essential for the development of brain Power, has not been known yet. There is a belief among people that fish contains a lot of phosphorus, so it is an excellent food for increasing brain power. But scientific tests have proved this to be wrong.

The second thing is about rice. Rice is a brain nutrient. World-renowned Indian scientist Dr. N.R. Kar, once told that the substance called amino acid present in protein are two types one is essential and the other is non-essential. A special type of food is absolutely necessary for the development and nutrition of the body and brain. The protein in Milk, fish, Egg, etc. contains essential amino acid. Although wheat contains more protein than rice, the essential amount of amino acid in rice protein is more than that in wheat. According to the opinion of Dr. Kar, the main reason for the intellectual development of the eastern countries is the high-quality protein found in rice and that is why rice is cultivated here in a special way. People who get angry at rice should try eating rice; it is possible that when their knowledge intensifies, they will come to know that the misconception they had about rice was due to not eating rice.

Regarding the effect of food, it is universally accepted that the body is formed by its essence. The mind and along with it the nature and character are also formed; because nature, character and mind are related to the body. That is why ancient scholars have praised the greatness of Sattvik food. There is no doubt that a person becomes what he eats. Some Sanskrit philosopher has said that just as a lamp consumes the darkness and produces the blackness of kajal, similarly a man reveals his Persona according to what he eats.

(xi) Other aids to health

Now, apart from food, consider other important contributors to health. Food alone is not everything in life. There are some other things which are as important as food for longevity and health or even more so in some ways. Air is the most important among them. A man can live without food for a month or two, but cannot live even for a few minutes without air. All-natural life **Works only** on air. This verse from the scriptures is absolutely true:

VAAUNA VE GAUTAM SUTREANAYAYNCH LOKAH PARSCHA LOKAH: SARVAANI CH BHOOTANI SAMBADDHAANI BHAVANTI...

Hey Gautam! Air is like a thread. Just as beads are strung on a thread, similarly all the environs are strung together in the thread of air.

The general nature of air is to give progress to nature and to pulsate life and transform things by being all-moving and the supreme soul. Its second main nature is to ignite the fire of life in living beings. The scriptures have called air the brightness of fire and the soul of fire. Modern science also considers it to be combustible because combustion is accomplished by its main element oxygen. That is the life air. The third nature of air is Tissue development and nourishment. Dhatu -fibers are formed and developed by its part called nitrogen. Nitrogen controls the combustion action of oxygen.

(xii) Relation of air with the body

In a healthy state, the human body needs about four gallons of oxygen per hour. Most of it goes in through breathing, the rest through the pores. The lungs absorb oxygen and mix it with the blood. The heart functions with it. As the energy of the body is spent, more oxygen is required and it is made available through the lungs. Oxygen produces bodily heat and digestion takes place with it. Blood gets new life through it, strength, expansion and glow increase in the body and the toxins produced in the body are destroyed. When food items are cooked in the stomach due to the heat of air, a toxic gas called carbon dioxide is released from it. Carbon (ember) is present in abundance in the body. When oxygen combines with it, they burn and this gas is produced, it comes out through exhalation. When oxygen enters the lungs through inhalation it binds to hemoglobin and in the process, carbon dioxide is released through exhalation.

It is important to know something about carbon dioxide. It is a gas that is usually released when coal is burnt. It is so much poisonous that sometimes people who burn fire in closed rooms and sleep are found dead or unconscious in the morning. This gas is present in nature from the decay of dirty objects, from the dirty drains of cities, from swamps. It is produced from the smoke of smokestacks and mills and factories. When any object starts rotting, it comes out in abundance from it. Sometimes sleep by keeping ripe fruits in closed rooms it causes their rotting at night and people faint or die because of inhaling the carbon di oxide, emitted by rotten fruits.

This is a deadly gas. Accumulating in the body, it causes not only disease but also death. Till the age of thirty, it is released in large quantities from the breath of a man. Then it gradually starts decreasing. It is present in less quantity in the breath of women. It is released more during the day and gets mixed in the atmosphere; it is less in the evening. It is the natural quality of the sun rays that they pull out carbon dioxide from all objects. Due to low temperature outside at night and slackness in physical activities, it is released even less by breathing, and it becomes very less at midnight. In the morning, this gas is present in less quantity in the atmosphere; because firstly it is released less by the breath of a human being, secondly due to the effect of the sun's heat, it does not get released from other objects and spread in the air. The importance of morning air is more because it contains oxygen in abundance due to which special enthusiasm and strength is obtained.

According to the natural system, plants drink this poison and donate nectar in the form of oxygen to living beings. This is the quality of plants that they eat manure and produce fruits. Therefore, people who live in open spaces in contact with plants remain alert because they get more oxygen. The hard work and life force of villagers is strong due to this reason.

There is a lack of vegetation in cities; many people live in cramped places and due to the high population, carbon dioxide is released in large quantities through breathing in a limited area. It increases even more due to the dirt in drains, smoke from mills etc. and the Shiva trees that drink that poison do not live there, due to this this toxic gas remains constantly present there. Its quantity is more in the air people breathe. As a result, the lungs become weak. You can understand this secret in this way that when many people sleep together in a narrow room, they become lethargic or unwell in the morning because they do not breathe pure air but keep drinking each other's breath throughout the night.

The same is the condition of those who sleep with their mouths covered, because they keep on inhaling the polluted air they exhale all night. When oxygen is not available from outside, naturally carbon dioxide gets accumulated inside. It is a natural rule that when oxygen reaches the lungs like a policeman, then the polluted air runs away like a thief. When vital air is not available, only destructive air gets mixed in the blood. It should be remembered that carbon dioxide is produced more inside the body due to special functioning of muscles, high fever and intensity of emotions. Therefore, to remove it, it is absolutely necessary for the hardworking, sick and people suffering from emotional distress to consume clean oxygen air.

Scientific research shows that carbon dioxide has a bad effect on the brain in particular. Its excess causes fatigue in the brain, loss of concentration and the mind becomes unstable and restless. Anesthesia, nervous weakness-and headache are its main consequences. This is why the breathing becomes very difficult when one sleeps with one's mouth stung. When one suffocates, the symptoms of insensibility appear first, because carbon dioxide spreads inside when oxygen is not available from outside.

(xiii) Effect of oxygen on the brain

Oxygen is the life force of the nerves. An experienced doctor (Dr. E. Podolsky) has written that as far as the consciousness of the intellect is concerned, oxygen is an essential element. Oxygen is the most important element in the brain as far as intelligence is concerned.

It has been scientifically tested in a modern way. Two famous scientists Glaisher and Coxwell flew in a balloon and reached a height of 28,000 feet in 48 minutes. Due to low air pressure there, oxygen was available in very less quantity. As a result, Glaisher lost his knowledge power instantly. He could not even tell the time by looking at his watch. Estimating his inertia, the balloon was lowered a little and as soon as he got oxygen, his mind became alert again.

Two other scientists have tested it in a different way. They entered a small chamber made of iron in which the air pressure was maintained with the help of a machine as much as it is at a height of 24,500 feet. The result was that one of them soon became confused. His ability to read, write and recognize objects was destroyed. His confusion was evident when he looked through the small window of the chamber. Whenever he was asked anything, he would say, "Enough, let us lie like this." His mental development had completely stopped. After this, the air pressure was increased. He became somewhat conscious. One of them picked up the mirror kept nearby, but he did not know how to see his face in it. He tried to see his face at the back of the mirror. When the air pressure was increased to 14,500 feet, they regained consciousness due to getting adequate amount of oxygen, but both of them did not remember what they had thought and what senseless things they had done during this time. Both their thinking power and memory had vanished due to lack of oxygen.

From the above examples, it can be understood why the ancient sages gave so much importance to dawn. In the morning, oxygen is available in maximum quantity to everyone, so thinking at that time matures the brain and sharpens the thinking power. In the past, morning was the golden time of the day. People, mainly students and intellectuals, used to make full use of it. The result was also good. Now it is the opposite. People waste their time in the morning and at ten o'clock, when the atmosphere becomes particularly polluted, then they go out to use their brain. As a result, their brain gets tired.

These qualities of pure air are clear- it keeps the breathing process in order, the body's ability to work is activated. There is an increase in enthusiasm and consciousness in the mind, the mental attitude remains fine, the body and senses are nourished, the elements of the body get movement, the heart, blood and the flow of the entire life works regularly.

(xiv) Air intake

Pure air should be taken in through breath as well as through pores. The best way to take in air through pores is to keep them clean and open. Pores open up by bathing, then pure air enters through them and the polluted matter inside also comes out in the form of sweat. Therefore, bathing is very necessary. As far as possible, the body should be kept open or loose clothes should be worn. This ensures a good touch of air. The importance of this touch can be understood from the fact that after a hard day's work, when you enter in an open field, a wave of happiness and energy surges within you. You should remember that this wave is generated by natural air and not by artificial air. The air from the fan is air-stimulating.

When natural air gives so much consciousness to the body by mere touch, then it must have special properties when mixed with the blood inside. In fact, when cool, mild and fragrant breeze is inhaled, the entire health is stimulated. The fragrant air carries the elements of the deities and of the flowers; therefore, the Vedas have praised it and said that O Air! You are the medicine for the world, you go as the messenger of the gods: **'TVA HI VISHVABHESHAJO DEVANAM DOOT EYASE.'** Many diseases are cured only by changing the air and for this people go to healthy places. It is convenient for the general public that they should take in as much air as possible in the morning in an open space and avoid impure air even during the day. As much as possible does not mean that one should take in air while standing in the sweltering air. It means that one should clean the lungs with pure air. Air intake is not possible properly while standing, therefore lungs should be made more active by walking so that they can take in clean air and throw out the polluted air inside.

(xv) Swarodaya-Vigyan

In this context, it would not be inappropriate to introduce Swarodaya-Vigyan. The order in which air is held in the body through breathing and what effect it has on bodily functions, is the main subject of this ancient Indian science. Many people have tested its truth. According to this scripture, at the time of sunrise, breath comes in and out from each nostril in the order of two and a half hours each. Twelve times a day and night, one nostril works and twelve times the other, and sometimes both for some time. On the Pratipada, Dwitiya, Tritiya, Saptami, Ashtami, Navami, Trayodashi, Chaturdashi and Poornima of the Shukla Paksha, at the time of sunrise, the left nostril of a healthy person is the source of inhalation and exhalation.

The right nostril starts functioning on these dates of the dark fortnight and on Amavasya. If there is any abnormality in it, it should be understood that there is some disease in the body, either secretly or openly. When the left nostril is breathing, one should do steady work and when the right nostril is breathing, one should do difficult work and when both are working, one should do meditation.

In case of any disease, the nostril which is working at that time should be closed with a cloth. This opens the other nostril soon and the left lung, which is inactive and causes disorder, starts functioning properly. We have seen that in case of headache, it is really beneficial to close the side where the breath is flowing. When the right breath is flowing while eating, the food is digested properly. Even after eating, it is beneficial to have the right nostril working for ten to fifteen minutes. Therefore, the rule of lying on the left side after eating has been told, because by lying on the left side, the right nostril opens automatically, this is the natural rule. Lying on the right side makes the left nostril work. According to the above scriptures, the immediate work done by the organs of the nostril from which the breath flows is done more smoothly. Loosening the lips and slowly drawing air and releasing it slowly from the nose is very beneficial. By practicing this two-four times, blood, indigestion and phlegm disorders are cured.

(xvi) Pranayam

It is also necessary to discuss Pranayam in the context of breathing. Pranayam is the ancient Indian practice of controlling your breath to control the movement of life force ("prana") through your body. The term "Pranayama" is derived from the Sanskrit terms "Prana" and "Ayama", translating to "breath" and "expansion". "The real meaning of Pranayama, according to Patanjali, the founder of Yoga philosophy, is the "gradual cessation of breathing, the discontinuance of inhalation and exhalation". Pranayam is not only an exercise for the lungs, it is also a great activity that strengthens the body, purifies the blood, nourishes the brain and energizes. It is not only useful for yogis but is a useful practice for every health-loving person.

To understand the importance of Pranayam, first of all we should know that breathing is closely related to age. Age is measured by breathing. In a day, the process of breathing takes place 21,600 times. This means that one day's life is spent in these many breaths. In a year, its number is 78,84,000. If the breath is stopped for some time every day, then it means that life will not be spent for that long and in a little more than a year, that much breath (and it is related to Aayu) will not be spent, as much is spent in a single year in the natural state. In this way, Pranayam saves life or reduces the loss of life. The second thing is that the lungs get filled with pure air and their germs die due to it. By purifying the lungs, the blood of the body gets purified and by the purity of blood, health is formed.

The direct benefit of Pranayam is that it strengthens the body's strength, thinking power and mental state. In case of illness, anger, impatience and fear, any physical or mental infirmity, the speed of breathing increases. This means that the increase in breathing is a sign of internal excitement or weakness. If the opposite is done, that is, if one practices to stop the breath and make it steady, then definitely the excitement and weakness will be eliminated. It can be seen from personal experience that when the mind is agitated, the speed of breathing increases and when it is calm, the breathing is slow. From this, it can be easily understood that control of breathing will definitely have an effect on mental health. Another direct benefit of Prana-Yam is that concentration of mind increases with its practice. Because when the excitement of the mind is controlled by stopping the breath, its restlessness also stops. This makes the personality alert and the intellect becomes stable and pure.

A German Jewish doctor has given importance to another activity related to Pranayam. He says that the lungs should be made airless by exhaling the breath and they should be kept in this state for a longer time. By doing this, due to the lack of air, the harmful bacteria inside die. He says that it provides amazing benefits in phlegm related diseases (asthma, cough, cold etc.). This seems to be logical.

(xvii) Brahmacharya (Celibacy)

Semen is also a major protector of health. Even after eating good food and getting plenty of oxygen, if semen is not protected, health can never remain good. Semen is the keeper of the vitality and expander of all the energy of the body. It is from it that manly efforts are established and increased and manly efforts are the true happiness of life. What can be a stronger proof of the importance of semen than the fact that life originates from it. It is the Brahman that makes man and the life-giving element. Such Brahman power staying in the body will definitely increase the self-power. Semen is that thing which has the quality of doing a special work, that is, which is the main functional quality of any thing: **'PRABHUT- KARYAKAARINI GUNE VEERYAM' (Sushruta).** Semen is the main element of the human body. It nourishes the body; protects it from external attacks of diseases; fills the mind with patience, peace, enthusiasm and a feeling of valor. We see clearly that in comparison to the wicked people, self-controlled people are naturally patient, enthusiastic, intelligent, strong-minded and brilliant. Such things are not seen in the wicked or sexually aroused people. This proves the potency of semen.

To be healthy, it is necessary to follow celibacy. It does not mean that one should become a celibate from childhood. This is impossible and unnatural. Health is harmed by the accumulation of more semen than required. When any energy in the world is not used, it gets destroyed either by itself or destroys the thing attached to it. Semen must be used but only as per the need. It should be considered as the main asset of the body and should be used for good work like an asset. This is called Brahmacharya in the practical world. In this context, the following things should be kept in mind:

1. **'ANNADRETAH: SAMBHAVATI'**(Sushruta) Semen is formed from food (Ann). That is why one of its names is also Ann-Vikaar. Purity of the food form purity in Semen, and it remains naturally in that pure form. It gets distorted by taking stimulants and due to this, restlessness in the mind and disorder in the body are born. Therefore, as much as possible, pure and simple food should be taken.

2. The condition of semen is affected by the desires of the mind. When the desire arises in the mind, sexual arousal occurs. If it is stopped at that time, then the body is harmed and if it is spent repeatedly on the arising of desires, then the physical strength is lost. Therefore, mental restraint is necessary to protect celibacy.

3. When the blood becomes contaminated or reduced, the semen also becomes contaminated and reduced. When the blood becomes contaminated due to adultery etc., the semen also becomes defective. When there is a shortage of blood due to lack of food etc., the semen composition also reduces. In both the conditions, the permanent strength of

the body is reduced. Therefore, one should pay attention to purity of character and dietary restraint.

4. The brain has a close relationship with the semen producing organs. Therefore, it is necessary to keep it well organized, strong and healthy. Scientific research has shown that enthusiasm, courage, patience, consciousness and masculinity vanish as soon as the sex glands are weakened. It has also been observed that by reviving or revitalizing the worn-out sex glands, waves of youth come in the minds of old people and they become physically fit too. Those whose sex organs are weak, behave like old people even in their youth. The strength, robustness and satisfaction of the sex organs have an immense impact on human nature and thinking. In this regard, it should be known that the genitals have direct connection with the brain. There is a thick vein attached to the spine which is called the semen-carrying vein. That vein is connected to the brain through the spine. Therefore, when the genitals become diseased, deformed or disabled, the brain is affected like that. Also, the condition of the brain has a complete effect on this organ. Therefore, this energy-producing organ should be protected and used carefully and in a natural way.

5. **ATI SARVATRE VARJAYET**: Excess must be avoided everywhere - If there is a need to follow this principle in any work, then it is in relation to physical pleasure and luxury. Excessive involvement in physical pleasure and luxury leads not only loss of semen, but also to many other diseases. Adultery may cause Aids, syphilis, or many other STDs, in which there is not only physical torture, but even more terrible mental torture. This is a major cause of insanity, because Aids & syphilis (syphilis,

heat) makes the micro fibers of the brain become completely useless. Therefore, in mental disorder cases, experienced doctors first check through blood test whether there are Aids or syphilis germs in it or not. If the test is not done and the mad person is actually suffering from Aids & syphilis, then he does not get any benefit by giving any medicine.

(xviii) Effect of mental condition on the Body

We have already mentioned the effect of the mind on diet etc. Here we will discuss how and to what extent a healthy mind is helpful for health. For fear of expansion, we will divide this topic into the following parts and see which mental attitudes have what effect on the health of the body.

(xix) Psychology

Health cannot be built without concentration. If you are not focused on your health, any diet or exercise, will not have its full effect on the body. For improving health, a little walk in the morning and evening seems to be beneficial. Postmen walk all day long. But their health does not appear to be better than others, as they do not go for a walk with the feeling of improving their health. With concentration, will power becomes strong and will power can do the biggest miracles. When a person decides to be healthy, he definitely becomes healthy. Powers are collected and combined only with concentration.

(xx) Faith

The belief of the mind affects health in many ways. Self-confidence naturally strengthens the nervous system and its weakness weakens the senses. Self-confidence leads to the feeling of immense strength in the body and accordingly the strength of the body increases. It is said about many ancient great men that they had the strength of ten thousand elephants. We understand it to mean that they had their mental power and morale. Self-confidence makes a person stronger than many people.

Those who lack self-confidence are seen to be suffering from many kinds of imaginary diseases. Such diseases are not cured by medicines but by removing doubts from the mind with logic.

Sometimes self-confident people become really sick due to false beliefs getting established in their minds. Some American doctors tested this in the following manner. A doctor said to a completely healthy man, 'You seem a little weak today.' After some time, the second doctor met him as per the pre-planned plan and said, 'What is the matter, your face looks pale, eyes are red and you seem unwell.' Later, the third doctor met him. He said, 'You seem to have fever, don't move around.' On hearing the words of all three, that healthy person started thinking that he was really sick and when he was checked with a thermometer, he had a very high temperature.

Another example of the impact of the faith of the mind. It was published in a foreign newspaper. A child had a strange type of rickets. The diagnosis did not reveal the cause. Then an experienced doctor suggested a strange medicine. He said that this child should be loved every third hour. This was done and the child started becoming strong & Healthy. He started believing that he is loved. We can see examples of this everywhere in Indian families. Children brought up by lone- widows or stepmothers become wither away, because they have this feeling in their mind that no one in the world loves them. Love comes from trust and love nourishes the mind and body. In its absence, there is pain, separation and loss of health. In beautiful families, mutual trust keeps everyone healthy and happy.

(xxi) Security: Rest Assured

There is no doubt that Security increases age and health. Worry makes the body weak. It is also said that **'CHINTA SAMAN NASTI SHAREER SHOSHANAAM'**. There is no other thing that drains the body like worry. A Sanskrit moralist has written that Chinta (Worry) is ten times bigger than the Chita (Pyre) because the pyre burns the dead body and worry burns the living body. Everyone must have experienced the insomnia and fatigue from worry.

Worry usually arises due to lack of money, despair, doubt etc. When a person feels insecure and sees his future as dark, then only he gets worried. This worry may be false but it affects health. A report supporting this subject was published in an American newspaper (Guardian). After Germany's defeat, the physical health of German children started deteriorating. There was shortage of food, but the biggest thing was that a doubt had arisen in the minds of those children whether the food they were getting today would be available to them the next day. **Thinking about** the uncertain situation of the next day, they could not even sleep at night due to worry. Then after studying their state of mind, their parents took this measure that before going to bed at night, each child was given a piece of bread. The children used to hug it like a doll and sleep with the peace of mind that they did have the food for the next day. To remain healthy, it is necessary not to worry about what has passed: **'GATAM NA SHOCHAMI'**. And not to unnecessarily and disappointingly imagine the future.

(xxii) Mental Disorders

Apart from anxiety, there are many other mental ailments which after some time erupt in the form of physical ailments. In this regard, this statement of a learned doctor (Dr. S.B. Whitehead) is noteworthy. *"In many subtle ways, mentality reflect themselves through your body. Your hot temper sends up your blood pressure. Your sulks depress your nerves. your fear inhibits your digestion. In thousand- and one-ways mental health reflects itself in your physical health and the way you react to people and circumstances":* "Mental disorders show their effect through the body in many subtle ways. An excitable nature increases the circulation of blood; depression or anxiety weaken the nerves. Fear disturbs digestion. In hundreds of ways, mood affects physical health and the behavior and conduct of human beings."

Generally, some people keep a secret hatred for someone from their own family, due to which they feel guilty. These ill feelings settle deep inside and after years they appear in the form of eczema, asthma, high blood pressure or vision problems. Hidden inner pain results in the physical symptom of the feeling of exhaustion and fear. When you feel tired and languid without any physical ailment, then understand that some bad feeling has entered your inner mind which keeps on waking up and torments you. Tiredness (or restlessness) is an indication of a disorder-induced conflict. **Fatigue is the red flag of emotional conflict-** Curtis Reed

It is clear from these quotes that to remain physically healthy, it is extremely important to be mentally healthy. The sins of the mind are reflected on the body, just like: **JEEBH TAU KAH BHITAR GAYI, JOOTA KHAT KAPAL'**-(Tulsi). The tongue went inside and the skull got hit by the shoes'

(xxiii) Company Effect

Company also has a physical effect on health because one person's illness can spread to another person, but it has a special mental effect. Company of a healthy person brings enthusiasm because one gets to see the vibrancy of health and after seeing that vibrancy, the feeling of becoming healthy, naturally arises. Thus, Company of healthy people gives rise to the mentality of improving one's health. This is why wrestlers keep the idol of Lord Hanuman in their wrestling arenas. Therefore, to be healthy, it is necessary to keep an ideal in front.

Health and Exercise

Exercise is necessary to stimulate the natural strength and vitality of the body and mind. Exercise does not mean wrestling. Exercise can be any activity by which the permanent strength of the body is sharp, active and strong. Its purpose is to obtain natural vitality. That vitality cannot be obtained by drinking tonic or consuming alcohol, because even though it is nutritious, it is not long lasting and natural. Exercise is the only means by which muscles get strengthened; nerves become healthy; The heart, lungs, brain and digestive system become active and unnecessary fat does not increase in the body because a lot of the polluted waste from inside is expelled through breathing and sweat. Every organ can remain fit through proper exercise. Blood circulation remains proper, enthusiasm and self-confidence are felt in the mind. The electrical energy of the body is activated and the body becomes spirited due to the friction and movement of the organs through exercise. These are all the benefits of exercise and one should exercise for these benefits.

There are many types of physical exercises; such as: Yogasan, sports, sit-ups, running etc. Their methods and benefits are well known. The simplest among them is walking, because everyone can do it easily for entertainment. It is also the best in many ways.

Whatever exercise is done, it should be done regularly and with full concentration. Morning time is the most suitable for it. At that time, only those physical activities should be done which give energy to the body. It is not necessary to jump around. Those who cannot do this can awaken their strength by stretching hands and legs on the bed, taking deep breaths and moving the muscles a little.

Even taking a short walk at home is a simple exercise, but only when the will power is strong. Similarly, when you are tired from work in the office, stretching hands and legs a little on the chair brings new energy to the muscles. At that time, closing and opening the eyes tightly two-four times and stretching body two-four times brings fresh energy. This, too, is a good exercise; at least for railway travelers and intellectual businessmen. But these do not give permanent benefits. For permanent strength, some kind of regular physical exercise should be done and with caution, because **"ANTARE – KHOTRE KASRAT KARE, DEV NA MARE AAP MARE"** 'if you do exercise intermittently, God may not kill you but it will' - that is, irregular exercise leads to physical destruction.

(i). Brain Exercise

It is necessary to know something about the exercise of the intellect. Though the intellect is exercised by thinking properly and doing creative work, but there are some other means for it. One means is playing chess. It is a pure Indian game which develops the intellect along with entertainment. It is said that Ravana invented it for Mandodari. Later, the diplomat Chanakya taught this game to Chandragupta to sharpen his intellect. After that, its popularity increased in Buddha-era India, because it was considered a good means of extinguishing the warlike instinct of man. Its non-violent war system was very much liked by the Buddhists. Without giving a complete introduction of chess, we definitely want to say that it is an entertaining and intellect-enhancing exercise.

(ii). Worship is the best exercise for intellect

Gods may or may not grant boons through prayers, but the mind certainly becomes stronger by establishing their radiant form within itself. This increases the strength of self-power and concentration of the mind. Instead of believing in the sympathy of an almighty God, man begins to consider himself powerful and his mental strength leads to intellectual and physical development.

(iii). Rest and Sleep

Like diet, exercise etc., rest is also necessary for health because it is through it that the lost energy of the body is regained and the body system does not become worn out. Rest is the means of reducing the workload on the muscles and nerves due to mental and physical exertion. Rest strengthens the nervous system. Both the body and the mind become healthy, the nerves get revitalization and are again capable of fighting for life. Therefore, it is necessary to take rest after hard work and the rest should be such that it gives complete peace to the body and mind, because this is its real utility.

Mental relaxation is achieved to a great extent by changing the topic of interest and by joking with wife, children and friends. Laughing also relaxes the mind, because laughter increases the circulation of blood, the speed of blood flow increases and mainly the blocked blood of the brain flows properly. It opens the lungs and the polluted air comes out from every vein. This brings peace to the mind; many worries fly away in the air of laughter. Any kind of entertainment relaxes the mind.

Sleep is the main means of complete relaxation. Natural, mental and physical peace is obtained in full from it. Therefore, deep sleep in appropriate quantity is the most important 'tonic' for the body. It is necessary to know something special about sleep.

1. Natural sleep at a fixed time is the healthiest sleep. To achieve it, a beautiful bed and bedding are not as necessary as natural food and hard work. Keeping the digestive system healthy and doing some physical work during the day helps in getting good sleep at night.

2. Sleep is not a physical activity but mainly a mental activity. Sleep comes only when the mind is lightened; it runs away when there is worry in the mind. Therefore, while lying down, one should not worry about any such work which requires the mind to think to solve. Think of some old subject; think of such a subject in which you have got success; engage the mind in some sweet memory. This will ensure that the mind will not have to think; it will enjoy the already solved things and will roam in the known streets only. It will not be pressurized by new thoughts and you will fall asleep engrossed in it. Psychologists have suggested this as the best way to sleep. Another way is to read an entertaining novel, story or poem before sleeping, or to chat with relatives. This will keep the mind from getting entangled in any serious worries. Ancient scholars of Ayurveda say that sleep is achieved only by removing the mind from the senses.

3.	Scientists have told the causes of insomnia and some good ways to cure it. Insomnia is a dreadful disease. If it is not cured as soon as possible, then both the body and the mind become unhealthy and later it cannot be cured by any treatment. The number of insomniacs among suicides is quite high. This disease usually occurs to those who do intellectual work and businessmen.

Insomnia is caused by excessive mental exertion and worry. The secret behind this is: in the normal state of sleep, a large portion of the blood in the brain drains out and the blood vessels contract. But during the waking state and mainly while thinking, the brain veins have ample blood, so they expand. These functions of both states are natural. Sleep comes only when the blood drains out of the brain and the veins contract. Due to excessive worry, staying awake at night and continuous hard work, the brain remains constantly filled with blood and the result is that the veins expand and become loose and their natural contraction does not occur.

In such a condition, they become incapable of expelling blood from the brain and sleep does not come due to the heat of the blood. If immediate care is not taken, the nervous system remains weak and cannot be cured further. Mostly Idiots, Stoics, Carefree and Insensitive people do not suffer from this disease because they do not do any work and do not have tendencies that puts pressure on the intellect. A fool sleeps whenever he wants, because his brain is always empty of blood due to lack of thinking. He suffers from the disease of excessive sleep. **This disease occurs because the nerves of the brain remain constricted.**

It is beneficial to take maximum rest in insomnia. With restlessness, the nerves start functioning normally again. Sea air works like magic in this disease. Sleeping during the day, breathing in the cleanest air, staying outside the house, exercising, all these are very beneficial in this. Drinking any hot drink, especially milk, before lying down, causes the blood of the brain to descend from there after getting heat. Drinking hot milk before going to sleep and when you wake up is very beneficial. By drinking hot milk and then keeping the feet in hot water for a while, the blood circulation of the brain decreases and you fall asleep.

In whatever way possible, taking natural and adequate rest is extremely essential for health. After a good sleep, double the work is done even in a short time. If you do not get sleep, half the work is done even in double the time.

Medicines

We also include medicines among the 'health-protecting and health-enhancing' things. By medicines, we do not mean only tablets, Injections, drops, Ras-Bhasms etc... According to ancient scholars, the thing that gives health to the body is a medicine. According to them, water, air, fasting, are medicines. Even Mantras, Penance are medicines for mental Health. Sun rays are the best medicine. Three types of rays emerge from the sun - heat-giving, light-giving and chemical-producing. All three are healthy. Similarly, air etc. have qualities which we have mentioned above at appropriate places.

1. In reality, food is the best medicine. As far as possible, no disease occurs due to diet control and digestion and if it occurs, it can be cured easily by changing the diet. Some simple food items do wonders if taken properly. Take salt for example. Two tolas of roasted salt taken with Hot Water is helpful to the patient of malaria. Drinking water with salt mixed in it, in case of weakness after fever, restores the body very quickly, because, the salt lost through sweat in case of fever, is replaced. In case of fatigue or restlessness at any time, drinking lightly salted water provides relief before sleeping. In case of tooth diseases, rubbing with salt and any bitter oil has amazing benefits and if one part of soda ash is also mixed with it, it works even better. Besides this, salt is also an easily available medicine.

Among the edibles, take bitter gourd. The outer peel of bitter gourd has a strange power to regulate the level of blood Sugar. Therefore, bitter gourd is beneficial for diabetics in every form. If a 'Diabetic' wants to preserve it, then peel its peel with a wooden knife (not a metal knife), dry it in the shade and eat it throughout the year. This experiment was done by an experienced Egyptian. He had experienced it and published it. Similarly, take papaya. It is a panacea for constipation. No matter how chronic constipation is, drinking a teaspoon of sugar mixed with ten to fifteen drops the raw fruit with Milk in the morning cures indigestion. There is no need to pluck the fruit for grass. Milk drips out by pricking it with a needle. Lemon also purifies the stomach and blood when taken in a cup of warm water in the morning.

Among such small but extraordinary things, we cannot forget 'garlic'. Vagbhata has considered it to be the nectar-like **RASAYANRAJ:** **'SAKSHADAM**

RITSAMBHOOTER GRAMANIH: SA RASAYANAM.' Maharishi Sushruta also considered it power-giving; Useful for intelligence, voice, complexion, eyes and Broken bone joiner; and downsizes the risks of heart disease, chronic fever, colic, leprosy, tumor, loss of appetite, cough, swelling, leprosy, indigestion, worms, Gas, and phlegm. In fact, it is amazingly beneficial in lung diseases, even in tuberculosis, weakness, stomach worm disease and paralysis and other rheumatic diseases. It completely justifies its names like "Vataari" "Shrimast" "Maha-aushadh", "Rasayankar" and "Asthisangdhankar" etc. In the initial stage of tuberculosis, eating one to ten raw garlic cloves in the morning restrics the said disease. We can say this on the basis of the experience of a couple of people.

In paralysis, cooking ten garlic cloves in milk and eating them for forty days gives amazing relief. This too is widely experienced. Generally, eating four garlic cloves on an empty stomach in the morning keeps the stomach clean and increases energy. Mahatma Gandhi used to eat garlic regularly every day and was completely healthy till the end. It is also a medicine for the elderly, because they suffer from Vata disorders and it removes Vata from the bones. Some people consider it an aphrodisiac, but Gandhiji once said that he never had experienced such a thing by regularly consuming garlic.

Prescribing medicines is not our subject. We have mentioned some proven experiments to show that even simple household items can cure major diseases; only wider understanding is required. Even Sankhiya (Arsenic) becomes Amrit if used properly and Madhu (Honey) becomes poison if used foolishly.

2.   We also consider **fasting as a form of medicine**. Fasting improves the health of the body. Cleanliness of body is achieved and the digestive organs get rest. Fasting is especially beneficial in indigestion etc. It should be remembered that during fasting, the Dhatu fibres are destroyed and their place is taken by the stored Dhatus of the muscles. There is more dhatu expenditure from the common organs of the body; for example - during the time spent in fasting, the weight of muscles reduces by 40%, but in the same time the weight of heart reduces by only 30%. Therefore, this myth that fasting weakens the heart should be discarded. Nature has made provision for the protection of essential organs.

3.   Mantras are also considered to be among the kind of yogic medicine. Whether one believes in them or not, it is true that they have the power to give strength, faith and determination to the heart. The peace and hope that they generate in mind is definitely beneficial for health. Words attack the heart. If you express good wishes for someone in sweet words, it swells up. If you say a scolding word to someone, it is cut off without any pain. This proves the power of words, mantras. Words touch the inner core the same way as you can experience how much power there is in touch by the touch of cold or hot air. When the auspicious and well-arranged words of mantras touch the heart with the air, the heart definitely gets excited. There is only a feeling of well-being in those mantras. The body also benefits from the touch of auspicious substances along with mantras. This touch should also not be considered ordinary. Men and women get thrilled by the mere touch of

each other. Similarly, a mother experiences heavenly bliss from the touch of her son. Chanakya has written that the touch of sandalwood is definitely cool, but the touch of a son's body is even cooler than that. Whatever thing a person loves, it gives him pleasure.

4.   It is said that gems and metals like gold also have an effect on the health of the body. According to classical opinion, planets have an effect on the body and gems and stones accumulate energy from the same planets. They also have a negative effect. **We cannot say to what extent this is true**. When the touch of a common substance like cold water brings coolness to the body and shrinks the body parts, then the touch of a shiny substance like diamond can also have an effect. Shukracharya In his ethics, has written that women who desire a son should never wear diamonds: **'NA DHARAYET PUTRAKAAMA NAARI VAJRM KADACHAN.'** In rich families, there is often a problem of not having a child. It should be seen that wearing diamonds in jewelry does not affect the ability of women to conceive. It is said about gold that it connects the body with natural electricity. **Whether this is true or not**, but it is certain that when the worn gold, touches blood through the skin, it produces a healthy effect.

5.   We can also take water, oil massage etc. as medicine. We have already written about water. Regarding oil massage, it should be known that it is extremely nutritious. Bathing and massaging the body is as beneficial as Watering a tree.

6.   It would be unnecessary to write anything about the use of medicines here; that is a matter for doctors and

Vaidyas. However, it should be remembered that the use of medicines is beneficial according to the strength; that is, the medicine given to a young person in a certain quantity will be different from the medicine and its quantity given to a child or an old person. Also, it should be kept in mind that medicines taken in an unnatural way do not have permanent effects. The medicines of the country in which a person belongs naturally benefit him.

Reasons to Health Damage

In brief, we should consider some common reasons for loss of health. The main reason is disease. Disease is that which causes pain to a person: **'TAD DU: KHA SANYOGA VYADHY UCHYANTE'** (Sushruta). This definition is very broad. It includes all kinds of things like food, unfavorable climate and bad company etc, about which something has already been written above. Here we will only point out some important things.

Tridosha- According to Ayurveda, Vata, Pittta, and Kapha are the three main carriers of the body. Without them, the existence of body is not possible. If they are in equal proportions, the body remains healthy. If even one of these increases or decreases, the body becomes diseased. Increase in Kapha causes many diseases of Kapha, increase in Pitta causes blood disorders and Vata causes stomach and brain diseases. One or the other of the three elements is dominant in the nature of a human being from birth. They keep fluctuating due to Food, climate, outdoor activities and mental status. It is not possible to describe all of these in detail here. For example, we will mention some things about Vata because it also has a special relationship with the brain. The brain and the nerves coming out of it are made of this Vata-dhatu. Thinking, reasoning and sensation-related functions are done with its help. All air-related activities are carried out by the Vata element in the body.

Those whose nature is dominated by Vata are impatient by nature, this is the opinion of Sushruta: **'VATALA DHYAAH SADA ATURAH'**. According to Vagbhata, people with Vaat nature are short-tempered, restless, talkative and suspicious by nature. Such people are rude, loquacious, alert and fond of imagination. The direct proof of this is that when there is excess of Vata in a person's body in old age, these things are visible in his nature.

Having Vata Prakriti does not mean that a person is born with these bad qualities. What happens is that when the nature is Vata Prakriti then due to any reason Vata gets agitated and these desires flare up. Even if there is no Vata Prakriti, a person becomes Vata-affected due to bad food or impure air intake or bad living habits. According to medical opinion, Vata excess is mainly caused by these reasons- eating bitter, dry, astringent, cold food, dry vegetables, heavy food, excessive fasting, indigestible food, under-eating, excessive exercise; travelling, sexual intercourse, worry, stroke, bodily pain, night awakening ,by forcibly stopping urine, stool, semen, vomiting, hiccups, tears, outbursts etc. and in the rainy season and during the third part of the day and when the speed of the wind is strong.

Due to the outbreak of Vatta, pain, breathing problems and arthritis can occur in the body along with, mental damage in particular. When it increases, anger arises and when anger increases, it heats up the blood and there is a great waste of breath. Not only this, it leads to madness. At least Sita knew this. She could not believe it when she suddenly saw Hanuman in Lanka and started thinking whether it was a delusion of her mind or a disorder of the wind or a disorder caused by madness or a mirage:

KIN NA SYACHCHITTAMOHYAM BHAVED VATA GATISTVIYAM. UNMADJO VIKARO VA SYADIYAM MRIGTRISHNIKA- (Ramayana)

When Vata gets angry, a person becomes angry and mad and starts blabbering, uttering meaningless sentences:

SWADEHAKUPITAD VATAD SAMBANDHAM NIRARTHAKAM, VACHANAM YENNARO BRUT SA PRALAPAH: PRAKIRTITAH:

In that state, thoughts become unstable and intellect is lost. Anger leads to attachment, attachment leads to loss of memory, loss of memory leads to loss of intellect and loss of intellect leads to total destruction. In a fit of anger, many people get fever, many go mad and many get paralysis. In a state of anger, the temperature of the body naturally increases and due to the increase in temperature, the air gets irritated because it itself is combustible and then the person starts blabbering, as in case of fever.

Angry people are often found to be suffering from diseases like Vatul (madness) or paralysis because their nerves get agitated repeatedly and become weak. According to the Hindu Karma Vipaak Shastra (Karmaphalodaya), paralysis is considered to be the divine punishment for those who hurt others, do injustice in the assembly, deceit and accuse others without any reason. A person does all these things only when he is suffering from Vata disorder. Kautilya has written in his Arthashastra that angry kings have often been heard to be destroyed due to natural anger: PRAYAH: **KOPVASHA RAJAN: PRAKRITI KOPAIRHATAH**:

These natural angers are such sudden diseases. To avoid this, one should avoid Vaata- disorder. The Ayurvedic remedies to avoid this are- keeping the stomach clean, regular consumption of ghee and oil, fasting, light diet of sweet, sour, salty and cooked substances, oil massage, renunciation of worry and fear. When the wind rages on the brain, it is usually pacified only by showing fear. This is a proven fact. When a person starts doing some wrong deed in a state of unrestrained rambling or anger, then he becomes calm only due to the fear of punishment. People say that he has come to his senses. This happens because the Vaat calms down. People say in colloquial language that when he was scolded, the wind got tightened and started moving away. Ayurvedic experts had already discovered this secret. Even today, new mad people are treated by showing fear. Doctors scare them by giving them electric shock treatment and many people get cured by this.

After understanding all these things, we should protect ourselves from being affected by Vata. Similarly, we should also protect ourselves from being affected by Kapha and Pitta. Now we will take up other health-destroying topics.

Consuming Poison

By poison intake we mean those poisons which we consume daily due to addiction. Alcohol has already been discussed. The second major poison is tobacco. A Chicago physiologist "Dr. Steinhans has written that if less than four hundredth part of an ounce of Nicotine were injected into a man's blood, he would die; and there is about one-third of this quantity in every cigarette smoked. Nicotine excites the heart to go faster. In the course of 24 hours, a smoker's heart may have to beat 10,000 extra times". It is written in the famous English encyclopedia on sexology that tobacco reduces sexual power. When many impotent men did not get cured by any method, they were asked to give up cigarettes. As a result, they became virile again. Therein a popular saying is mentioned, which means that tobacco and women are enemies of each other. Love for one destroys love for the other.

Tolstoy had experienced that tobacco destroys the power of reasoning. According to him, most of the murderers in Russia had the courage to commit murder only after smoking cigarettes. Nicotine mainly destroys memory, corrupts lungs and causes difficulty in digestion. Teeth lose their shine and mouth becomes foul-smelling by eating or drinking tobacco. At least cigarette is a terrible addiction. There is an authentic book in English on the erotic life of the World War-1 (Sexual Life during the World War) It is written in it that when cigarettes became scarce in countries like France etc., the young women there, used to rent their chastity to the cigarette sellers by taking one cigarette each. Cigarettes awaken feelings of both insolence and shamelessness.

We can consider PAAN as one of the poisons. To a certain extent, it is not only a mouth freshener, but also a beauty enhancer, a stimulant and a blood purifier. But when the addiction increases, it kills the appetite, makes the blood dry and weakens the teeth. The root of betel leaf contains a dangerous poison. It is well known that by consuming the powder of the roots of betel leaf, the woman loses her power to conceive forever. In such a situation, eating paan must have an ill effect on women at least. In medicine, it is forbidden for women to eat paan during their menstrual period. Women who indulge in sexual pleasures eat paan more. It must have an effect on their ability to conceive.

Vanaspati ghee is also a type of poison. But Pure ghee is considered nectar. It can even neutralize snake poison. It increases longevity. Its Sanskrit name is Ayu. It is incomparable in increasing health, radiance and intelligence. Vanaspati ghee cannot replace it in these matters, though it may replace it in sweet shops. This artificial ghee automatically digests the digestive power, the essence of manhood is lost and vision gradually disappears. These things have been scientifically tested on living beings. After two-three generations, their descendants are found to be impotent and blind.

Laziness

Laziness is also harmful for health because it leads to unnecessary obesity, the heart becomes incapable of circulating blood, and the body becomes heavy. A lazy person lies down all day, which reduces his life span rapidly. Scientific research shows that the heart does not beat as much when one is standing or sitting than as much as when lying down. One of the Insurance Companies had calculated and published that the main reason for suicide is laziness. Suicidal tendency arises from laziness and inactivity. According to the calculations of the company, the number of obese suicide victims is more than that of thin people.

Laziness and obesity can be eradicated by simple diet and hard work. Drinking honey or lemon mixed water in the morning is beneficial. Squeezing a lemon in the bath water and taking a bath is also beneficial. Another benefit of this is that it does not cause stains on the skin and the skin color shines.

Constipation

We have already written something about constipation. This disease contaminates the blood and rots the body while it is alive. It is the mother of fever etc. The saying **'AAANT BHARI TO MATHA BHARI'** is well known. Triphala intake is a good remedy for this. In modern treatments, the use of 'enema' is the best.

Anorexia

Not getting food on time or to the extent of hunger also destroys the body. There is no need to prove this because in India there are numerous people who are deprived of food, from whose condition its ill effects can be estimated.

Similarly, health is destroyed due to many reasons, one of which is unclean living conditions and dirty food in the market. The destruction of health is also directly caused by polluted climate. It should be remembered that climate has a great impact not only on the body but also on the brain. It changes the nature of man. It has been observed through scientific studies that excessive cold makes the nerves restrained and shamelessness comes in the persona. Hot climate causes harshness, irritation, laziness, fatigue, restlessness and nervous laxity in the nature and destroys the concentration of the mind. This is the game of oxygen.

Health Examination

In the end we would like to say that keeping all things in mind, Health should be protected and the body should be made so strong that it can bear its own burden, if not that of others. For this, one should take care of the three vital organs - heart, brain and lungs - because they are the main operators of the body; and blood should be protected because in the words of Sushrut, blood is the root of the body; it sustains the body. In fact, it is life. The nervous system should be kept strong because it is they who weave the body's net. Health should be tested daily with various measures. For example, if the head is heavy, the tongue is dirty, then it should be understood that there is heaviness in the intestines. Excessive excitement or lethargy should indicate nervous weakness, red-yellow or burning urine should be considered unhealthy and urine without foam should be considered destruction of manhood.

Chapter-4

Rich have all the Virtues

The famous ethicist Bharthari has written that the one who has money is considered to be of high family, learned, virtuous, orator and handsome; money provides shelter to all the virtues. In reality, money is the giver of prosperity to humans, helper, friend, troubleshooter and Aladdin's lamp. It provides livelihood, increases prestige and fulfills desires. The much-experienced Vyas has rightly said that absence of money is the death of a man: **'PURUSHASYA'DHANAM VADAH'** [Udyog-Parva]. Which mortal being will deny this statement of policy that poverty is the most painful: **'SARVOKASHTA DARIDRATĀ.'**

Earning wealth is a personal duty of man, because without it life cannot go on. This earth is called Vasumati (of wealthy people). One who does not get Vasuta in this earth cannot enjoy material life. One who is Vasumat (rich) enjoys Vasumati; one who is Vasukit (beggar) spends the life of hell even on Earth which has so many things to enjoy 'NAANARATNA VASUNDHARA' [Kalidas]. Such is the system of worldly life.

Earning money is not only a big selfishness but also a charity. It is a great national duty. Nations are made of individuals. Therefore, the collective prosperity and poverty of individuals affects the condition of the nation. When a country is rich in wealth, its civilization and independence develop, the nation becomes powerful, capable and peaceful. Economic conditions are found standing right behind the political situation. Even in wars, the financial strength of the nation becomes the backbone behind the military power. If the economic condition of the country is not good, then the armies cannot stand in the field for long. When people remain hungry, then the nation's **Rules get flouted, public decorum breaks down**, rebellion takes place, insurgencies increase. Weak & Poor do not have mercy **'KSHIṆĀ NĀRĀḤ NISHKARUNA BHAVANTI'**,

The accumulation of wealth from all points of view is the ultimate duty of man. The philosophers are of the opinion that wealth leads to religion and happiness - **'DHANA- DHARMA TATH: SUKHAM'**. To consider wealth as the root of sin like the ascetics is wrong. Wealth is not the father of sin, but its absence makes a man commit sin. Sin grows in the mind of the poor, because then there is a shower of tears arising out of pain. A useless man does wrong not only to himself, but also to the country and society, because he himself consumes the wealth of others without earning anything and depletes the national wealth. One who is ready to accumulate wealth, with his bravery, does some good to himself and to the country and society. Believe that only wealth brings welfare to the public life. Nature wants that you do not become poor. In the words of Sheikh Saadi: 'The Sun and the Moon are all busy working so that you can earn and keep getting bread to eat.

(i) Means of Earning Money

Now consider the means of acquiring wealth. Wealth is seen to be obtained by luck too, but luck is such a force over which no one has independent control. Therefore, it is not right to become inactive by relying on luck. Tulsi is of the opinion that troubles are not destroyed by hanging pictures of Kalpataru and Kamdhenu in the house: **'CHITRA KALPATARU KAMDHENU GRIHA LIKHE NA VIPATI NASAAVE.'** Kautilya is also of the opinion that wealth is produced by wealth only, how will the poor stars help: **'ARTHO HYARTHASYA NAKSHATRAM KIM KARISHYANTI TARAKAH:'.** We should believe that wealth is produced by intelligent work and when produced, it increases. After all, labor is the father of money.

Work or hard work can be in the form of business as well as job i.e. in the form of service. Though scriptures have considered service-attitude despicable. There is no doubt that earning and spending enough money can be done only in business. One who wants to enjoy the wealth to the fullest should make business the means of earning money. Business, even if small, is more profitable and lucrative than a job. Job involves dependence; therefore, one has to adopt a very artificial persona to make oneself agreeable to others.

(ii) Keep these points in mind

Due to the circumstances, whether you do business or job, if you want to progress then keep these things in mind:

1. <u>Do not sell your self-respect and morality to anyone</u>- whether you are doing a job or business or have set out to do it, do not forget your human ideals. Humanity degrades as soon as morality degrades. Do not do such work which is against the soul. Everything can be bought with money, but the honour and dignity of a good man cannot be bought.

2. <u>Do not depend on the mercy of others</u>- Among others, we also include luck. Luck can help you get a good job or a good opportunity for business, but its (luck's) help will not help in doing it. Only self-competence can help you get a good position or a good opportunity. Among others, we also include friends and elders. They can help you only to a certain extent. If you do not have self-confidence, they cannot become your backbone. There is a saying in English that. **"God helps those who help themselves".** God helps only those who are self-reliant. This experiential statement of a famous foreign thinker (Sir William Temple) is worth remembering in this regard: *"A man that only translates shall never be a poet, nor a painter that only copies, nor a swimmer that swims always with bladder, so people that trust wholly on others' charity and without industry of their own will always be poor."*

So be self-reliant and don't look at others' faces; looking at others is a dog's instinct. Sometimes one feels compelled to look at others' faces, but then it should be done with preparation, that is, someone should look at your usefulness and you look at his pocket with a true eye. Rahim's wors should be kept in mind **"TAKI, PRABHUTA NAAHIN GHATI, PUR GHAR GAYE RAHIM".** Going to others' house does not lessen your nobility.

3. <u>Do not be content even by mistake</u>- In the eyes of sages, **SANTOSHAH: PARAM SUKHAM'**, 'contentment is the ultimate happiness' may be a good principle, but for a worldly man, contentment means sitting idle. At least Lakshmi (Goddess of wealth) does not like idleness or stagnation. She is very fickle. Only when you run with her, you can get her company. Only then hope remains and a life full of hope is the happiest life. Do not become contented and pessimistic or contented by being pessimistic. Keep your willpower strong and alert.

4. <u>Look into the future</u>- If you have even a spark of hope, then look into the future, because you have to spend every moment from today onwards in it. You have some right over it and it can be created by you. Only a leader who thinks ahead of his time is considered a pioneer. Therefore, if you want to become a leader in your field then make a plan for ten years from today and then move ahead with that plan. Move like you do when you travel by train from one place to another, having prepared all the details of the route and having a ticket for the desired destination. Look into the future, but not the dark future.

5. <u>Catch the time</u>- Time is the biggest businessman. He is such a businessman who walks with long hair but is bald at the back. He can be caught only when caught from the front. Running after him makes the opportunity slip

away and the person who is behind time can do nothing except sitting and regretting. There is a saying in English that **time is money.**

In our scriptures, the great glory of Mahakaal has been sung. Its meaning is that time is very powerful, it should be respected. Respect and welcome are given only from the front, behind the back there is usually criticism. The power of time is proved by the fact that it changes and passes everyone. It enjoys Age. Time-lord Sun sets every day only after taking a day of everyone's life. When it takes something from you, it is wise that you also take the right price of your life from it, do not let your thing go to waste.

Therefore, seize each hour and each moment. Seize means to keep doing something every moment. To keep doing something does not mean to do mischief, but to do some useful work. Those moments will become valuable for you. One hour of a wise man's life is considered equal to the entire life of a fool, because a wise man knows and does use that one hour appropriately. Therefore, do not let even a minute go waste. In essential tasks, give more importance to 'now' than 'later'. The world moves very fast; in a minute it goes from one place to another. Therefore, as far as possible, do not postpone tasks by promising. Do the tasks immediately, that needs to be done immediately. Believe that Tomorrow will bring with it many troubles. Adopt the policy of **'SHUBHASYA SHEEGRHAAM'.** Do the (auspicious) work Immediately.

Do not wait for the golden opportunity. Golden opportunity cannot come on its own. If you sow its seeds today, then only it can be harvested tomorrow. This is the law of nature. If the creator or father of tomorrow is weak today, then his son tomorrow will also be weak by birth. It is foolish to depend on the future. A little part of the future is immediately attained after every moment and every hour. You should not consider it to be far away from you and you should start walking towards your goal from where you are standing. A scholar has said that the path of life's journey begins exactly from where you are standing. The future can become a golden opportunity only when you find yourself ready for it. Former Prime Minister of England Disraeli has said that **the secret of man's success is to be ready when the opportunity comes.**

This preparation can be completed by starting from today itself. If you run to dig a well in case of a fire, then your house cannot be saved from the fire. It is wise to prepare before the situation arises. By accumulating resources from today itself, they can be used at the right time. Therefore, be farsighted. Eyes are kept at such a height so that Humans can see far away.

6. Recognize the time- Along with respecting time, practice recognizing it as well. It is not easy to recognize or read time, because it does not always remain the same, it keeps changing. Recognize its speed based on its effect, not with the help of almanac, calendar or clock. Being clairvoyant is a great quality, that is why ancient scholars were called KALDARSHI OR TRIKALDARSHI.

Only the one who recognizes the time and behaves accordingly is successful. Only the one who recognizes the time and the situation quickly is astute & quick-witted. One should recognize it properly and make changes in his life accordingly. This does not mean being an opportunist, but being time-follower. Thinking, behaving and working according to the time is the means of success. Therefore, read the time. The main means of reading it is your discretion; the external means are the newspaper, TV Channels, social media etc. Instead of getting the knowledge of time from the almanac, get it from the these. Almanac is the work of the pundits, whereas the newspaper, TV Channels, social media are Granths for awakened citizens, businessman and public at large.

Why should we read time? Understand its essence from the following sentences of Sardar Patel.: "The modern world is different from the ancient world. Earlier everything used to move slowly at a fixed pace, so there was more time; now one day has become equal to a century. In no time, so many states, so many empires have been destroyed and vanished. Who can say that time does not have wings and in view of this, who would like to wait for time or waste it?"

Look at the modern times in which you have to live. Look at them from the point of view that this is the age of airplanes, space crafts and not the age of bullock carts. The more work you can do in a short time by using your brain or power or both, the more your value will increase. Be aware not only of this large division of time but also of its new circumstances. In short, be microscopic - not only in relation to time, but also of every useful thing. Look at the place and time minutely; look at every task from the point of view of timeliness and usefulness.

7. <u>Keep the powers of the mind alert</u>, even if you are a businessman or an employee, always keep your self-

confidence strong. Do not consider yourself incapable. The biggest mistake of life is when a person becomes hopeless by considering himself incapable and helpless. Give up the attitude of giving up and become enthusiastic and decide that you have to become successful, you have to achieve something. Only by being determined does a person get self-confidence. Use your imagination, but with a purpose. Imagination also has great power. It finds the next step. After that, take recourse to discretion. It will be able to decide the right step among the steps found by your imagination. Make your memory strong - but not for remembering useless things. Keep in mind the useful things proved by experience with discretion. Make your thoughts accustomed to it so that they can immediately recognize the true form of a thing. For success, it is necessary to take recourse to the three things: -1) Accurate knowledge, 2) Faith in success and 3) High imagination power.

The most important thing is- Courage. Maharishi Vyas has written in Mahabharata that Lakshmi resides in courage. Cowardice is a destructive emotion. Whatever big businesses are standing today, they were established with courage. If more caution was taken than necessary, not even a single factory could have been established. Courage is required both in the battlefield and in the business sector, because there is a feeling of struggle and competition in both. A person who takes special care of self-defense cannot go very far. If you want to be victorious, then stand in the field of work with courage, raise your arms, fight with the circumstances and at the same time remain firm with patience. Courage and patience never fail. Make your mind so strong that your concentration does not slacken until you achieve your goal.

Know It To Shine

8. <u>Be tolerant and hardworking</u>- Tolerance comes from patience. It does not mean that if someone insults you, you should swallow poison and sit down. Its purpose is to be steady-minded and listen to everything peacefully, understand everything and avoid any controversy. By being tolerant and hardworking, the work gets completed without any obstacles.

9. <u>Be well behaved</u> - Business is mainly run by behavior. Its Sanskrit synonym is **'vyavahar'**. A businessman is also called a 'Vyavaharak'. Always keep truth and trust in behavior because the world's business is run by these. Deceitful behavior is economic ruin. When the reputation of a business is established, then only its name is sold. When the reputation is lost, its goods are not sold, but are auctioned. Reputation is established by true behavior. Mix artificiality in business only up to the extent it is necessary. Cheating is like beating Lakshmi with a stick and driving her out of the house. Trustworthiness is Lakshmi's mother.

Being personally well behaved is also the first step towards achieving wealth. Who is not influenced by politeness of behavior! Someone asked a well-known businessman that by which business did he earn so much money? He replied that by trading only one thing, which you too can do; that is politeness, humility. America's rich man Rockefeller once said that politeness is a purchasable commodity just like sugar or coffee; and I am ready to pay more for that ability than any other thing in the world. To earn money, it is not as important to be learned as to be well behaved.

10. <u>Become a master</u>- Wealth is not obtained by knowledge, but by the use of knowledge. Therefore, instead of becoming a knower, become a worker (karmayogi). In short, become a Yogi, a Rishi, an Arya, a Shakt– only then can you get wealth. This does not mean that you should sit in a temple and ask for wealth from Ram, the giver of all. There is no need to get angry at these words. Efficiency in work is called yoga: **'YOGAH: KARMASU KAUSHALAM'**. And according to the Gita, the name of physical activity for sustaining life is karma. Yoga is not magic. Rishi is made from the root 'Rish', which means motion and according to grammarians, motion means knowledge, movement and attainment. Arya is also made from the root 'Ri', which means motion. That by which work is accomplished – ability, strength – is power. The one who practices it is a Shakt.

Knowledge and power can be advertised through work and at least in this age of science, wealth can be earned through it. Therefore, do not just believe in the superiority of knowledge. Work according to the plan and keep in mind the principle of the learned Vyas that there is no doubt that a working man is strong and rich: **'PAANIVANTO BALAVANTO DHANVANTO NA SANSHAYAH:'**

11. <u>Do the work diligently according to your interest and ability</u> - The first thing is that you should choose such a profession as far as possible which is in accordance with your interest and ability. If this is not done, then you will appear like that person who goes to see a fair wearing a loose coat of engagement. Therefore, wear clothes of your size only. Secondly, whatever work you do, do it with diligence, concentration and perseverance. Just as a pearl is

obtained by diving into the sea. Similarly, money is obtained by immersing or being absorbed in work. While doing every work, keep in mind the elegance and perfection. Man is beauty lover by nature.

Every work done with good taste and concentration is praiseworthy, noble and rich. In concentration, keep the ideal of Edison in front of you. Edison had patented 1500 new inventions in his 70 years of life. He always remained engaged in one thing or the other and did not participate in any society events. Despite being a millionaire, he did not worry about money and prestige, although both ran after him. Solving problems was his addiction and he worked continuously for it with full concentration. The result is well known. A man who is constantly industrious can do everything, and the work itself becomes easy out of fear of the person's persistence working -: **Job fears the craftsman**

12. <u>Collect virtues and become extraordinary</u>- If you are poor but still have virtues, you will surely find someone who appreciates virtues. Even God, whether in the form of Ram-Krishna or Jesus-Muhammad, is more revered by the people when He has virtues, then what to say about humans! Collection of virtues is always beneficial. Virtues are the birthplace of money. Collect new virtues and become an expert in one subject, only then you will be considered superior to the common people and will be the center of attraction. By being skilled in some work, there is no fear of livelihood. Self-confidence, ability and practice - these are the proven steps of Lakshmi-mandir.

13. <u>Adopt the spirit of service</u>- Whatever be your situation, you can benefit from others by subduing them

through service. Service is definitely valued in society. Service proves the usefulness of a person and one gets prominence accordingly. Shukracharya has written that by rendering proper service at the right time, even an unimportant person becomes Important and by being lazy or making mistakes in doing something, even an important person becomes an Unimportant;

APRADHAN: PRADHAN: SYATKALEN AATYAN TSEVNAAT PRADHANOAPYAPRADHANAH: SYATSEVALASYADINA YETAH:

Even if you are an independent businessman, do not give up the spirit of service. Henry Ford had said in a speech that the big businessmen of this era can only remain 'servants of the public'. Because only when the public appreciates their products will they be consumed in the market; the public itself becomes the owner and gives them money. Now that era is coming to an end when businessmen could suck the blood of the public by becoming money-vampires. Now business can develop only under the protection of the public. If you do a job, then service is your capital.

14. <u>Consider financial purity as religion</u>- According to the ancient shastra writers, financial purity is the main purity. It is really very difficult to remain spotless in matters of money. Not stealing is not the only thing that comes under financial purity. It means not misusing money, not being greedy, not being lazy and not trying to collect money through unfair means. If money is not pure, then money never stays, consider this to be true. Those who are not clean in matters of money are usually money-slaves, not money-masters. You can test this by the fact that no

thief, dacoit or bribe-taking government officer is found enjoying his sinfully earned money.

15. <u>Hold your position, seat firmly</u>- The power of the place is a great power. You can understand this from the fact that as long as the hair is on your head, you groom it, apply oil on it, and enhance your beauty with it. Not only this, the father smells the head of the children. When the same hair is cut, it is considered as impure and dirty and thrown away. Same is the condition of human beings. As long as he is sitting on a post, on a throne, on a chair, his dignity remains intact, he is respected. As soon as he leaves his position, his seat, his glory decreases. Therefore, the scriptures advise that do not give up your position and place. **"SANSTHAN NA TYAJAYATE**. The author of Mahabharata has written that wise people move the other foot forward only after keeping one foot firmly; they do not leave the previous place without examining the next place:

TISHTHATYEKEN PADEN CHALATYEKEN BUDDHIMAN NA PARIKSHYA PARAM STHANAM PURVAMAYATANAM TYAJET. (Maharshi Vyas)

16. <u>Churn the ocean of life</u>- Consider it to be true from a practical point of view that even an almighty being like Vishnu got Lakshmi by churning the ocean. Wealth cannot be obtained without hard work. It is written in the scriptures that one should pray to fire: **'DHAN-MICHHET HUTAASHNAT'**. Fire is also called Dhandaayi and Dhananjay. This does not mean that if you sit in front of the fireplace with folded hands, money will start pouring down. The meaning is clear. If you look, you will know that many wealth-enhancing activities are done

with the help of fire. The second meaning is that wealth is obtained only when the body is ignited by fire, that is, the fire of hard work. Money has heat, this is the only proof that it has fire. Do not go by the words, look at the meaning and spirit. Only the money that is earned by shedding sweat can be digested. The heat of money obtained without shedding sweat becomes unbearable, it makes the head dizzy. In essence, understand that wealth cannot be obtained without melting. Therefore, be humble and soft-hearted and use your body to shed labor. Hard work increases a man's wealth; not only wealth, it also increases the feeling of co-operation. Psychologists say that hardworking people fight and quarrel less. The root cause of quarrels are addictions and inactive people. Therefore, a hardworking person is also a social reformer; is this not a small matter of pride?

Do not rest more than necessary, because it destroys the working power. An American writer has written that the reason why the cities of America appear so prosperous is that there is "No place to sit Down". What we mean to say is that standing in the field of work increases prosperity.

17. <u>Give importance to success of the task</u>- Do not give much importance to difficulties and obstacles in the task. Even a simple task seems difficult when you start because nothing is easily achievable and even big problems seem easy when solved. There are two German proverbs- one means that the beginning of every task is difficult. The other means that the problem seems easy when solved. Keep these in mind. In this world, only success is accepted- whether it is a race between the Hare & the Tortoise, a task or a human being. Therefore, try to succeed. If someone other than you have succeeded in any task, then you will

Know It To Shine

also definitely succeed- if you work hard! 'By practicing again and again, a dull-witted person becomes intelligent!' **KARAT KARAT ABHYAS KE JADMATI HOT SUJAN**

18. Think about your daily income and expenditure- Do not develop the habit of reconciling your accounts at the end of your life or at the end of the year. Every day, see how much your income is, how it can be increased; how much your expenditure is, how it can be decreased. Think about this in the morning and prepare your programme and work according to that plan the whole day and in the evening see whether you are in profit or loss. Weigh your situation daily. That part of your income is more valuable which reaches the bank after proper expenditure. That is useful in times of crisis and the scriptures say that money should be protected for a crisis: **'APADATHE DHANAM RAKSHET'**. If you have money, then learn to save it, and if not, then learn to earn and save. This is possible only when you think about this question every day. In this regard, this verse of Chanakya Muni is worth keeping in mind:
KAH: KAALH: KANI MITRANI KO DESHAH: KAU VYAYAGAMO KO VAAHAM KA CHA ME SHAKTIRITHI CHINTYAM MUHARMUH:
What is the time like? Who are the helpers? What is the country like? What is the income and expenditure? Who am I? How much capability do I have? One should think about these things again and again.

19. Be cautious in Money transactions. Shukracharya has written that giving of money leads to friendship, but taking it back leads to enmity: **'DHANAM**

MAITRIKARAM DAANE CHADANE SHATRUKARAKAM.' This is what happens in loan transactions. The proverb 'give loan and make enemy' is not only very famous but also very much experienced. Therefore, as far as possible, neither give nor take loan. As soon as you take loan, Tulsi's saying: **'AAB GAYA AADAR GAYA, NAINAN GAYA SANEH'** -Honor gone, respect gone, affection gone from the eyes- is completely vindicated.

20. <u>Donation increases wealth</u>- It is a supernatural but proven truth since ancient times that donation increases wealth. No matter how little your income is, if you give some of it to a deserving person, it definitely accumulates self-confidence if not virtue and the mind feels that the money was used for some charitable purpose; secondly, public prestige is gained. If you look at it on a larger scale, you will find that donation brings economic benefits indirectly. Take the example of Tata, Birlas, Bill Gates, Ajim Premji, who are famous for donation. The advertisement of their names through donation creates love for their business among the public. They could not have earned this much love and fame by just advertising. Many of their business adventures succeed because of their donations for philanthropic purposes.

21. <u>Do not disguise yourself as a rich person like:</u> Do not falsely advertise your wealth like a big businessman and "The Talukdar of Awadh". Rather, make your lifestyle according to your income status.

22. <u>Be like a Bania (businessman)</u>- If you want to earn money, then Instead of becoming a Pandit, & emotional and arrogant like Thakur, become a Baniya (a person of an

Know It To Shine

Indian mercantile caste that is mainly found in Gujrat and Rajasthan, and spread all over the world doing business and Trade and considered to be miser) simple, sweet, cautious and knowledgeable of 'Arthakari Vidya'(Economics). Money comes not from philosophical wisdom or knowledge of Dhanurveda but from business mindedness. Hold on to every penny the way Baniya holds on to it. If you don't like becoming a native Baniya, then become like an English Baniya who came to India from 'across the seven seas' and while doing business became king from Trader.

23. Five principles to be kept in mind:

1 **SHRIMANGALATPRABHAVATI PRAGALBHAYAT SAMPRAVARDHATE, DAKSHYATTU KURUTE MOOLAM SANYAMATPRATISHTHATI.** - (Vidur)
Wealth is generated by good deeds, increases by Pragalbhata (courage, ability, keenness, speed, determination), flourishes by cleverness and is protected by restraint.

2 **YATHA MADHU SAMADATTE RAKSHAN PUSHPANI SHATPADAH TAVDVADARTHAN MANUSHYEABHYA AADYADAVIHISYA.** - (Vidur) –
Just as a bumblebee takes honey from a flower without destroying it, similarly man should also take a part of wealth without destroying the original source of wealth.

3 **KARANAAT PRIYATAMETI DVESHO BHAVATI KARANAAT; ARTHARTHI**

JEEVLOKOYAM NA KASCHITKASYA CHITPRIYAH: (Mahabharata) –
Love arises among people due to reason and hatred arises due to reason only; In this world of "Businessmen", no one purposelessly is dear to anyone.

4   **PRASARAYATI KRITYANI, SARVATRE VICHIKITSATE; CHIRAM KAROTI KSHIPARTHE SA MUDHO BHARATARSHABH** -(Mahabharata)
One who makes the work long, doubts everything, delays the important work, is called a fool.

5   **KARYAE KARMANI NIRDISHTE YO BAHUNYAPI SADHAYET: PURVAKARYA-VIRODHEN SA KARYE KARTUMARHATI: NA HYOKAH: SADHAKO HETUAH: SVALPASYAPEEH KARMANAH: YO HYARTH BAHUDHA VED SA SAMARTHO ARTHSADHANE -** (Hanuman in Lanka)
After completion of his duty, the one who performs other tasks without conflict with it, is a good worker. The one who knows many ways to achieve wealth is the one who earns money. There is no need to write anything specifically on the above shlokas. Yes, it should be understood that here meaning of wealth is work. Wealth or respect is the price received for the success of work.

Keeping all the above points in mind, we should now consider some other important things that are useful for those who earn money through different means.

1...If you are a businessman

1.   Capital, hard work and ability- Business requires either capital and hard work, or ability and hard work. If you have capital, then see in which work it will be put to fruition. Think with a creative mind. Look at the needs and interests of people. Awaken hope, faith and enthusiasm and put your wishes into action and combine your and others' hard work with the capital. If you do not have capital, then with your ability you can get others to invest money and with your own hard work you can start the business. Try to become a businessman. If you have a lot of capital, then use machinery; if you have only a little capital or ability, then adopt home based industries and grow gradually. Remember Gandhiji's advice that **if you want to grow, "start from the bottom."**

2.   Be prepared for competition - There are many similarities between military work and business methods. One can be called a violent war and the other a non-violent one. The country is captured by the army; the market is captured by business. Both require organization, discipline and skill. The armies march ahead playing the band and the business grows by advertising. Just as there is competition between two armies facing each other, the same is the case between two businesses. The opportunity is also used in the same way in both, as different parts of the army move towards a goal by cooperating with each other to achieve a single objective. Understanding these things, you should enter into business with military enthusiasm. Just as victory is achieved by new types of weapons, similarly economic success is achieved by the invention of new things,

production of attractive and useful things. Only by manufacturing a new product at the right time with new ideas and advertising it in a new way, its publicity can be increased. Remember that this is the age of propaganda. The basic secret of propaganda is repetition. By publishing the same thing again and again, it gets embedded in the minds of people. Keep one special product of yours and try again and again to prove it to be the best. If you try to make or tell all your products to be the best, you will fail. Make only one product special and concentrate your energies on its promotion. Other products will also follow it, just as Gandhiji got all the public approval behind his service to the nation. Pay more attention to their sale than their production. Money comes from sales.

3. <u>Business grows with popularity</u>- To expand your business, gain the sympathy of the public. For that, first of all, take care of the demand of the public. Do not try to loot the public by giving goods according to the demand and on the pretext of their price. The public is satisfied only when it feels that it has got a product more valuable than its money or has got the right product according to the price. That is why sacrifice a little. The more discount you give to others, the more profit you will get. If you take the least profit from people, their money will be saved and that money will reach you again indirectly. Once satisfied, they will become your permanent customers. Keep in mind how more sales can be made with less profit. It is essential to sacrifice momentary greed for permanent profit.

4. <u>Utility in all things</u> - Anything can be made useful. If you understand the current needs and interests of people in time and trade according to them, then you can use anything. During the world war, when there was a shortage

of things, clever people made a lot of money by making even small things useful. A person named John Trail had bought old papers worth thousands of rupees as soon as the war broke out, because he understood that soon due to non-availability of paper, they would be needed for packets and paper bags. As a result, he earned lot of money from those newspapers during the war. Similarly, seeing the shortage of pins, some people started business of acacia thorns. There are hundreds of such examples. The above-mentioned John Trail is of the opinion that money can be made from everything, if you know who needs it. This is how a businessman uses an opportunity. There is a saying in English that **He who hesitates is lost**. one should make a firm decision and jump into the field with whatever 'weapon' is available.

5. <u>Management</u>. It is necessary to keep in mind some more things about the internal management of the office. The first thing is that every business has a definite program, a well-organized work system. If there is chaos in it, there is no unity. Success always comes from the strength of the power of union. A big business should be divided into departments and capable people should be given responsibility and they should also be trusted. Only efficient planners can get work done from hardworking people and the ability of a manager is considered to be that he can get the work of three people done from three people.

By treating employees well, we can get their full cooperation. They should not be given false hopes and should be given respectful salary according to their ability and hard work. They should not be made to feel that you are doing them any favor. Everyone should be encouraged by giving rewards as much as possible without unnecessary cuts in salary. It is better not to divide too much in small business. In every situation, employees should be instilled with the feeling that it is their own work and if the products presented by them are appreciated well, they will also get a share in the profit. Where everyone comes together for money, everyone can be satisfied with money. By engaging even, the smallest person in suitable work and making him satisfied, profit can be taken from him. Business is organized with cooperation in the same way as a knot is tied with the fingers of both hands.

Producing more products at the lowest cost and preventing wastage is also an important part of management efficiency. By using all By-products somewhere, their wastage can be saved.

Accounting and correspondence can be done only under management. Your accounting is the mirror of your business, do not forget this. It is very important that it is well organized and correct. Correspondence is the life of business. In letters, in emails, in social media, it should be kept in mind that they should be clear, simple and full of truth. There is no place for sentimentality in business; whether it is correspondence, emails or conversation, keep in mind that less words and more work is the universally accepted principle in the business field. In business, only those ideas are valued which are logical and meaningful.

6. <u>Meditate like a sage</u> - If you have opened a business, be farsighted, do not expect immediate profits; like a sage, wait for money with hope and faith, do sadhana. Sit with a tight chest, big shocks can come. All the big businessmen of today are not standing in the market without any reason. Big waves of the world ocean hit them

every day, but they do not move from their seat. The bigger a person is, the stronger the shocks of time he faces. The flow of money becomes unbroken only by continuous hard work and that is the purpose of business. If you give up even once and sit down in front of the circumstances, they will attack you mercilessly because their enmity with you continuously run every day.

7. <u>Increase National Wealth</u>- Increase national wealth through Industries or business or Trade- The biggest public work done through them is that it can serve the country at a much high level. Keep in mind that the money that reaches the country from outside in exchange for goods increases national wealth. Therefore, produce such goods that can be sold abroad. Also, produce such goods which are demanded domestically and are imported. This way the wealth of the nation will remain safe in the country.

2...If you are an officer or an Employer

If you are an officer in a business organization or a government position, then keep these things in mind.

1. <u>Lead</u>- An officer should have all the qualities of a leader. Influence and subjugate people, gain their sympathy, not by terror but by your ability, your courage and your efficiency. Only a person who has the ability to make a plan thoughtfully and work accordingly can lead others. Therefore, set a goal with a steady mind and move towards it firmly. People follow the one about whom they know that he is going in a certain direction and going in that direction is auspicious. First make everyone your followers, after

this they will automatically follow you. This is how you will get their cooperation. Do not show inexperience and powerlessness. Do not show lightness and inferiority complex.

2. <u>Be fair and trustworthy</u>- Your dependents will show their trust in you only when you are impartial, strict and firm in justice and truthful by nature. People should be impressed by your justice, dedication and intelligence. You cannot sit on the throne of everyone's heart just by sitting on a chair.

3. <u>Be serious, calm and mysterious</u>- Be as serious and calm as possible in work, in management and in dealing with employees. Silence increases authority. A French thinker (Aéandre Maurice) has written in one of his famous books (The Art of Living) that **"an officer should be so serious that his persona appears mysterious to his dependents to a certain extent."** Till there is no intimacy, a person, who is far away, considers high officials to be strange, supernatural and accepts their authority. When he is close, he brings to life the saying **'Ghar Ki Murgi Daal Barabar'** (Heavenly chicken is as good as a chicken). 'Too much familiarity leads to disinterest and disrespect.' Being serious does not mean that the person should remain silent like a statue of Gautam Buddha. It means that he should not be unruly, should not be gullible, should not be talkative, should not be romantic and should not be sentimental. Disorganized mind is terrible A person who is of fickle nature and keeps getting happy and unhappy every moment, people consider his happiness to be dreadful:

KVACHIDRUSHTHA: KVACHITTUSHTO RUSTASTUSHTA: KSHANE KSHANE. AVAYAVASTITCHITASYA PRASADOAPY BHAYANKARA:

4. <u>Be simple in nature and speech</u>- be strict only in the discharge of your duties; do not show your arrogance in your nature and speech. The sages of the Vedic period also prayed to God that a person with harsh words should not be our Lord: **'MA NO DUH: SHANS ISHAT'** (Rig Veda). Do not give anyone an opportunity to doubt your gentlemanliness and kindness. Praise the qualities of others wholeheartedly and show your appreciation to people. Show personal sympathy in people's difficulties and also intimacy in personal problems. The intoxication of power is more maddening than wine. Do not forget your goodwill and modesty in power- induced madness. Remember that your colleagues are also human beings, they also have hearts, they also have compulsions and personally they are weaker than you. Do not threaten them and get work done from them in a humane manner. Try to settle people instead of destroying them. Instead of being an exploiter, be a nurturer of those dependent on you.

5. <u>Be above others</u> - Be an ideal for everyone in persona, in dress, in work, in knowledge and understanding so that people can respect you. Persona has an immediate effect. Understand the effect of dress and attire from the fact that even an ordinary person becomes impressive as soon as he wears police uniform. Unless you are an expert in the work, how will you inspect and control the work of others? An officer should be an

expert in his subject. He should know some things which are not known to the general public. He should have the ability to keep the secret. Only by having special qualities he can become an ideal and guide for everyone. An officer can handle his responsibility only by knowing the exact details of all the works of his department and understanding the work process. The rules related to punctuality and discipline which you want others to follow, first follow them yourself, so that people can learn from you and do not question your strictness. In this regard, remember Hitler's last sentence, probably on the last day. When the shells were raining on Berlin and Germany's defeat was certain, people advised Hitler to leave the place for self-defense. Hitler replied self-respectfully that "'If I die, it is for the honor of Germany -It is because as a soldier, I must obey my own command to defend Berlin to the last, I myself had ordered to protect Berlin till the last breath, so how I can run away."

6. <u>Above all, be courageous</u> – **"Fear destroys self-respect"**, this is the opinion of Napoleon. Another statesman is of the opinion that by showing courage you can defeat even those who are greater in number than you **"Courage overcomes numbers"**

    Do not get influenced by the circumstances and criticisms. This is possible only when the person remains steadfast in his duty. While performing your duty, make a firm resolve that your efforts cannot fail. This firm resolve will give you courage. Be courageous, not adventurous. Start following the definite path after taking a decision. Do not stop, equip with self-power and make your own extraordinary way in whatever field you are in.

7. <u>Know how to work and how to get the work done-</u> Unless you know how to work yourself, you will not be able to get proper work done from others, nor will you be able to motivate them to work. Getting work done is a great art. Some of its secrets are:

(A) One should be assigned the work for which he is suitable. In this regard, Shukracharya's policy is valid that there is no letter which cannot be used in mantra-composition, there is no tree which is not a medicine for some disease or the other; there is no person who is not suitable for some work or the other - it is difficult to find a coordinator for all:

AMANTRAMAKSHARAMNASTI, NASTI MOOLAMA KOUSHADHAM AYOGYAH: PURUSHO NASTI YOJAKSTATRA DURLABHA:

Work can be taken from even an ordinary person: 'Where a needle is useful, what is the use of a sword.' Even if a person is physically thin, he can be very useful. Sheikh Saadi has said that even if an Arabian horse is thin, it is better than a whole stable of donkeys. In fact, after giving work to someone, one should see its result after understanding it and then decide about his ability or inability.

(B). Care should be taken that no one should sit idle. Socrates has written that not only a person who keeps sitting idle is considered idle but also a person whose capabilities and skills are not used fully. **Not only he is** idle, who is doing nothing but he too that might not be employed better -Socrates.

(C) As far as possible, regular control should be maintained on the work of the employees by giving written and definite orders regarding the work. A foreign writer has written that the eyes of the employer work more than both of his hands. Everyone will agree that more work is done under supervision. If there is any problem in front of the eyes and someone knowingly violates the rules, then prove his crime and punish him so that others get a lesson. It is better to reveal it immediately rather than keeping a grudge against someone in mind. Vyas has written that getting burnt in a moment is better than smoldering for long time: **KSHANARDH JWALITAM SHREYO NA CHA GHOOMAYITAM CHIRAM.**

(D). One should not deliberately blame his colleagues. One should not look at their ordinary mistakes. A foreign ethicist (Fuller) has written that **if you are a master, then sometimes become blind**.

(E). Give this true assurance to those from whom you need work that the doors to their future are open and they can showcase their abilities, skills and that you can progress further with this. Man's life becomes interesting only when he has some work to do and a peg to hang his hopes on. Remember this, 'If vendors are tied up, there would not be any market.' Keep everyone enthusiastic'.

(F). Take full responsibility of your dependents. They should not have any illusion that you will back out at the last moment and they would be made responsible for any mistake.

(G). Do not use your special rights repeatedly. If a storm blows every day, in a few days people will become so accustomed to bear it that they will start considering it as a normal wind. Do not let people become shameless.

(H). Even by bowing down tactfully at some places, the workers get fascinated: **'SABAHIN NACHAVAT RAM GOSAI, APUWA RAHAT DAS KI NAAI.'** (Tulsi). Wherever some important work has to be done quickly, one should bow down in the same way as Hanuman bowed down before Surasa.

(I). The fame of an officer influences the workers. If you are famous and influential, people will naturally try to get the honour of being called your capable colleague. Therefore, keep such a reputation that it can fill the nerves of others with excitement in your absence.

(J). Gravity is the reason for downfall - When you take charge, remember that only the heavy object falls to the earth. There is a greater risk of rolling down from a high hill. **When the hair grows too long, the barber's scissors are ready.** So be careful. Walk carefully.

3... If you are an employee

If you are an employee, then apart from the above-mentioned useful things, keep the following things also in mind:

1. <u>Keep your ambition strong</u> even while holding an ordinary position and keep trying to uplift yourself by

keeping in mind that in this world one gets rights according to one's ability; **a half-liter glass cannot be filled with a litre of milk.** Enthusiastically improve your ability every day, that will be your main asset. Apart from work-related knowledge, keep accumulating other useful knowledge as well. Don't remain a follower of the same routine. Being knowledgeable is beneficial. Keep accumulating experience every day. Do not rely too much on your memory, use your notebook.

2. <u>Do not work only for food</u>. Do not earn only keeping in mind how to get food in the evening. Make the evening of your life your goal and not the evening of your day. It would not be inappropriate to say that you should get yourself insured because you never know when the evening of your livelihood or the evening of your life will come. Save something.

3. <u>Do more work than what you are paid</u>. Do not let your work become less valuable than money. Complete your work completely and do the same every day. Do not show good work for a few days and gain the trust of your superiors and then become lax. When you eat the earnings of work, do not pollute or destroy it. Only mad people or animals break their things. Be true in performing your duties. Keep shining your qualities. There is a saying in English. **Let your stars shine**. You will show more success than expected, only then your stars will shine. Remember this. Hard work does not have as much respect as good hard work. Only that successful hard work is accepted whose sequence of success is not broken.

4. <u>Do not think yourself to be irreplaceable</u> or best suited for any task. Believing so increases pride and you

may remain in delusion. Work with the belief that there are others who compete with you and you still have to become more suitable. There should be neither worry nor uncertainty while doing the work. Do not trust yourself or others more than necessary. Keep accumulating more self-confidence for the competition.

5.   <u>Just be like a seed in the soil</u>, be absorbed in your work. This is the natural way to success. You may become a multi-faceted person in due course. In simple words, be absorbed in work while working. Focus all your attention on your work. Keep your personal matters far away while working. Avoid personal matters of others as much as possible. Make this your principle and know the key to success of honesty, hard work and unity. Success will not be achieved in a day; success and progress are achieved only by continuous daily practice. Push the difficulties behind, utilize and promote your strength and take interest in work. This is how you will be able to prosper.

6.   <u>Follow the rules of the place</u> where you work properly. Be grateful to the person under you, consider his profit and loss as your own; be honest in your accounts; do not spend more than required in connection with work; do not delay work; do not procrastinate; do not do any work with the greed of reward; do not expect any favours, because you get salary for getting work done; do not criticize anyone behind their back and even when leaving, take leave with good intentions so that future relations remain. The tendency of ungratefulness is self-destructive.

7.   <u>Do not be action-hating</u>, stubborn or obstinate in any work and have the courage to accept your mistakes

immediately and take full responsibility. Understand the reality by testing and not by guesswork. If a task is impossible for you, then do not give false assurances of doing it.

8. <u>Show your talent in your work</u>. Whatever work is assigned to you, show your talent in it; complete it as quickly as possible and in the best manner and keep showing your services intelligently. Understand the usefulness of the work, make a plan and do it properly. Do not wilt in between; remain green, otherwise how will you bear fruits?

9. <u>Be careful in your conduct</u>. Treat your seniors like fire. Go near them only when necessary; otherwise stay away. Respect the views of colleagues. Keep asking them, keep taking their advice. Be as useful to everyone as possible, Be polite and civil in the situation; **cold iron cuts hot iron.** Show yourself to be calm, virtuous and clever in your behavior.

10. <u>Do not be overly hardworking</u> and cautious in work. One harms health, others harm selfishness, because these make work burdensome. To collect money by destroying health and selfishness is like burning your own house and collecting ashes to become a recluse.

11. <u>Spread your roots like a tree.</u> Wherever you live, make new friends and try to involve your old acquaintances in your work. Those roots will support you in the storm of adversity. Do not get uprooted by the jolt. Then stand up again as before. If you are a fatalist, then remember this statement of the learned Vyas that just as unsolicited

sorrows keep coming, happiness will also come, then getting scared of sorrows and getting anxious for happiness is only showing your helplessness:

APRARTHITANI DU: KHANI YATHAIVAYANTI DEHINAM... SUKHANI CHA TATHA MANYE DAINYAMATRATIRICHYATE.

12. <u>Engage yourself in some interesting activities.</u> Besides being an expert in work-related knowledge, participate in some interesting game, competition etc. to increase your popularity so that you can attract people towards you after work.

13. <u>Do not become a servant of two masters</u>, that is, do not accept the authority of two equal officers at the same time. Do not ignore the officer who is above you. Even if the supreme officer has special favour on you, then also respect the officer above you completely and do not let it appear by any act that you have or want to have a direct relationship with the supreme officer. Ignoring the middle officer is very dangerous. In this regard, consider Hanuman as an ideal. He was the recipient of special favour of Ram, yet he did not forget his master, Sugreev. After showing his prowess in Lanka, he did not forget to maintain his dignity. While chanting Jai Ram in the kingdom, he said- "victory to the King Sugrieve who is protected by Ramchandar" "victory to the most powerful Ram", victory to Mahabali Laxman",

JAITYATIBALO RAMO LAXMANSHCHA MAHABALHA: RAJA JAYATI SUGRIVO RAGHAVENABHIPALITAH ॥

14. <u>Keep looking for suitable Opportunity</u>. If your future does not seem bright in any work, then do not keep doing it out of helplessness. Rather keep looking for suitable opportunity and place for yourself. But wait for some days and then change the place. An experienced person has said that **he runs far, who never turns**. Its other meaning can also be: he who does not look here and there has to run a long race. Accept the meaning which suits your situation.

4... If you are an Unemployed

If you are unemployed, the first thing that is required is that you should not become indifferent. The era of indifferent people has ended long ago. This is the era of optimists. As soon as a person gets discouraged, his consciousness is lost. When a person sees his future as dark, then only the feeling of suicide germinates in his mind. Self-confidence and self-power are most needed in the condition of unemployment, otherwise a person's back breaks, he starts wavering and wants to sell his personality at a cheap price. Fear increases in inactivity.

1. <u>Eliminate fear and despair</u> from the mind and believe in this verse of the scriptures, proven by hundreds and thousands of examples, that nothing is impossible with perseverance: **'NAA SAADHYAM TAPASA KINCHIT'** (Mahabharata). Believe this, it has been proved in worldly life that every person is his own mint, for making money.' If you are disappointed thinking that you are too old and hence the opportunity has slipped out of your hands, then

remember that sixty-four percent of the people in the world have achieved great successes at the age of forty-five to sixty-five years.

2. <u>Resolve to become self-reliant</u> and do it with hope and enthusiasm. **Do not become like a motor with a weak battery that starts only when your wife and children push you from behind.** Be alert yourself. Do not sit like a homebody. The world's great assets, like light, air, money, your wife, come from outside; they are not born at home! Therefore, resolve to enter the field of work, make a firm resolve. Being stagnant while being alive is an unnatural act. Make a firm decision that you are capable, you will definitely do something. Keep the ideal of some great industrialist in front of you and take inspiration from his life story.

3. <u>Make a plan for the future</u> according to your situation. Keep in mind that what you have or what you are - your income will depend on one of these. If you do not have money, then accumulate and develop virtues. Make your character and nature beautiful because these are the wealth of the poor. Practice the art of impressing others and expressing yourself properly. Acquire qualifications. Acquire special qualifications in the art in which you have special interest. Make yourself an expert in that. Any useful knowledge or skill is the basic substance of a worker. Adopt professional knowledge and practical art, not poetic art. Set a goal and **make yourself capable and choose only such work which is feasible.** In short, in the words of a well-known writer on this subject, the first business, Dharma or duty of a young man who does not have money is to make his own personality as valuable as possible. If you want to do business, then imagine setting up your

office by making self-confidence as the root, intelligence as the management, and hands and feet as the laborers.

4. <u>Increase your acquaintances</u> as much as possible, they will give you work ahead. Associate with people who are elder to you. Participate in meetings and societies, never fail to serve others in a voluntary manner, give speeches, write articles or display any skill to become popular. Keep walking on the path, you will find someone who may be impressed with you.

5. <u>Do not sit idle. Get out to work</u>. Sitting at home will not do the job. Remember the advice Vidula gave to her lazy son Sanjaya. She said that tasks that are not started can never be completed: **'ATHA YE NAIVA KURVANTI NAIVA JAATU BHAVANTI TE.'** Do not hesitate to go out for work: **JAB NACHAN NIKSI BAVRI TAB GHUNGHAT KAISA**' When the dancer came out, how can she wear a veil?' (Kabir). Yes, do not go out like a beggar. Do not consider yourself to be someone's slave. To have a begging attitude while going for a job is foolishness and cowardice. Go with the intention of selling your qualities at a fair price. As much as possible, meet the officers who are hiring. Do not rely solely on the application form. It does not give a complete idea of your ability and personality. That is why every employer wants to meet the applicant in person. Do not tremble in going in front of him. Do not think that you have gone to take a loan or donation from him. Just think that you have gone to sell your ability. Meet with effect. Have Self-confidence. Being non-confident will make you show yourself poorly.

Keep a few certificates of reputed persons with you and your application. They will be your lawyer in your case. The officer will not be impressed by self-praise, because he is smarter than you, that is why he is an officer and you are unemployed. Do not write such things in the application as auspicious words and sentiments that if you hire us under your protection, we will pray to the Almighty God for your long life in all births. Mention only your qualification and experience in it and use practical language, not ornate.

6. <u>Keep bouncing like a ball.</u> If you fail somewhere, do not fall like a lump of mud. Keep knocking the door of destiny again and again. Even if it is sleeping, it will open the door once, albeit with irritation. When the door opens, enter inside with authority. Gandhiji has written that no matter how small an opportunity you get, you should not let it go. **No opportunity should be missed however trifling.**' Disraeli has written that continuous effort is the mantra of success. **The secret of success is consistency to purpose.**

7. <u>Spread your wings and keep flying</u>. There is a saying that even a sitting eagle remains sitting, does not move forward even by a single step; whereas a walking ant reaches many yojanas in some time. Do not sit with your abilities. They will get rusted. Believe it to be true that most people suffer not because of their karmic faults but because of their inaction. Memorize this advice of Vidula mentioned in Mahabharata: "Do not follow the behavior of men who are devoid of servants, poor and living on the food of others, and lack effort. Just as birds get life from ripe fruit trees, similarly the life of the one who has many birds under his shelter is successful."

Chapter-5

Conversational Skills

The power of speech

In Kishkindha, enchanted by the words of Hanuman, the wise man of speech, Ram had said this to Lakshman - "His words are free from all sorts of complications, His words are free from the doubts of letters & sounds, His words are neither too fast nor too slow, He speaks the words memorized by heart and he speaks the moderate sentences in the moderate tone. He utters the words that are cultured, in a sequence, without haste, without delay, auspicious and charming. Whose mind cannot be satisfied with this (sweet, sounding right coming from throat & head), picturesque speech ......? Even that of a sword-wielding enemy can be satisfied!"

Rama was particularly impressed by Hanuman's eloquence and we know that due to that the friendship between Rama and Sugreeva was established and strengthened. Even by writing hundred letters, Sugreeva could not have obtained the friendship of Rama which he easily obtained by sending his eloquent minister. Even after this incident, we see many such incidents in Ramayana where many tasks have been successful not only due to

Hanuman's bravery but also due to his eloquence. Going to the Lanka of the mighty Ravana and being imprisoned there, and then return after achieving the purpose.

Hanuman alone was able to escape due to the effect of his power of speech When he got imprisoned, he had taken only the recourse to his power of speech. Through that, he had not only protected self-respect but also without hurting Ravana's Royal Honor. When Ravana asked him the reason for creating a ruckus, he said that I was desirous of seeing the king; it was difficult to reach you in normal condition, so I destroyed the forest; thereafter, your warriors eager for war came to me and I had to fight for the self-defense and this way I was able to see you in person which is very rare. After this Hanuman again humbly said, "I have come here on royal work. Your brother the monkey king (Sugreev) has asked about your well-being and has sent a message for your benefit."

Thus, with his polite and timely speech Hanuman impressed Ravana a lot. He also spoke intelligently to Sita and strengthened her faith and patience. When Sita was disappointed thinking about Ravana's strength and Ram's helplessness, Hanuman consoled her and said, "O Goddess, the monkey king Sugreev will soon come here with millions of monkeys. All those monkeys are more than me or equal to me, no one is less than me. When I myself have come here then what to say about them; only the small ones are sent to do work, not the big ones: **'NAHI PRAKRISHTAAH PRESHYANTE: PRESHYANTE HITARE JANAAH:'** Thus, with his eloquence, Ramadoot accomplished both his purposes - on one hand, by entering the city of the demon king, he displayed the might and glory of Rama and Sugreeva and even after the display, he kept his life safe and on the other hand, after finding Sita, he not only conveyed Rama's message to her, but also strengthened her self-confidence by removing her doubts. This not only made Rama's task successful, but Hanuman's prestige also increased hundredfold. When he returned after being successful, the waiting monkeys held him in high esteem: **'HANUMANTAM MAHAVEGAM VAHANT IVA DRISHTIBHIH:'** Hanuman's importance increased in everybody's eyes.

To show the effect of the power of speech, we have given the example of Hanuman above. Even in the present times, we see that major problems of politics and business are solved by dialogues. Major problems which cannot be solved even by writing and war are solved by the meetings of clever orators. Man's public life runs only by speech. In our daily life, we can see directly how much people are affected by words. People start laughing on hearing a few sentences of humor, they start boiling on hearing words of anger and contempt and they start melting on hearing words of respect. Those words neither hurt anyone physically, nor do they cause any financial loss or gain to anyone; yet they have a great effect on man, this is clear.

Both Vashikaran (Attraction) and Uchchatan (Aversion) are seen to be accomplished through words. Therefore, who will not accept the power of mantras of words? By using beautiful words, people get bound in each other's love. Good speakers mesmerize the listeners. On the contrary, harsh words cause big quarrels, people die without being killed and people with soft hearts sometimes even commit suicide. Words have as much effect on man as a stick has on an animal. The reason for this is that man is an emotional creature. The words carry the inner nature and knowledge of the listener and penetrate the emotional sphere of the listener. Just as the fragrance of a flower reaches from one place to another through air, similarly the feelings of one person reach the inner self of another easily through speech. Being basically emotional, man gets agitated by the impact of the emotions carried by speech. If this were not so, then no one would start dancing or get agitated by the ordinary air of words. Being thoughtful and emotional, man gets affected in his innermost place by understanding the essence of the words. Only the foolish and bewildered among humans are not affected by words.

The personality of a person is identified through his speech. Knowledge, nature, state of mind, ideology, all can be known through speech. Just as an earthen pot is knocked to check if it is broken or not, similarly, through conversation, it is checked whether a person's brain is mature or not. Speech opens the window to a person's inner self., His character can be measured. Statements, expressed in written words are not as much effective as the vocal speech. It is because of our voice, our tone which contain the essence. Voice itself is a power. It stirs those sound waves which touch not only our body but our inner self too.

For example, take the sound of Veena or any other musical instrument. That sound has no meaning, yet it has an impact on the heart. When meaningful words are combined with sound, then emotions, which are the basic elements of speech, are especially aroused. Speech, combined with sound, moves the air waves and reaches the listener's heart through its natural path - the ears, leaving a deep impression.

The mantra-power that comes in words comes from the combination of sound with word formation. Understanding this scientific truth, the sages have told the method of reciting stotras loudly. A sleeping man wakes up and becomes conscious with sound, then why will his emotions not awake? Written language is deprived of this help. It enters the field of knowledge in an unnatural way and before accepting it, one has to arouse his emotions. Like a language with sound, it cannot open the emotional building of the listener with its own impact. That is why we see that letters do not have as much impact as talking together. The words of letters or writings do not strike as hard as the words of speech or conversation.

We can understand this secret in another way - a woman may be extremely beautiful to look at or in a picture, you may be attracted to her beauty, but if she turns out to be harsh and shrewd on meeting her, then only you can understand your disappointment and pain. On the contrary, if an ugly woman is sweet-spoken, then probably you will not give as much importance to her beauty. Just as a beautiful picture or figure alone does not reveal the simplicity or cunningness of a particular person, similarly, written speech also cannot bring out the feelings until the reader himself acts accordingly in his mind. Therefore, we should believe that the pure offspring of life, that is, language, is born from the womb of Voice & Speech. (In Sanskrit, **voice or speech is called Pran-Patni**) It is in the voice that our feelings come alive and they are very lively and are especially impressive. Whereas a memorial of feelings is created in the written form and seeing which, people have to put efforts to awaken their feelings.

Having seen the importance of speech from different perspectives, we should now consider its art. No one can have any doubt about its effect and no one can be mistaken that it is the main tool of worldly conduct. Personal success or failure to a great extent depends on the eloquence or inarticulation of people. Therefore, now we should see which qualities or characteristics develop the power of speech. In other words, how can a man use this power of his successfully, or what are the methods of good conversation and how can they be used.

It should be remembered that talking or expressing feelings through speech is a great art. Like other arts, it is perfected only by practice. Its practice is not done by merely memorizing the dictionary and grammar. Even after learning many subjects, this art does not develop automatically in a person. It has been observed that even great scholars sometimes cannot advertise their knowledge properly through speech. On the contrary, practical and clever people with limited knowledge express their intelligence beautifully on the basis of whatever they know and successfully encash the cheque of their feelings in the bank of society. The great poet Bharavi has rightly written in **'KIRATARJUNIYA'** that among scholars, those are the best who can express their mental feelings through speech; their place among them is even higher who can express their facts with deep meanings in clever words. But such people are very few:

**BHAVANTI TE SABHYATAMA VIPASCHITAAM,
MANOGATAM VACHI NIVESHAYANTI YEH.
NAYANTI TESHWAPYUPPAN NAIPUNAH:
GAMBHIRMARTH KATICHIT PRAKASTAM.**

Actually, it is not possible to make a rule to speak the same words on all occasions. The form of speech also varies with the place, occasion, purpose and person; there is a difference not only in its words but also in its tones. Therefore, its principles cannot be determined like mathematics. For it, knowledge of human nature, knowledge of circumstances and self-knowledge are also necessary. It has no special relation with classical knowledge; because it is a business art which changes like the phases of the moon. It changes according to place, time and subject.

It is true that no definite rules can be made in relation to conversation, yet there are some things which are worth keeping in mind in social conversation. Their practice and use as per the occasion give strength to speech. It is necessary to take recourse to them for clear and meaningful expression of feelings. Briefly, we will discuss them further.

(a)...Mental restraint and ability - Speech is a part of intelligence and hence it is formed according to thoughts. No matter how sweet the voice is, if it does not emanate thoughtful speech, it is useless. A skilled speaker can be one who is a good thinker, who is adept at making a picture of thoughts in his mind and who is capable of understanding the essence with a subtle vision. The tone of speech is formed according to the maturity, clarity, order, alertness, seriousness, sweetness and vigour of the thoughts.

An English scholar has written that **words are the** 'Labels" **of thoughts.** Just as the label on a bottle or parcel shows what is in it, similarly words show what and how the thoughts in the mind are. Broken Sentence or instability in words shows mental dearth and instability of thoughts. Half sentences show mental weakness. To strengthen the power of speech, it is necessary to first build the power of thoughts. Speech becomes clear due to clear thoughts. If there is doubt, ill will or arrogance in the mind, then the same is reflected in the words. Speech becomes simple and clear only due to the simplicity and clarity of thoughts and it should be remembered that simplicity and clarity are its special qualities. Its significance is lost due to not being balanced and understandable.

Therefore, first strengthen your knowledge Centre; make your imagination, reasoning and memory strong and alert. After listening to every topic and understanding its essence, practice thinking over it with logic and judgment. Whatever the topic is, think over it with a decisive mind, keeping the reality in mind and then see its purpose and result. The wider your field of knowledge and perspective, the wider your field of behavior will be. By being very knowledgeable, you will be able to enter many fields and talk on many subjects, due to which your influence will also be wider. Therefore, it is necessary to accumulate life-related knowledge from the point of view of usefulness. After estimating the reality of that knowledge, accept only the essence and forget the useless.

You should try to become a capable speaker by eradicating the negative thoughts of doubt, pessimism, intolerance and self-inability in your mind. If there is doubt in your mind, you will often speak doubtful language. You will speak in a harsh tone and neither you nor your listeners will develop a feeling of sympathy. You will not be able to succeed in talking with despair and will keep groping for reality in the dark. If you are intolerant, you will not be able to tolerate the truthful speech of others and will not be able to argue on any matter.

If you consider yourself incapable, you will not be able to express your thoughts freely. Self-confidence is the first quality that a skilled speaker should have. When you meet someone, keep this belief in mind that you are not insignificant, you will impress him and will be successful. If your self-confidence is shaken, then whatever is there in your mind will also be forgotten in time and you will probably start stammering or you will start struggling to escape from there somehow. Self-confidence brings firmness, and we should keep in mind Napoleon's opinion that firmness brings success in practical work. **"Firmness prevails in all things"**- Napoleon

When you meet someone, trust others with confidence - trust that they too have thoughts and can be influenced by thoughts - trust that they too have intelligence, so if you speak artificially, they can sense it - and believe that they too can be as emotional as you are. Therefore, create a welcoming space for them and their thoughts in your mind - and then talk to them. If you yourself are narrow-minded, where will you give space to their thoughts? Therefore, keep your field of thought open.

Listen to everyone, later you may do whatever you want to do. **"SUNIYE SABKI CHAHE KARIYE MUN KI"**. Do not meet anyone with negative thoughts about them in advance. Talking with good intentions even towards a bad person always leads to success. By having bad intentions, a person sees only the bad qualities of others, which does not benefit him in any way. A thoughtful English writer has said that, **"The fewer faults we possess ourselves the less interest we have in pointing out the faults of other people"**. Our tendency to unnecessarily judge others decreases when we have fewer faults. We blame others only when our own attitude is corrupt.

Therefore, it is necessary to purify one's nature first. Along with this, it is also necessary to keep one's nature under control. If the person has a habit of lying or distorting facts, then the person's words will become trivial. In that condition, the person will make a mountain out of a molehill and will not be able to discern what the truth is. Napoleon has written that **"The man who habituates himself to the distortion of truth and to exultation at the success of injustice will at last hardly know right from wrong"**. The person who becomes habituated to saying straight things in a roundabout way and getting happy after achieving success in a crooked manner, can hardly differentiate between right and wrong, that is, he becomes addicted to achieving the task by being untruthful.

By developing such a nature, you may be able to speak at a few places, but later, when your words are proved to be untrue, their value in society will decrease. It is necessary to make your talks entertaining, but not by coating them with lies. It is better to adorn them with the natural beauty of thoughts, beauty of words and attractiveness of voice.

(b)... Authority over Voice- Apart from knowledge, thoughts and nature, pay attention to your voice. If the instrument is out of tune, a singer cannot sing well. It is the voice that gives strength to the thought of speech. According to it, the speech becomes powerful, sweet, heart-touching or effective. It is from it that the self-power of a person is known. The direct proof of this is that when a sick person becomes weak due to illness, his voice becomes weak. A healthy person's voice is stentorian. The fluctuations in the voice create a difference in the meaning of the words and the intention of the speaker. Only by having control over the voice the ideas can be properly advertised.

It is not necessary to shout to show your strength. Shouting at the top of your voice does not give a sense of bravery. Children and weak people usually shout. Shouting is a sign of inability. The pronunciation in the voice should be clear and audible. It should be serious, but not harsh; it should be vigorous, but with softness. It should be raised only till its naturalness is not destroyed. It should not be lowered so much that half the words remain in the mouth. Clearness of pronunciation and pleasantness of the ears are the special qualities of speech. Ambiguity and harshness are its main defects. Neither fire a cannon of words nor rain hailstones. Make it soft, serious, loud or slow according to the thought. Those who do not have control over the voice, even when speaking politely, appear as if they are scolding someone. Remember that people often judge others by the sweetness or harshness of the voice and then like or dislike. Good or Bad all are same till they speak- If it is Crow or Cuckoo, you know in spring season.

BHALE-BURE SAB AIK SE JAB TALAK BOLAT NAHIN, JANI PADAT HAI KAK PIK RITU VASANT KE MAHIN

(c)...Words and Grammar- Words are the hands and feet of speech. Only by having sufficient knowledge of words can the right expression be done. The right word for the right expression can be found only when your knowledge of words, meaning and vocabulary is vast. If you are careless in this, you may say something wrong and you will have to correct your language again and again. Those who are not very good at words have to say again and again that I did not mean this, I did not mean that. By having knowledge of words that express the right meaning, you can make your speech meaningful and also reach to a right decision. Similarly, by knowing the exact meaning of words, one can understand the intentions of others correctly. Word power is considered a special quality of a person. It has been observed that people who hold high positions have a larger vocabulary than ordinary people. In other words, knowledge of more words is necessary for self-improvement. Without it, man cannot express himself properly nor can he dominate others.

Just like the collection of words, their selection and structure are also necessary. It is not necessary to have a dictionary; it is necessary to have knowledge of its useful and popular words. The choice of words and the construction of sentences by them reveals the good taste and intelligence of a person. Good poets make the feelings alive by increasing the intensity of the feelings only by the choice of beautiful words and their systematic composition or style. When the choice of words is not right and a person is not able to tie them in a chain, only then he creates a cloud of words or uses the word axe.

While talking to someone, keep in mind that you are not going to catch fish but to subdue a thoughtful person. No intelligent person gets trapped in the net of words. No one is impressed even by using a barrage of difficult words. Others can be impressed or defeated only by irrefutable arguments expressed in sweet and simple words. The speech of only that speaker has an impact who can fill maximum thoughts in few words. The number of words should always be less than the number of expressions and they should only reflect the unity and order of the expressions. In fact, success is achieved only by choosing the right words for the right occasion and speaking in a pithy voice. The subject gets lost in meaningless words and the listener never gets enough time to sit and discern what the speaker is saying.

Choose simple, touching and thought-provoking words and acquire the ability to use them at the right time. Use the words of the language in which you speak. Though sometimes the hybridity of the language increases the impression. Polite and restrained vocabulary enhances the nobility in a person. Dirty words first dirty your mouth, whether they dirty the mouth of others or not. A beautiful speech is made of bright gems of words. Paying attention to grammar through word arrangement also makes the speech healthy. There is no need to write much on this, because everyone knows that without grammar the language cannot be organized properly and it becomes disorderly. Pure and idiomatic language is more heart-warming.

(d)...Knowledge of Human Nature- Even if the language decorated with thoughts, tone and words is against the nature of the listener, it does not affect him. For example, the description of the heroine's gestures may be liked by a connoisseur; but a working person will find it extremely unpleasant. He will like the discussion of market prices more than that. By knowing the interest of the people, keeping in mind their situation and talking to them accordingly, even ordinary things seem to be liked by them. Therefore, be penetrating. Be insightful. Become allegorist.

In addition to the above. for a meaningful and impressive conversation keep the below mentioned important things in mind while speaking: -

(e)...Don't talk big with a small mouth - While talking have Self-confidence and self-respect and be aware of your actual situation and your dignity. Above all, be aware of the dignity and self-respect of others. It is good to advertise yourself according to your inner strength. But Unwarranted efforts to promote yourself become disgusting.

(f)...Don't say 'I'-"I" Many people become so obsessed with themselves that they talk about themselves in everything and use the word 'I' more out of the habit. 'I did it', 'I said', 'I knew it' etc. are present in their every talk. They cannot talk about others and even if they do, it is with blame. Due to such a nature, they become accustomed to bring others down with their words and start showering self-praise. Keeping this in mind, a foreign scholar (E.F. Christ) has said: *"You may have become a knocker and unconsciously slipped into the habit of finding fault. It is* *also easy to acquire the 'I' habit and to become self-centered and to incessantly talk about your own affairs."*

Its meaning has been given above. In a civilized society, saying 'I' too much is a sign of being a goat or a cat. Giving others a chance to speak more about them is a good way of talking. Your play may be a Ramleela for you, but in the eyes of others it will be less valuable than a drama. Therefore, to attract someone towards you, let him talk more. And you stimulate his right thoughts. Telling others the way they think of themselves is eloquence and attracting them towards you by telling them the same is deftness in behavior. Do not try to get your work done by bringing them down and becoming a burden on their chest. Braggarts may be considered cowards.

(g)...Do not be a pain in the ass- do not try to force something down the throat of others by repeating it over and over again. The listener gets bored of it and he gets a terrible indigestion of your talking. Repeating one thing again and again shows narrow-mindedness. Those who are very talkative are usually whimsical and suspicious.

(h)...Do not try to show off by starting a fire- Do not try to get your work done by inciting someone's thoughts or by creating a rift between two people. It is a great folly to make yourself someone's spy without any salary. There is no permanent benefit in talking about this, on the contrary, your self-esteem decreases.

(i)...Do not pluck stars from the sky- Do not rely too much on imaginary things in your conversation. Keep your feet on the ground and talk about things that are possible. Do not fly in the air while talking, otherwise the person you are sitting next to will go far away from you. Talking too much shows triviality.

(j)...Do not praise or criticize yourself - If you praise yourself, first of all no one will believe it, because even the lowest of the low praises himself. Secondly, no one will take interest in it, because self-praise from one's own mouth is not naturally liked by others. If you criticize yourself out of stupidity or cleverness, then people will think that when this person himself considers himself so bad, then who knows how bad he must be in reality. Criticism and praise are the same which come from the mouth of others. Why should you try to put flowers on your head or hit a shoe on it with your own hands? This is unnatural.

(k)...Don't be a theoretician- Don't become as rigid as a piece of wood by considering even small things as principles. People who advertise their principles through words and then sit behind them usually do not remain steadfast on principles. Principles are followed by action, not by clever words. Keep a scope for changing your thoughts according to the fair thoughts of others and then exchange ideas with people. Success is not achieved in pretense and hypocrisy.

(l)...Do not rush to slur- Even if an unpleasant situation arises, do not destroy the sweetness of the tongue as much as possible. Remember this quote by Tulsi: **TULSI MEETHE VACHAN TEIN SUKH UPJAT CHAHUN AUR BASIKARAN EIK MANTRA HAI, PARIHARU BACHAN KATHORE.** Meaning "sweet words produce happiness in all the four directions, Mesmerism of sweet words is a spell, hence Harsh Words must be avoided". One teaching of Kabir is also worth remembering: **EISI VANI BOLIYE MANN KA AAPA KHOYE, AUIRAN KO SITAL KARRE AAPAU SITAL HOYE,** "Speak such words, which remove your ego and sorrow, and which not only cool yourself but others too". By cooling others, you also cool yourself. Avoid being arrogant and adversarial. Apart from stupidity and wickedness, these are the two reasons why people talk nonsense. Only thoughtless people are loudmouth.

(m)...Do not become a judge or critic- In conversation, neither have the attitude of giving a judgement in measured words like a judge nor of scrutinizing others like a critic. This will destroy the naturalness of the conversation. Mere preaching does not impress anyone. Accusative or objectionable speech is always intolerable. Do not even try to become a great preacher.

(n)...Keep knowledge by heart - Do not sit down to talk in long form and do not depend on books. Knowledge is that which comes to the mind to be revealed when the need arises. If this does not happen, then you will not be able to confirm your opinion at the right time. Beautiful sutras and authentic sayings, if kept by heart, are very useful at the right time. They become your advocate.

(o)...Keep originality and topicality in mind - To be a successful speaker, it is necessary to be quick-witted, sharp-witted and talented. Everyone respects new ideas. Borrowed ideas do not have much impact. It is necessary to keep topicality in mind; because: even if it is good, but it may seem dull without any occasion. Like in a war, words of beauty and decoration does not look good.

Understanding of timing is the key to success. The form of language changes according to the context. Where poetry is discussed, speech with embellishments and full of emotions is considered most popular. Where politics is discussed, only logical words and measured words in business and work are considered important. Vague words are not enough there.

(p)...Speak with Purpose and Impact - Whatever you say, speak in a logical tone keeping a purpose in mind. Just as a lawyer prepares his case and speaks carefully in support of his side, similarly you should prepare your topic and express it in a proud manner. Do not panic, do not exert and do not become pessimistic. Use your power of speech by being hopeful with a steady mind till the end and try to present the facts in logical words. Speak on your topic authoritatively but in a polite language. Polite language does not mean to say 'yes-yes' but to speak words politely.

Like a lawyer or a trader, weigh each word before speaking. Using words in haste is often harmful. Give evidence to support your opinion like a lawyer and keep in mind that your own statement does not contradict what you had earlier said. Do not take all the qualities of social eloquence from lawyers. Resorting to fabricated stories like many of them can be a loss of reputation. It is also not right to adopt their cross-examination skills. Asking riddles in a conversation stops the flow of the conversation. Do not create a storm like lawyers. Yes, be attentive like them.

(q)...Speak Fluently-to form a definite opinion on a subject, speak vigorously and do not get agitated quickly. Fluently does not mean that you start mumbling and the subject and grammar get swept away in the flow of speech. It means keeping the chain of thoughts connected and the thread moving in a definite direction.

(r)...Speak Chitravaani – Chitravaani does not mean that you talk in a dramatic way by winking your eyes and eyebrows. An example of Chitravaani can be found in the part of Ramayana that we have quoted in the beginning of this chapter regarding Hanuman's speech. Chitravaani (Picturesque Description) means expressing your feelings and expressions in a natural and entertaining way; along with speech, the appropriateness of the figure and body gestures, i.e., making the expression pictorial.: **AKARAYARINGITARGATYA CHESHTAYA VACHNEN CH, NETRAVAKTRVIKARESHCH LAKSHATEYANTARGATAM MUN:** The figure, movement, gestures, speech, expressions of the eyes and mouth reveal the thoughts correctly.

To make your speech interesting, take interest in the subject and avoid dull and unnecessary discussions as much as possible. Language expressed in an artistic manner by laughing, giving similes, coloring it with imagination is especially effective. Modesty and courtesy are the natural ornaments of language like the modesty and good conduct of a woman. Humor and sentimentality also make it pictorial. By having interest in a beautiful art, the speaker can talk about that subject in a beautiful manner. The purpose of pictorial speech is that the listener should also see the described subject with his imagination:

(s)...Be an admirer of virtues- Even if you are virtuous yourself, respect the virtues of others. Just as you remove your shoes while praying, similarly, while talking to others, remove the faults of others that are held in the feet of your mind. With the attitude of a fly, you will only get the pus of others, but if you have a bee-like attitude, you will be able to collect honey from the Flowers.

A critic is not respected anywhere. Take the essence of the words of the person with whom you talk and praise him wholeheartedly whenever you get the opportunity. Do not be stingy in praising him. Your praise will give self-satisfaction to the other person and he will consider you as virtuous. In this way, both will remain attracted towards each other and only then will the purpose be successful.

Instead of building bridges of praise, show to the other person in a natural way that you are understanding the essence of his words. Be friendly to him and give your suggestions so that he understands that his words are awakening your feelings. If he says something beneficial, do not miss to thank him immediately. If someone does you a favor, express gratitude to him humbly as soon as possible. If others talk about themselves, do not ignore it, show your personal affection in it and encourage the speaker, make his right aspirations stronger. Try to agree and be of same opinion with people, but keep in mind the appropriateness, purpose and result. Do not attack anyone's principles, customs and religion. Show sympathy with others to gain sympathy. Only by being tolerant you can be connoisseur and popular.

(t)...Speak Beneficial Words- It is necessary to keep the truth in mind while talking, but at the same time it should also be kept in mind that it should not be a harsh truth. Where there is a compulsion to tell a harsh truth and there is a question of justice, only then should an unpleasant truth be told, otherwise speaking truth, while keeping in mind your own and others' interests is the true form of truth.

In this matter, keep in mind the advice of Maryada Purushottam Ram, which he had given to Sumantra at the time of going to the forest. When Ram sat in the chariot and started leaving Ayodhya, King Dasharath became impatient and ran after the chariot and started calling Sumantra from a distance to tell him to stop the chariot, but Ram ordered Sumantra to speed up the chariot. Seeing Sumantra in a dilemma, Ram said that "On returning, if the king angrily asks you why you did not obey the king's order, then tell him that due to the sound of the chariot moving, you could not hear him" Keeping this principle in mind, be a sweet talker, but not too sweet talker. Being too sweet talker leads to become a Machiavellian.

'PRIYAVAADI BHAVATI DHURTAJANAH'. Speak the truth as humbly as possible and bow down when the situation demands. By being stiff, there is a fear of breaking like a tree in a storm.

Learn to bow down when you see the strong force of others because when their force calms down, you will be found standing again. **Stoop to conquer.** 'Winning over others by bowing down yourself' is considered a special tactic of today.

(u)...Do not show inexperience- Do not show inexperience to others in any matter that you are completely naive. If you are naive, then remain silent as much as possible **(MAUNAM SARVARTHA SADHANAM)** and let the other person reveal his knowledge. You will get material for your talk from his talk. Keep agreeing with him in between. If you are very intelligent, then talk like a realist and not an idealist, otherwise the dryness and uselessness of your knowledge will be revealed.

Do not show the universal acceptance of your intelligence to others. Exchange your views freely, but do not reveal all your secrets to others. In this regard, an experienced writer has written that **"Be wiser than other people but do not tell them so."** Do not let them know the depth of your intelligence. Do not break their modesty by any gesture or other and talk to them with caution after quietly understanding their intention. Do not understand the depth of someone's complete feelings with his words only. Shakespeare has written that a Devil can even read religious scriptures to get his work done. **The devil can cite scripture for his purpose.** Therefore, do not get caught up in words too much. Read the mind of others and talk accordingly.

Getting entangled in words or quarreling also shows inexperience. Usually, those people quarrel who do not have the ability to reason or who are intolerant. Argue with your opponent and assure him that you are arguing after understanding the facts of his statement. He will definitely be pleased with your appreciation. Getting surprised by revealing your ignorance in some ordinary subject will prove your smallness. Remember this statement of

Goldsmith that small things appear great only to those who are small themselves. **Little things are great to little men.**

(v)...Meet elders and Seniors- As far as possible, get the chance to enter and talk with your elders and seniors. It is more beneficial to spend an hour with an experienced person than to spend your whole life with a fool. When meeting your elders, take care of courtesy, take care of their dignity, obey their simple requests and do not go around sharing their words after meeting them. Whatever promise you give them, follow it later to the letter & Spirit. Neither interrupt their words during the conversation nor let it be unanswered. Keep them on your head and eyes.

(w)...Impress with your Personality - Personality has a great attraction. Etiquette and attire also have a great impact in conversation. When you meet someone, meet them by stimulating your personality. That is called 'personal magnetism. Everyone is subdued by gentleness, politeness and pleasant speech. Be fearless when you meet someone; talk to the listener by his name or title from time to time. This will be a good advertisement of your personality. Take the minimum time of the listener and do not take more than ten minutes for the first introduction. Do not discuss any personal matter in that ten minute; inquire about the new acquaintance only. Even if you meet an old acquaintance, ask about his health etc. As far as possible, meet people at their homes; meet in the office only for work. Wherever you meet, do not make sarcastic remarks. Reach the main topic as soon as possible without making much introduction and if you come up with some new thing on that topic, then do not take the credit for that thought yourself but let others take it. This will only reveal your greatness. Even by giving credit to others with your mouth, you will be the one who will get all the credit in the minds of others.

If you are in a position, do not make your personality easily accessible. In that case, not mixing too much, but staying more serious will strengthen your authority. In this connection G. B. Shaw used a sarcasm **"I talk a great deal. I have never set up to be a strong silent man"**. By remaining silent and taking the words seriously, certainly, the Authoritative-Strength increases.

(x)...Listen carefully- Listening carefully is also an important part of good conversation. Sometimes listening carefully to others is more effective than speaking yourself. This is the best way to impress others. There is a small poem in English in which the importance of this art has been described. It is this:

"Would you know the way to woo him..?
It is simple- Listen to him !
Listen graciously and sweetly,
Listen subtly and discreetly
Listen with Intelligence,
With wide-eyed awe and eloquence,
He'ld find endless fascination,
In such brilliant conversation!"

To charm others is very simple - listen to them carefully. Listen with fascination, simplicity, subtlety and with a patience, with understanding, surprise and with wit or flattery. This kind of charming way of talking will give them immense pleasure, i.e. in this way they will be extremely attracted to you. There is no doubt that listening to others with fascination is the best way to satisfy others. Use this method when you have to deal with an arrogant person. In that context, also keep in mind that the listener should not be a fool or narrow-minded to believe everything heard.

Summary

Knowledge of human nature can be gained only through experience. It should be remembered that every person is selfish and self-respecting to some extent. Everyone has a different point of view. You cannot expect everyone to accept your words as the authority of Vedas. If you want to win them over even if they oppose you, then you will have to keep in mind their nature and personality.

These are some important points regarding the effect, use and manner of conversation. It is appropriate to use this power with decisiveness according to the place, time and person. Conversation has great importance in human life, because everyone sees this in every matter and wants to know what people say.

Chapter-6

Behavioral Efficiency

Being a person of practicality or methodology gives more worldly success than being an expert of a subject. Even if someone is well-educated, if he is not clever in practical matters, then his knowledge remains at home. On the contrary, if someone does not have vast knowledge but has practical intelligence, then he can accomplish a great job even with his ordinary ability and becomes popular. The whole world runs on the basis of business and practical matters.

No single framework of practical knowledge can be made. Its art varies with place, work, situation, time and person. What is considered improper and unrighteous at one place, becomes appropriate, and therefore duty, in another context. In daily life, there is no religion greater than truth, but in politics and business, only sensible behavior is universally accepted. Some tact is definitely mixed with deceit. Shukracharya has written that tact is often deceitful: **'YUKTI: CHHALAATMIKA PRAAYAH:'** And it is also written that where both tact and power are combined, there victory is achieved from all sides: **YATRA NITIBALE CHOBHE TATRA SHRIS SARVATOMUKHI** (Shukraniti) Therefore, it cannot be said that pure truth is the only practical religion. At times, true religion is protected by Tact. This can be understood correctly from the life story of Krishna. The same Krishna who preached the Geeta-Dharma to Arjun at the beginning of Mahabharata, the same Krishna, due to circumstances, told Arjun to abandon his religion for victory: **'DHARMAMUTSRIJA PANDAVA'** (Drona Parva). This proves that the best practical religion is the welfare-oriented conduct according to the time.

Brihaspati has said that only on the basis of ancient scriptures, 'one should not judge one's duty'. Thoughts devoid of tacts lead to loss of Dharma, that is, duty is not decided: **KEVALAM SHASTRAMASHRITYA NA KARTAVYO VINIRNAYAH: YUKTIHINE VICHARE TU DHARMAHANI: PRAJAYATE**

In other words, one should be realistic and not just an idealist; one should be time-smart (opportunist) and not become an incarnation of Dharma. One who is time-smart is one who knows when, where and how to behave with whom. Even though that behaviour is logical, but it is successful only when it is based on morality. Without firmness on the side of truth, only intellect or tact cannot win. That which ultimately establishes truth is the best tact and that is the Dharma of man.

Without going into much detail on this subject, we will point out the basic principles of behaviour in different spheres of life. This subject will become clearer from them and it will also be known where pure and simple behaviour is **VYAVAHAR-DHARMA** and where tactful, rational behaviour protects the dignity of true-dharma.

1 …. Home Policy

Home is a place where pure truth, non-violence, faith and balanced behaviour is pleasurable. Home becomes heaven only with mutual goodwill and good behaviour. It becomes hell with lies, intolerances, quarrels, deceits and tricks. Pay attention to these important points related to home policy:

1. <u>Family does not belong to just one person</u>, but to every family member. Everyone is a king in his own house, everyone wants to protect his rights. In that self-rule, no one wants to be insulted or despised. People tolerate insults outside, but cannot tolerate insults done by family members in their own house. One can live as a poor person outside, but no one wants to live as a poor person among brothers and relatives: **'NA BANDHU MADHYE DHANHEEN JEEVANAM.'** Such is human nature. This is why when the dignity of even the smallest member of the family is protected and his selfishness is fulfilled, he remains satisfied and the house remains well organized. Ignorance and injustice spread poison within. The dignity of the house remains intact only with mutual sympathy, sacrifice and loving behavior.

At least these days, there should be democracy in homes as well. Due to the arbitrariness or autocracy of one person, the atmosphere of the house becomes like that of north Korea. Now householder cannot keep his wife as a maid. This is the age of equal rights. In the changed of TIME, the entire atmosphere is filled with the feelings of self-rights, equal treatment and independence. Therefore, there should not be free rule or tyranny of any one person over others and the house should be governed by consensus and mutual cooperation. There is no insignificant person in the house. The cooperation of the younger people of the house is also very necessary, because according to Chanakya, rice cannot grow without husk: **'TUSHENAAPI PARITYAKTA NA PRAROHANTI TANDULAAH:'**

2. <u>There must be a Mukhiya in a home</u>. Ethics says that a family in which all members are arrogant or all are proud or all desire importance, that family gets destroyed: **SURVEY YATR VINETARAH: SURVEY YATRABHIMANINAH: SURVEY MAHATVAMI CHCHANTI KULAM TADVASIIDATI**. Mukhiya does not mean police captain. Many householders or fathers seem like police captains. They have a natural fever of anger 24 hours a day. They want to dominate everyone by force of terror, display arrogance and want to find out secrets of everyone by placing spies behind each other in the house. Such a government type head is not needed in the house. The Home needs a Head of the family, who adopts truth, non-violence and service spirit, that is, the head of the house should behave in such a way that people naturally respect his authority. What is the need of military behavior in the house? creating the atmosphere at home of arrogance or suspicion is like **turning the house into a drill ground or an office of the secret police.** A Sanskrit word for father is **'Kshantu'**, which mean...Patient, Enduring The beauty and power of the father i.e. the head of the household lies in his tolerance and forgiveness. His saintly behaviour helps in maintaining the household and his arrogant behaviour leads to the destruction of the household.

3. <u>There are three types of behaviour</u> with the main people of the house. It is appropriate to treat children with pure affection and simplicity. According to the scriptures, the Tirtha of a son is considered to be the best among all the Tirthas. Regarding women, the scriptures say that if they are disrespected, Lakshmi does not stay in the house. Hindu scriptures consider them to be Griha-Lakshmi. The third type of main people are the elderly. One should be very careful in dealing with the elderly, because due to weakness, their nature is dull, dejected, hatred towards the youth, lack of enthusiasm; therefore, they see the world with these perspectives through their tired eyes. The perspective of the youth is usually not match with them. Perhaps, seeing this disparity, ancient psychologists had made the rule that after a certain age, they should become forest dwellers. Now this is not possible. For domestic peace, it is necessary that the elderly should be treated properly. This English proverb should be remembered that **old age is the second childhood.**

4. <u>Special attention has to be paid to hospitality,</u> in household affairs. It increases the prestige and dignity of the house. Chanakya has written in a verse that "Come, sit here, this is the seat; you are seen after a long time, what is new; are you well with your children? I am very happy to see you" - one should go with a free mind to the house of a person who welcomes a visitor with great respect like this.' The best religion of a good householder is that he should consider a small person who comes to his house as his elder. Even if a Vaman (Dwarf)comes as a guest, he should be treated as Virat (Grand) and with respect.

Know It To Shine

2…... Friend-policy

1. <u>There should be mutual Trust and Rapport</u>, in the practice of friendship. It should be remembered that friends are adopted relatives of each other. Therefore, it is appropriate to behave like brothers with each other. Humanity achieves a great victory in making a stranger one's own. It is achieved only when mutual goodwill and sympathy are expressed and selfishness of both sides is suppressed. Friendship lasts only between people with similar nature.

2. <u>Do not become friend abruptly</u>. One should neither make friends nor become friends of anyone suddenly. Many people become friends in front of others due to selfish motives and behave like enemies behind someone's back due to selfish motives or due to their nature. One should remember this English proverb that **"an open enemy is better than a doubtful friend".** One should not be deceived by beauty and sweet talk. This saying of Tulsi is often true:' **"MUN MALIN TAN SUNDER JAISE, VISH RAS BHARA KANAK GHAT JAISE".** "A beautiful body with the polluted mind is Like a golden pot filled with poison". Therefore, one should first become acquainted, then know each other, then become friends. Considering everyone as an intimate friend and behaving like friends is fatal. Wise people prefer to stay away from those who are friends only for time and selfish motives. That friend is the best who behaves the same in prosperity and adversity. The friendship that remains strong in the days of adversity is the only everlasting one. Tulsi has also said that a friend is tested only in times of crisis **"AAPATTI KAAL PARAKHIYE CHARI, DHEERAJ,**

DHARAM MITRA ARU NAARI": 'Test all four in adversity: patience, religion, friend and woman.'

3. <u>Qualities of Good Friends.</u> According to the scholars, these are the characteristics of a good friend: he stops his friend from committing a crime, engages him in useful works, hides his secrets, proclaims his good qualities, does not abandon him in times of trouble and also helps him financially in times of need:

PAPAN NIVARAYATI YOJAYATE HITAY...., GUHYAM NIGUHATI GUNAAN PRAKATIKAROTI. AAPADGATAM CH NA JAHATI, DADATI KALE SANMITRALAXANMIDAM PRAVADANTI SANTAH:

To remain a good friend of someone, one should adopt these qualities. A friend should have so much faith in the other that he can say with pride in the language of Vedic sages that a friend of a person like you can never be a curse: **'NA RISHYETTVAVATAH: SAKHA.'**

4. <u>Help Friends in their days of Troubles.</u> People living in similar or similar adverse situations usually have more intimacy and mutuality. Post election alliance of political parties is the best example of this. Friendship of difficult times usually does not break. Therefore, if you want to completely win over someone's heart, you should help him in his days of sorrow. That is where humanity awakens and when humanity awakens, there is definitely unity.

5. <u>Do not take unfair advantage from a friend</u>. It is easy to make friendship but it is difficult to maintain it. To

maintain it, some special things should be kept in mind. The first thing is that one should not try to take unfair advantage from a friend. The giver becomes big and the receiver small. In this way, due to the loss of the feeling of equality, the scale of friendship starts going up and down. The second thing is that one should not interfere in the personal life of friends and should not ridicule them on any occasion. No one loses his personality because of being a friend. Apart from this, one should be more tolerant. No one will like the company of people who get angry easily. One should not try to control a friend by being obstinate or deceitful or by showing arrogance in any matter.

No matter what kind of friend he is, too much cannot be expected from him. Everyone has independent interests and independent compulsions. Remember Even a very good gentleman friend can sacrifice his selfishness only up to a certain extent. Therefore, one should not make his friendship a burden for the friend. This statement of the scriptures is valid to some extent that **one should not trust a friend too much,** because even a friend has friends to whom he can reveal secrets or sometimes he himself can become an enemy and misuse those things.

6. There is no consideration of high or low in friendship, but this does not mean that if a friend becomes a high official and you remain a clerk, you should still claim equality with him or start exerting yourself on his strength. In this regard, this English proverb is valid that a high-ranking friend should be considered as your lost friend. **A friend in power is a friend lost.** Not everyone is lost, but most people are definitely lost by getting mad or carried away by the intoxication of position. If such people remain friends due to gentlemanliness, then also you should not

become blind on their strength. No one deliberately takes poison trusting a doctor friend! No one becomes strong on his own by the strength of others.

7. <u>Always be cautious in dealing with friends</u>. Even a little doubt destroys its root. It remains alive only by meeting again and again. But it fades even by meeting too much. **"ATI SARVATR VARJAYET"** 'Excess should be avoided everywhere.'

3......Public Policy

There is a great need of good behaviour in the public sphere, because there one has to be in contact with people of different nature and class. Some important points related to public behaviour are as follows:

1. <u>Politeness is the soul of public behaviour</u>. The display of politeness and courtesy reveals the nobility of a man. In this context, we remember an incident that happened after the Ram-Ravana war. Ravana was lying on the battlefield; Ram said to Lakshman: *"The demon king is a great scholar of politics, public policy etc, Go! and get his comments, sermons before his death."* Lakshman went to the battlefield and went near his head to get some advice. When Ravana asked him, he told the reason for his visit. The ethicist Ravana said with self-respectfully, 'You, even being a prince, do not know the public etiquettes; the one who begs for education does not stand near the head of the teacher, but at his feet and until you do not follow the decorum of the students' etiquette, I cannot impart knowledge to you. Lakshman immediately became alert and humbly came near his feet. Ravana advised him that

"Never promise to do any work without the intention of doing it. Do not postpone anything for later".

It is equally important to follow etiquettes not only with elders but also with younger ones. The famous scholar Carlyle has written that **"A great man shows his greatness by the way he treats little man"**. In this regard we should keep the ideal of Ram in front. He never violated the decorum in his conduct. For example, he was the architect of Vibhishan's fate, but after Ravana's death, when Sita had to be brought from Ashokvan, he asked Hanuman to enter Lanka with the permission of King Vibhishan and bring Sita. He also requested Vibhishan to give him permission of bringing Sita. All this was not necessary for Lanka's conqueror Ram, but even after being victorious, how could he abandon the decorum of his natural politeness!

2.   <u>Do not become Selfish, Arrogant, etc.</u> One should not become blind anywhere in the social world, neither be selfish, nor arrogant nor bigot, nor willfully ignorant. One who is night blind cannot see even the stars in the sky. One should put oneself in the situation of others and see things from their point of view also. Do not involve personal matters in public matters. **Even if one considers the social etiquette to be a false etiquette, one should still consider it to be a good etiquette**. No matter how pure the social etiquette is, from a personal point of view it is somewhat artificial. One has to mold oneself according to the interests of the society.

3.   <u>Strive for the Peace in the Society</u>. We should express our love for peace in society. Our speech and behaviour should not be such that people consider us to be the descendants of **"Narada"** (A travelling, storyteller &

disseminator of news Sage, as per Hindu mythology). Popularity makes public wealth easily available: **'JANANURAG PRABHAVAHI SAMPADAH'** (Bharavi).

4. Self-Respect and the Respect of others. In our conduct, we should take care of our self-respect and the respect of others. We should keep in mind Gandhiji's advice that **"no person loses honour or self-respect but by his consent"**. No person loses self-respect without his own approval. One should not do any such act which makes oneself ludicrous or humiliates others. One should express his pride through his laughter, behaviour, lifestyle, attire etc. If someone wants people to congratulate him without being deserving, then this is not possible. People bow down to the one whom they consider more capable and stronger than them. False pride leads to humiliation.

5. Protect the Dignity of the Women. Mainly, raising eyes and hands on women is considered uncivilized. Even cruel treatment of women is intolerable in civilized society. Valmiki is of the opinion that gentlemen never torture women. When Lakshmana came to Kishkindha after getting very angry with Sugriva, Sugriva remembered this policy. He told Tara that you go ahead and meet him because your going will calm the anger of a great man like Lakshmana: **'NAHI STRISHU MAHATMANAH KVACHITKURVANTI DARUNAM** His guess turned out to be correct.

6. In Anger, show Strength not Unruliness. If there is a need to get angry somewhere, then one should show brilliance and advertise one's strength but not unruliness. The motto is that one should keep displaying the brilliance;

everyone ignores the fire in wood, but nobody ignores the burning fire nearby. Therefore, the fire of power should be kept displaying, but with a purpose and good thoughts. Unjustified anger, which is born out of obstinacy, perversion or bad behaviour, is self-destructive. By getting angry again and again, the feeling of enmity gets strengthened.

7.   <u>Do not always find Faults of others</u>. You will not find a person with all the virtues in the society. Therefore, as far as possible, one should not try to find out the faults of others. The one who appreciates virtues is himself considered to be virtuous. One should take advantage of the good qualities of others, and let their bad qualities remain with them. The best advice is that before becoming a public reformer, one should reform himself by applying his own principles. A self-destructed or a wicked person in the guise of a gentleman cannot be respected by anyone.

8.   <u>Read the situation and circumstances correctly.</u> Only he is considered to be skilled in dealing with others who can quickly understand the feelings of others and can establish intimacy by expressing sympathy, joy or sorrow as per the situation and time. He is neither a person with a confused mind nor a person who speaks two different things. The sign of a gentleman is to be one in his thoughts, actions & words: **'MANASYEKAM, VACHASYEKAM, KARMANYEKAM MAHATMANAAM.'** The artificial expression of a chameleon has no value.

9.   <u>Avoid False Promises, deceit etc.</u> in social Life. Keep away these things: making false promises, putting someone in an ethical dilemma, getting things done through deceit, the audacity to strive to get something that is

beyond your reach and greed. Apart from these, there are two big social crimes, which every smart person should avoid. The first is the crime of ingratitude, the second is jealousy. Napoleon considered ingratitude to be the biggest social crime. Regarding jealousy, a western scholar has said that if. **If you want to punish someone, then teach him to be jealous of someone.**

10. Be careful in remaining silent and while talking. By remaining silent, seriousness is shown in the society, at the same time keeping mum when seeing some injustice shows low self-esteem and one becomes guilty of the injustice because **'MAUNAM SAMMATI LAKSHANAM'**. "Silence is equal to consent". Therefore, one should be careful in remaining silent, like while talking, one should remain silent as much as possible in relation to his personal problems, "**RAHIMAN, NIJ MUN KI VYATHA MUN HI RAKHAYI GOY, HANSI HI LOG JAHAN KE, BANTI N LE HAIN KOY**" "The sorrow of one's own mind, one should keep it to himself. People will laugh, no one can share that sorrow". The moralists are of the opinion that destruction of wealth, sorrow of mind, bad character at home, cheating and insult- these things, intelligent people do not say to others. **ARTHANASHAM MANASTAPAM, GRIHE DUSCHARITANI CH. VANCHANAM CHAPMANAM CH MATIMANN APRAKASHYATEY.** (Manusmriti)

Regarding secret things, this Saying is completely valid that they should be protected from falling into six ears: **'SHATKARNE VARJAYETSUDHIH:'**

4......Business Policy

For any behaviour which is done for a business and professional purpose, the following points should be kept in mind:

1. <u>Do not do work hastily</u>; working without thinking is a place of grave troubles. Virtuous properties accept those who works after thinking:
SAHASA VIDDHIT N KRIYAAM VIVEK: PARAM AAPDAM PADAM, VRUNUTE HI VIMRISHYA KARINAM GUNALUBDHAAH: SWAYAMEVA SAMPADAAH: (Bharavi)

2. <u>Work should be ready before the Scheduled Time</u>. One should always keep "Time" in mind while doing work. Whatever be the work, it should be ready before the scheduled time. By not reaching on time, not only the train but also the train of luck or success is missed.

3. <u>Show your Prowess in Meetings</u>. If you have to meet someone to accomplish a task, you should go at the appointed time and in proper attire. On meeting, you should make the first impression as deepest as possible. Do not be sheepish or arrogant, but be eloquent, demonstrate and push Subject-specific courage.

4. <u>Do some research of the person before you meet</u>. One should not forget that "the wise enter the pond and the heart only after knowing its depth: One who understands human nature can instantly read the minds of others. And only he succeeds in his task. Therefore, one should move

ahead after finding out the depth of the person whom one has to meet. Only after understanding his state of mind, one can succeed in arguing with logic, otherwise one has to grope in the dark.

5. <u>Put your arguments in soft Language</u>. Showing quick wit, showing natural curiosity towards the listener, giving constructive suggestions, showing an effort to agree with the listener by giving strong arguments in soft language, supporting your opinion logically, explaining your viewpoint correctly to the other person and giving an effective and quick reply after listening to his words carefully - these are the things that show practical ingenuity of a Gentleman. Explaining means that the direction in which your intellect runs, the thoughts of the listener should also flow in the same direction. If you can have the intellect of others for your work, then it is true practical cleverness.

6. <u>Do not show flattery and stubbornness</u>. In conversation, one should resort to eloquence and cleverness, not flattery and stubbornness. Conversation or behaviour should not reveal any deceit which would make one feel ashamed in the future. Business tact is necessary only to a certain extent. Selling an expensive thing by proving it to be cheap is not deceit, but calling a fake thing real is deceit. Such deceit is not acceptable. Reality should be kept in mind everywhere.

7. <u>Goal must be to accomplish the desired Task</u>. When you meet someone for work, you should use the opportunity to accomplish your work instead of talking about entertainment. The most appropriate thing is that we should use even the entertainment meeting to accomplish

our task. It means that we should not let even the opportunity of entertainment go waste. If we do not get success in one go, we should not lose hope, but should start afresh again. It is foolish to sever ties with someone out of disappointment. There is a saying in English **"It is easier to climb a mountain than to level it"** that it is easier to cross a mountain by climbing it than to cross it by making it flat.

8. <u>Avoid conflicts in business</u>. One should always circumvent conflicts in business. One should try not to interrupt and not allow the other person to interrupt. It is against respect of either side. Even if the matter gets worse, one should try to resolve it. Getting angry or threatening brings bitterness in the business. It is also said that one who has anger cannot have a shortage of enemies! One should not get carried away by momentary excitement but act with foresight.

9. <u>Special care in communication</u> and correspondence. One should decide one's opinion on a subject and then communicate in brief after weighing the words with lawyerly wisdom. Literary style is disastrous in work related communications. One should not write in such a way that the reader digs a mountain and finds a mouse.

In short, it should be understood that success in the workplace is achieved only by clear and rational behavior. Being well behaved in the business and workplace is the direct path to achieving success.

5.... Fool-Policy

1. <u>Be aware that there is No medicine for fools</u>. It is most difficult to deal with a fool, because he only talks about himself and even if he listens to others, he misinterprets the meaning of something by understanding something else. Ethicists have written that there is no medicine for a fool: **'MOORKHASYA NAASTYO AUSHADHAM'**. His nature cannot be changed by any remedy, because he becomes cold again like heated water. It is said that a Guru once told his foolish disciple that tying a turban on the head increases a person's respect. On hearing the Guru-Vachan disciple left for the market. On the way, he remembered that if he had tied a turban, everyone would have treated him well. So, as he had no other clothes, he took off his dhoti and tied it on his head and went naked with the belief that now whoever sees him will consider him a great Mahamahopadhyay. Understand the meaning of the story. In teaching a fool, one loses both his and one's own intelligence.

2. <u>Do not tease Fools</u>. The greatest skill in dealing with a fool is that one should not tease him. There is a saying in English - one should avoid the front of a bull, the back of a horse and all around a fool. If a fool is to be controlled, he should be given some food or a sweet story should be told to him for his entertainment. Doing something according to his wish is also a way of controlling him. But there is a fear of losing self-respect due to this. It is wise to stay away from such people. It is better not to touch them than to apply mud on them and then wash them off. There is also a semi-educated category of fools. People of that category become egoistic after

having a little knowledge. Ordinary knowledge makes them egoistic.

3. <u>Nourish the ego of fools to get the work done</u>. Bhartrhari has also written that it is easy to please a fool, it is very easy to please a learned person, but even Brahma cannot convince a person who has limited knowledge but considers himself to be very knowledgeable." **AGYAH: SUKHMARADHYA: SUKHTARMARADHYATE VISHESHAGYAH: GYANLAV DURVIDAGDHAM BRIHMAPI TAM NARUM NA RANJYATI.** The work can be done only by satisfying the ego of such people and making them proud and let them live in their own paradise.

6... Exceptional Policy

Not all the people in human society are good, there are also deceptive and evil people and they are in majority here. They are very powerful and therefore cannot be controlled by a single method. The great souls may be able to control the cunning creatures (humans) by yoga and self-power, but usually they can be controlled by the intelligent people who have to take recourse to tact, politics, diplomacy and punishment policy etc. Not all are of the same nature. Hence cannot be controlled by a single tact. According to the circumstances, the wise, intelligent and insightful people control evil people by different methods. Incidentally, we give some useful information in this regard here.

1. <u>Do not be too good for all the people</u>. Mahamuni Vyas says that do not be too simple. Go and look at the

trees in the forest; there you will find straight trees cut and crooked trees standing.
NATYANTAM SARALAIRBHAVYAM GATVA PASHYA VANE TARUN., CHHIDYANTE SARALAASTRA KUBJASTISTHANTI NEERUJAH:

Tulsi has said this in this manner:
**TEDH JAANI BANDAI SAB KAHU.
VAKRA CHANDRAMAHI GRASAI NAHI RAHU**

Even when Ram wanted to cross the sea with a saintly attitude, the sea was not ready to give him way. Then Ram gave up his forgiving attitude and picked up his bow and arrow and said – Shame on the One, who forgives that person who considers, the one incapable: **'ASAMRTHA VIJANAATI DHIK KSHMAAMI-DRSHE JANE'** (Ramayana). The sea immediately became humble. Shaw had said after Gandhiji's assassination that **"It is dangerous to be too Good"**. Being too straightforward is frightening at least in an ordinary society. Evil people consider a simple person to be a lamb and wolves naturally start chasing the lamb. Demons used to surround the ancient sages and saints, but they used to run away even on hearing the name of archer Ram-Laxman. It should be remembered that "'**a dog licks the face of a simple person.'**"

2. Collaborate with other Illusionists. The great poet Bharavi has written that those fools who do not become illusionists along with the illusionists are surely defeated:
VRAJANTI TE MUDHADHIYAH: PARABHAVM, BHAVANTI MAYAVISHU YE NA MAYINAH:

3. <u>Adopt the ways as per the circumstances</u>. The author of Panchatantra has written that victory should be achieved by saluting the best, creating differences among brave enemies, giving favours to the lowly and fighting with those of equal valour:
UTTAM PRANIPATEN, SHURAM BHEDEN YOJAYET.NEECH MALPAPRADANEN, SAMAM SHAKTI PARAKRAMAIḤ.:

4. <u>Do not stick to ethics</u>. Kalidasa's opinion is that taking recourse to only ethics is cowardice. And using only power is animality: **KATARYA KEVALA NITI: SHAURYA SHVAPAD CHESHTITAM.**

5. <u>Be diplomatic in dealing with enemies</u>. It is written in the Mahabharata that until the opportunity comes, the enemy should be carried on the shoulder; when the time comes, he should be smashed and broken like a pot is broken by smashing it on a stone:
VAHEDAMITRAM SKANDHEN YAVATKALSYA PARYAAH: ATHAINMAAGTE KALE BHINDED GHATAMI VASHMANI.

The lion goes backwards before leaping. But it is not good to lag behind everywhere. Where there is a possibility of harm from the enemy, it is wise to attack first. That is why ethicists are of the opinion that **attack is the best defense**.

6. <u>Have bigger Virtues than Enemy</u>. It is written in Kautilya Arthashastra that one should cover the faults of the enemy by one's own virtues and enemy's virtues by one's own good qualities:

PARDOSHAANSVAGUNAISHCHADAYED GUNAN GUNADVAIGUNYEN.

7. <u>Find flaws of enemies</u>. Kalidas has written in Raghuvansh that seeing the enemy's hole i.e. defect or weakness and attacking on it leads to victory: **'JAYO RANDHRA PRAHARINAAM.'**

8. <u>Do not worry about weaker enemies</u>. Panchatantra believes that intelligent people can increase those enemies who can be destroyed easily. Like the phlegm increased by jaggery (GUD) is easily released on its own and go away. There is a saying in Hindi that 'why should we give poison to someone who dies by giving jaggery?' **JO GUD DINHE HI MARREY, KYON VISH DIJE TAAHI**

9. <u>Know the Shelter of enemy</u>. There is a saying in English that **when the mouse laughs at the cat, there is a hole**. when a mouse mocks a cat, understand that there is a hole nearby.

10. <u>Do not be carried away by flattery</u>. Where there is unnecessary flattery, one should be apprehensive about the result being sorrow, because no one shows flattery without a purpose: **"ATYADARO BHAVED YATRA, ARYAKARANVARJITAH: TATRA SHANKA PRAKARTVYA, PARIAMEASUKHAVAHA**

11. <u>Do not dance before blinds</u>. Sheikh Saadi has said that "recognize the one who is your buyer". This is true because 'the art of dancing go waste if performed before blinds. **"ANDHE AAGE NACHATE KALA AKARATH JAYE"**

12. <u>Stand firm on your place</u>. A person who stands firm at his place is always strong. Even a pet dog has the courage of a lion. When in water, a crocodile can pull even an elephant, but outside it, it is despised even by dogs.

13. <u>Control inner conflicts</u>. A foreign scholar (Fransis Meehan) has written in one of his famous books ('The Temple of the Spirit') while discussing the causes of conflict that if you try to find the root of the destructive conflicts that take place between countries, castes and classes, you will find that the one who spreads all the bitterness is a talented person within whom a fierce struggle of opposing mental tendencies is going on. He will be suffering from his inner turmoil; he will be unable to overcome his mental conflict; he will be disturbed, egoistic or emotional; his soul will be in pain within. That is why he pollutes the outside environment with the poison from within, spreads his bitterness outside, spreads the doubt and jealousy of his nature among others, as a result of which there is strife outside.

We give such a person the opportunity to rise and attain high positions and let him occupy influential positions and then wonder why the thinking human race does not live in peace. There is a constant struggle between one and the other, because each person keeps struggling with himself. Men are at war with one another because each man is at war with himself. Such persons who do not control their mental conflicts and conquer their inner self will definitely spread the feeling of conflict in the society. External peace can be established only by eliminating internal unrest.

14. <u>Do not run away from difficult situation</u>. Running away from a difficult situation is the biggest mistake because generally the one who runs away puts himself in front of the same danger he wants to avoid as compared to the one who stays at his place. When we have to face a serious situation, nothing can be worse than running away from it, because a person who runs away exposes himself to that very danger more than the person who sits or stands, normally of course.

15. <u>Fight for the Rights</u>. One should always shout for one's rights. Without shouting, a child does not even get his mother's milk. At least in the political field, shouting relieves one of the troubles. Every government listens loudly because it sits at a height. One should shout but like a human being; not like a donkey, jackal, dog or crow.

Policy Brief

An Ethicist has given the essence of complete practical knowledge in one verse. He says that a friend should be treated with simple behavior, an enemy with strategy, a greedy person with money, a master with work, a scholar with respect, a young girl with love, relatives with equal behavior, a hot-headed with politeness, a teacher with salutation, a fool by telling stories, a learned person with knowledge, a lover with Romantic stories and all with the Modesty:

MITRA SWACHHATAYA RIPU NAYVALAIR LUBDHAM DHANAIRISHWARAM;

KARYEIN DWIJAMADAREN YUVTIM PREMNA SAMAIRVANDHWAAN;

ATYUGRAM STUTIBHIGURURUM PRNATI BHIRMURKHAM KATHABHIRBUDHHAM VIDYABHI: RASIKAM RASEN SAKALAN SHILEN KURYAD VASHAM;

Chapter-7

How is your Appearance

Who will deny that the appearance of every part of the body has an impact on others? A person's personality speaks for itself through his every part. A beautiful woman does not roam around with a certificate; her beauty itself attracts others. People start accepting the authority of a person with a well-built and strong body at the first sight. Therefore, it has to be accepted that a person's personality is reflected by his physical appearance.

Before discussing this topic, we should know that our appearance is not exactly the same as we imagine about ourselves. A man forms a false notion of his body's appearance according to his feelings and thinks that everyone recognizes him in that form. He sees his emotionally colored appearance even in front of the mirror. When he is in love, he considers himself beautiful even though he has the face of a Chimpanzee. When he is disappointed in love, he considers even his beautiful body to be ugly. In reality, he does not see his real figure, but sees his assumed mental image. He imagines that he must look like this and at the same time thinks that it would have been good if he looked like this. In this situation, his appearance becomes strange at least in his own eyes. In the eyes of others, he appears to be the same as he is from outside, but in his own eyes, he appears to be something else according to his mental attitude. Due to mental conflict, he also does unnatural things and remains under the illusion that everyone is staring at him with keen eyes. Therefore, he tries to hide his imagined physical flaws.

The framework of the mind has an impact. The feeling of femininity in the mind, a man acts like a woman and thinks that everyone is considering him a beautiful woman. He does not look like beautiful woman; he looks like a eunuch. Many people imagine their heroic form by twisting their moustaches, but in the eyes of others they look like clowns. When the morale is weak, a man considers his strong body as weak. Similarly, the lifestyle has an impact. When the clothes are dirty, a man starts considering himself small in the civilized society. Even a short person living in a grand palace considers himself very big. A first-class passenger considers himself a very big man in the eyes of sleeper-class passengers. On winning somewhere, even a short man walks with pride and thinks that everyone is looking at his great figure.

A well-known psychologist had said that in a state of mental conflict, a person mis-understands the weight of his own body. When happy, people feel that their own body is light and think that everyone is considering them light. When one is worried, the body feels heavy, but in the eyes of others it remains the same. A person in a high position never thinks over the smallness of his size. A strong peon considers himself to be small and submissive in his eyes and his boss, who may be weaker than him, to be brave and huge. The reason for this is that the mental attitudes of a person agitate his nerves and according to them, the mental image of the person appears before his eyes.

When a person forms an opinion about himself, he expresses himself accordingly. He tries to improve himself through various efforts. Thinking that his neck is longer than someone else's, he keeps his neck pressed down while going out and thinks that people will not be able to sense his imaginary flaws. But his artificial appearance becomes strange.

There is a similar misconception in the subject of speech. Many people consider their voice to be pleasant to the ears, but it sounds harsh to others. It is a scientific fact that our own voice sounds as sweet to our own ears as it does not to the ears of others. We create a false image of our personality in our minds on the basis of the sound we have perceived. After examining many people, otolaryngologists observed that they were shocked when they first heard their own recorded voice and said that their voice was not like that.

Many people are perplexed when they see their photograph because they see a different form in the photograph than what they imagine themselves to be. Many people become artificial while getting their photograph taken because they definitely try to suppress or hide some imagined ugliness of theirs and in such a condition their appearance becomes distorted and unnatural.

After understanding this psychological mystery, we should see the true nature of ourselves or someone else. The perceived form is usually not true; the truth is that which is perceptible. The perceptible form has certain characteristics of the body, which affect others. No matter how we consider ourselves, our form in the eyes of others is the same as is reflected in each and every part of our body.

Forgetting our imaginary form for a while, we should think about those Samudrik traits which reveal our real personality. Those traits which are not present in these should be adopted as far as possible. The main benefit of knowing these is that we can achieve practical success by correctly identifying others by their shape or anatomy. For this purpose, we give a brief useful description of the physical traits below:

Main Characteristics of a Perfect Body

According to Samudrika shastra, such body parts are considered good and attractive in a healthy and beautiful body...: -

1. Five long body parts- Arms, Eyes, Mouth, Nose and Chest,
2. Four short organs   - Neck, Ears, Back, Thigh,
3. Six Elevated organs- nose, eyes, forehead, teeth, head, heart,
4. Five subtle organs - finger joints, teeth, hair, nails, skin,
5. Seven red organs - palms, soles of feet, nails, palate, tongue, Lips and eyes,
6. Three deep   - voice, intellect, navel,
7. Three are broad- chest, head, forehead.

In the Valmiki Ramayana, the poet said this through the mouth of Narada regarding Ram who is endowed with all the good qualities:

VIPULANSO MAHABAHUH: KAMBUGRIVO MAHAHANUH: MAHORSKO MAHESHVASO GUDJATRURRINDAM. AAJANUBAHU SUSHIRAH: SULALAT: SUVIKRAM: SAMAH: SAMAVIBHAKT ANGAH: SNIGDHAVARNAAH: PRATAPVAN. PINAVAKSHHO VISHALAKSHHO LAKSHMI VANCHU BHALAKSHANAH:

Ram has big shoulders, big arms, a neck like a conch shell, a big chin, broad chest, holds a huge bow, has a hidden collarbone and is the destroyer of enemies. His arms are long upto the knees, his head is beautiful, his forehead is beautiful and whose presence is auspicious. His body-parts are neither too small nor too big. Each limb is well-formed. The complexion of the body is balsamic and he is radiant. His chest is plump, his eyes are large. He is adorned with auspicious features that are beautiful.

These are the main characteristics of the body, which attract your attention. Whether you are familiar with Samudrik Shastra or not, you like the person who has many of these characteristics. His personality is impressive. You are silently impressed with the influence of his personality.

Most of these characteristics are inborn, and this is where we have to accept that a large part of a person's personality is inborn. The saying **"HONHAR BIRVAAN KE HOT CHIKNE PAT"** 'A promising child has smooth soles' is true here. This inborn personality is called Prepossessing Personality.

It is a mistake to consider these characteristics as everything. These characteristics cannot be found in everyone because not everyone is the best of persons. Yes, many of these characteristics are found in the body of a wealthy man and when you meet a man with such characteristics, then believe in his personal greatness. But before trusting him completely, think about other things also because it is possible that he has betrayed himself. Nature may have given him a beautiful appearance and personality, but he may have changed his path with his traits. Just as you see a blemish on the moon, similarly look for blemishes in these organs as well.

There is one more thing to understand in this regard. If you do not find these characteristics in your body, then do not consider yourself inferior and get disappointed. If your mind is strong, your intellect is alert, then you can certainly do extraordinary work even with ordinary organs. A courageous person can face wild animals even with an ordinary stick. If a person who is physically strong but mentally weak, and goes with a cannon on his shoulder, he will fall unconscious on hearing the roar of some living being from a distance. So, first test the strength of your mind and intellect and do not consider the external characteristics of the body as the only criterion.

We will discuss the method of reading emotions after writing something on how much depth of human personality can be known from the different parts of the body. Just as your personality may be different if one eye or one ear is missing, similarly the presence or absence of certain characteristics on specific parts of the body has an impact…

1.... Head

First of all, we consider the head. You must have heard this saying **"SAR BADA SARDAR KA, PEIR BADA GANWAR KA"** 'A leader has a big head and a boorish person has big feet.'. There is truth in it. If a person's head is small in proportion to his body, like a kangaroo, then consider him a fool. A beautiful, well-shaped and big head definitely makes a person talented, whether he is educated or not. It is not necessary that you consider a person with a big head to be a gentleman. His intelligence can be sharp in any direction. If he starts doing evil, then he will show good use of his intelligence in that too. His intelligence is like a gun, which he can use as a soldier as well as a robber. Similarly, it is not necessary that you should consider such a person to be happy too. If someone is suffering from macrocephaly, then his head will definitely become big. Just believe that normally a person with a big head has a big brain. He has the power of thinking and reasoning.

A farsighted and thoughtful person has a long head. A person with such a head is talented, sincere, intellectual and a philosopher, and also a scholar. Such people are also fond of imagination. Therefore, if they go in the opposite direction, they become suspicious and fearful.

The head of an arrogant person hangs backwards. If the back of the head is pointed, then the person is of a curvaceous nature; if it is bulging on both sides, then the person is emotional, romantic and has an inspiring mind. A round head which is raised like the back of a tortoise is considered highly commended. People with such heads are hardworking, self-reliant, fearless, have a fertile mind and are tolerant of pain.

A person with a very small head is careless, delirious, lazy, foolish or miserly. A person with a awkwardly-built head is indecisive, fickle, cowardly and a flatterer.

A person is also judged by his hair. Soft and shiny hair reflects the softness and health of the person within, while rough or coarse hair reflects the ill health and dryness of the person within.

People with stiff and copper-colored hair are often crazy and addicted to travelling. People with curly hair like everything that is round, twisted or twisted. Such people like to wear round glasses, are fond of a mountain stick, shoes with slanting tips or a flared kurta. Their gait is also swaying, their speech is also spicy and their handwriting is also round. If you ask them to walk straight, they will get tired after walking a furlong. If you ask them to stroll for a while, they will roam around all the streets of the city.

It is not true that people with curly hair are pleasure-seekers. They are definitely addicted - whether that addiction is of knowledge or art or some immorality. When they are addicted to knowledge, they are fond of novels, stories, dramas and mystical poetry. When they are art-lovers, they show good talent in all arts. They are good at music and literature. When they are pleasure-seekers, they become the most shameless and daring. Such people can do masculine work; they are more energetic outside than at home. People with standing hair are arrogant. Such people may be sweet-spoken for some reason but by nature they are cruel, conceited or proud of themselves.

2.... Countenance

The best test of a person is his facial features. The entire history, character and nature of a person is reflected on his face. Since ancient times, not only Indian philosophers but also Western scholars and worldly scholars have been believing this. The shape of the face reveals our permanent personality; its nature and its deformity can also reveal our Character, **temperament and mood.** You must have heard that some people can guess the state of mind of a person by looking at his face. There is truth in this. A person can hide his true nature and character through his speech and behaviour, but not through his face. There are very few people who do not let the feelings of the heart show on their face, even then their inner feelings get expressed on their face. One can consider the face of a person as the mirror of his personality, but sometimes one has to be cautious. Some people are innocent by their face but are devious by heart. They practice that their feelings do not get reflected on their face. This can happen with the practice. But the real nature of ninety out of a hundred people can be known by their face.

This is how a person may be judged by the different parts of the face.

(i)... Forehead- The person whose forehead is elevated and large is intelligent, sharp-minded, thoughtful, progressive, fame-seeker, influential and trustworthy. If the forehead is half-moon-shaped and has a special shine, then the person is radiant, restrained and self-confident. If it is full of many lines, then the person is clever, thoughtful, suffering from some mental agony or a philosopher; if it is dull, small and sunken inwards, then the person is foolish or idle and arrogant. If the forehead is very small, covered with a thatch of hair from above, then the person will be careless, addicted and free from the feeling of honour and insult. If it is raised upwards and sunken towards the bottom, then the person will be dull-witted, lazy, a man struck by troubles. The person with a broad forehead is generous, calm, modest and skilled in behavior.

(ii)... Eyes- The true reflection of the soul is seen in the eyes. You must have heard something or the other about the effectiveness of different types of eyes. Some people's eyes look as if they will speak any moment. Some people's eyes look like a loaded pistol and some like a bottle of liquor. Some people's eyes drip with pity. Some have compassion, some have affection, some have anger, some have simplicity and some have restlessness of heart. Something like mother's affection drips from many eyes; the brilliance of a brilliant man emanates from his eyes like a spark. Eyes have a strange power of attraction, a strange power to produce effects, and a natural ability to reveal a person's entire personality.

Big and clean eyes like a blooming lotus are the best. If they have natural sweetness, radiance and simplicity, then a person with such eyes is definitely happy, fame-lover, generous, kind-hearted and influential. He is especially a lover, connoisseur and lover of knowledge.

The eyes of a greedy person are sunken, sharp and restless. The vision of an arrogant person is wide or torn, heavy and especially red. The eyes of a philosopher are large but covered by eyelids, and the eyes of a drunkard are usually small and slanted. The eyes of a fool are usually round like the eyes of an owl. The eyes of a cunning person are brown like a cat.

The eyes of a person with a restless heart, whether large or small, do not remain steady. The eyelids of such a person move rapidly. The eyes of a fearful, hungry and delusional person look as if they will fall down. The eyes of a poet and a person suffering from pain seem to be floating. The eyes of a clever, evil and untrustworthy person are dull, small like shells and are often uneven.

If both the eyes are very small and sunken, then such a person is considered to be one who casts a secret eye on the wealth of others and leads a mysterious life. The person whose eyes are close to each other is cunning, sly and a betrayer according to Samudrika Vedanta. The person whose eyes seem to be raised upwards is a virtuous person, a poet or is confused or incapable. The gaze of an honest person is straight and that of a wicked person is crooked. The gaze of a timid, criminal and a person of shy nature is lowered and that of an angry person is curved.

The more serious a person is, the less his eyelids move. You can test this yourself by sitting in a serious state for some time. The gaze of a serious person is also steadier. One who blinks a lot is unstable and weak hearted. The eyebrows of a conceited, greedy and stubborn person remain raised like a bow. The eyebrows of a thinker are thick and crescent-like in their entire length. Both the eyebrows of an individualistic, creative, person remain joined. He may have disregard for societal expectations. One with thin eyelashes is sharp-witted, one with long eyelashes is full of poetic power.

In short, eyes that are like lotus or deer-eyes, whose region is red, which are smooth and whose eyebrows are raised and wide are especially effective. Eyes that are like a cat, are curved, whose eyebrows are semi-circular or very different or uneven are inauspicious. The redness of the sclera region reflects the wellness of a person.

(iii)... Ears- The ears of an angry person are pulled back, those of a cautious person are erect. The ears of a home-loving person are also found erect. The ears of a suspicious person appear protruding and prominent. Fools and cowards are usually long-eared and the ears of a thief are like those of a mouse. The ears of a person who is very cautious are like those of a rabbit. The ears of an intelligent person are found pulled downwards. A person with small ears is a miser and a smuggler and a person with wide ears is rich and generous. A person with pointed ears is cruel and a person with fleshy ears is happy and healthy.

It should be remembered that ears do not only perform the function of receiving sound, they have a very close relationship with the intellect. Among the organs of the body, ears are the closest to the intellect. Some nerves go directly from the ears to the intellect. When you are engrossed in some matter, naturally you keep your hand on the ear and bend your head to one side, which puts special pressure on the intellect. As soon as the ears of the students are pulled, their intellect becomes alert and cautious.

Modern scientists have found that there are two pea-sized glands behind the base of the ears which generate and receive emotions. According to them, emotions are generated not from the heart rather from the above-mentioned sensitive spots. Whatever it may be, the structure of the ears reveals the inner strength of a person. The swaying and hanging ears definitely reveal the goat-like nature of a person.

(iv)... **Temples**-A person whose temples are prominent is considered to be studious, self-controlled, thoughtful and a person desirous of fame. A person with sunken temples is a pleasure-seeker, greedy, anxious and adventurous.

(v)... **Nose** - It is easiest to identify a person by his nose, because it is at the forefront and cannot be covered or moved in any way. It remains standing like the Ashoka pillar.

One whose nose is like that of a parrot is sharp-minded, clever and a politician. One with a long nose is serious, efficient and self-confident. One whose tip is radiant is radiant, has strong self-power, is self-controlled, enthusiastic and lucky. One whose nose tip is dull is devoid of talent, lacks self-control, dry and ineffective. If the nose is long and slightly raised or bent at the tip, then that person is prudent and observant. If it is bent at the tip or raised too much upwards, then that person will be clever and humorous. If the nose is pressed in the middle, then that person will be stubborn. One with a flat nose is miserly. One with a wide nose is greedy, one with a swollen nose is short-tempered, lustful and arrogant. One with a round and flat nose is desirous of others' wealth, one with a curved nose is cruel; A person with a thick nose and a pig-like nose, is snobbery, slanderous, lazy, of low IQ and has a dirty and dull nature and with a thin nose is a thief and the one with a nose like a samosa is a fool who is not affected by the movement of the world. **JINHAY N VYAPE JAGAT-GATI**

(vi)... Face- A face like a blooming lotus reveals the inner and spiritual beauty of a human being. A person with beautiful, well-shaped, even and soft face is of high spirits and happy nature. A person with a very big mouth is sad, beggarly and foolish. A person with a round face is dishonest, asymmetrical face is fickle and a person with a protruding face is a big fool.

A person with red lips is talented, soft and delicate. A person with thin lips is talkative, arrogant and suspicious. A person with small lips is poor and greedy, a person with pale lips is short-sighted and distressed. A person with curved lips is crooked-minded; a person with thick lips is lazy, foolish, short-tempered, cowardly and addicted. It is considered auspicious for both the lips to meet naturally. If they appear to be pressing inwards when they meet, then such a person will be silent, mysterious and timid. If they come together like a beak, then such a person will be unstable, irrational, talkative and a flatterer. If the lower lip looks like a lid of the upper one, then such a person will be conceited, hypocritical and selfish. If the upper one hangs over the lower one like a roof, then such a person will be devoid of humour, but sensual, sensible and calm. A person whose lips are dry will definitely be dry and timid at heart. A person whose lips meet in a curved direction will be cunning, a person whose both lips turn upwards near the ears on both sides will be stubborn, conceited and cruel.

(vii)... Beard -People consider beard and moustache as a symbol of manhood. If beard and moustache do not seem decorous on a man's face then consider him impotent. His nature will be restless, timid and indiscreet. Such a man will consider himself weaker than women. If there is very less hair, then the signs of feminine nature will be found in their nature. There are many women who have hair in the area of the beard. They are called Pota or Naramanini in Sanskrit. Such women behave like men and are cruel by nature. Western sexologists say that due to strong sexual desire in women and being constantly dissatisfied, hair grows on their face. Such women are naturally irritable and they become corrupt.

Those with pointed moustaches are of a brave nature. The moustaches of flatterers, misers, cowards and impotent people hang down like the pans of a scale. Pointed, smooth, soft and bent beards and moustaches are considered inauspicious by people. Beard and moustache are not a very good test of a person, because it can be moved around as per one's wish or can be banished from the face as and when willed.

(viii)... Cheeks-- A person with puffy cheeks is either a fool or a humorous or an addict or lazy. A person whose cheeks get dimpled while laughing despite having puffy cheeks, is an industrious person, a connoisseur, sharp-witted and has self-confidence. People with very small or very big cheeks lack self-confidence and are dependent. People with fleshy and soft cheeks will be of a delicate nature and people with thin and sucked-in cheeks will be thoughtful, hardworking, fame-seeker, woman-lover and harsh, unruly and courageous.

(ix)... Teeth-- Teeth reveal the electricity inside. Shiny teeth indicate that the person has energy in his body. Bad teeth reveal the internal impurity. Pearl-like, lightning-like, Jasmine-like white and lustrous teeth are indicative of good health. People with big teeth are usually happy, cheerful, simple-hearted and intelligent. It is auspicious to have dense and even rows of teeth. A person with curved teeth has a violent mind and a person with very small teeth is cunning, flatterer and treacherous. A person with very big teeth is lazy, foolish and wanders around helplessly. A person with uneven and scattered teeth is unruly. A person with a pointed tooth along the side teeth is sharp-minded and quick-witted. A person with dull teeth should always be considered as lacking enthusiasm and dejected from within.

(x)... Chin -- A particularly clever person has a pointed chin. A person whose chin is full and prominent is a happy person. A person with a small chin is homely, miserly, selfish and arrogant, a person with a thin chin is a lover and a connoisseur and a person with a broad chin is generous and more polite than required. A person with a big chin is courageous, hardworking and is trustworthy.

3...Face-Reading

A lot can be known about a person by looking at his entire face. By looking at the innocence in someone's face, one can easily guess the honesty of his nature. By looking at the gentleness on the face, one can know about his mildness, by looking at roughness, one can know about harshness, by looking at softness, one can know about simplicity and by looking at the crookedness, one can know about wickedness.

Cleanliness of the face not only indicates health, but also gives a feeling of the energy of the mind. The aura of all the virtues or vices of a person is found on his face. All the brilliance of the body is expressed through the face. You must have seen in ancient paintings that a halo of light is formed around the heads of great men and gods, it is 'Aura'. This halo is not created by imagination only. In fact, a kind of aura emanates from the blood of brilliant men, which has a special effect on the atmosphere for several feet. Every object that shines casts its aura. That aura emanates from the inner light of the person. The glow on Mahatma Gandhi's face is well known. Those who had seen Malviyaji were also familiar with that glow. What I mean to say is that by seeing the glow on someone's face, you can easily understand his brilliance and power of influence.

You will never find a glimpse of brilliance on the face of a person without self-control. Self-brilliance is found only in the body of intelligent, serious, self-controlled and calm people.

One whose face is prominent is fame seeking and clever in action. One whose face is sunken is wicked, miserly, deceitful, unlucky and having many bad qualities. A person with a hanging Face is sad, gloomy, dirty and always hateful towards others. The face of a simple-hearted person always looks as if he is smiling. The visages of the people with pure cheerful nature are shining. Agile and enthusiastic people have long face. A person with a big face is said to be sad, sorrowful and accident-causing. A person with a round visage is an owl and also a wicked person. A person with a small visage is said to be a victim of trouble, a square visage is said to be a sly but alert person and a bent face is said to be of a criminal. A person with a small mouth like a squirrel is miserly and does everything hesitatingly. It is written in **'Brihat- Samhita'** that those whose faces look like a cow, bull, lion or eagle are intelligent, conscious, intelligent, brilliant and progressive. Those with faces like those of a monkey, buffalo, pig or goat are disorderly, stupid, mean and weak respectively. A donkey-face has all the characteristics of a donkey.

There are no wrinkles on the face of a carefree, prosperous, calm and self-confident person. The lines on the face of a person who is tolerant of pain, hardworking, worried or weak mainly indicate the hard work, practice and thoughtfulness of that person. A person with a beautiful face is a connoisseur, a pleasure-seeker, a lover of art and music and an admirer of people. A person with a deformed face is an insidious, a harsh-spoken person who has many vices in his mind. A person's personality is revealed not by the colour of the face but by its structure and its naturalness and equanimity. You do not see the colour of an intelligent person. If the upper part of someone's face is narrow and tilted backwards and the cheeks and chin are wide and jutting forward, then you will sense that he is conceited, greedy and useless.

People have always been impressed by the shape of the face. Queen Elizabeth of England used to say that **"A god face is the best letter of recommendation."**.' World-renowned playwright Shakespeare has also expressed the same thing through the mouth of a character and said that **"I consider your face a map of respect, truthfulness and Loyalty"**.

The facial features certainly reflect the nature and character of a person, but sometimes it can also be misleading. Therefore, one should not judge a person as a good man or a bad man just by looking at his facial features. With practice and by using various things, people make different kinds of faces.

A good book was written long back by Peter Howard; its name was **'Ideas have legs'**, i.e., ideas have the power to grow. It is written in it that the famous speaker of that time, Churchill, had practiced making faces for years in his youth by keeping a mirror in front of him. By studying how the facial features should be while expressing any emotion, he learnt to make his face accordingly on the occasion and then he became a successful speaker. There can be many more such cunning people who hide their personality and show an artificial personality.

The famous Mussolini of Italy had done a strange practice to impress people. While talking to someone, he used to change his appearance in such a way that people would come under his spell. He used to do this change only with the help of his eyes. By making the eyes long, he used to place a black circle with the help of the pupil right in the middle of the eye circle. Due to this, a circle of white color used to surround the black part and if one stares at it for a long time, the person sitting in front of him became mesmerized. Mussolini also practiced this in front of a mirror for many days.

There may be many such cunning people whose facial expressions may deceive you; but ninety percent of people are revealed by their faces. One can test it accurately by looking at their faces while they are sleeping; or look at their faces carefully when they laugh. In that condition, their pretense will be revealed. You will find many such people who, even while laughing, appear to be weeing because their heart keeps crying.

4.... Torso

a... Neck--. The shape of the neck also reveals something about a person. A person with a long neck is foolish, wanders, talkative and eats too much. One whose neck is flashy is lustful and addicted. One whose neck is heavy at the bottom and very thin at the top considers the usefulness of life to be indulging in food and drink. If the head seems to be attached to the shoulders, then that person is hardworking, dry, arrogant and miserly. A neck that is dry or tied in many parts of the veins is a sign of poverty. One with a neck like that of a buffalo is strong. One with a neck like a conch is talented, desires fame and is self-respecting.

b... Chest-- - One whose chest is elevated, broad and full is happy, powerful and hardworking. Such a person is brave by nature. One with a narrow chest is coward, lazy and narrow minded. One with a high chest is courageous, enthusiastic and always powerful.

c... Shoulder --- The shoulder of a patient, hardworking and manly person is raised and muscular like a bull. The shoulder of a criminal is naturally bent and thin.

d... Stomach and waist---A person with a long stomach is gluttonous, unstable and has a peevish nature. A person with a round stomach is usually humorous, romantic. He is happy and satisfied in every situation and trustworthy. He may do less physical work, but he can be Ganesha in the field of intellect. When you want to make a good friend of a simple mind, then look for a fat man. People having thin stomach are the worst. The ideals are those whose stomach is slightly lower than the chest; neither too raised nor too long. A thin waist is the beauty of women but a little flashy waist is the best for a man. A person with a flexible waist should be considered to have a flexible nature. He will be fond of women and will run away from men. A person with a flat stomach will be a pleasure-seeker.

e... Hands-- - The hands of a great man reach up to his knees. We have heard that Gandhiji's hands used to reach up to his knees. Good hands are like an elephant's trunk, gradually thin from the top; they are longer and fuller. Such persons are famous, efficient, generous and powerful. Such persons whose hands are very short or unevenly covered with hair are usually unhappy and cowards, are prone to talk and do wrong things. Those whose hands are the same from top to bottom, that is, they are not trunk-shaped, they are deceitful, get angry without any result, and in cunning work they are clever and harsh.

f... Palms and Fingers--- The best criterion to judge a person is the palm. A well-known palmist had written that when you meet a new person, look at his hand while shaking hands. If you know even two-four important characteristics of palmistry, then you will know a lot about that person's nature etc. from them and can talk to him accordingly. As soon as you look at the palm, first look at the nails. If they are smooth, shiny, well-shaped and red or copper-colored, then you can certainly assume that the person is radiant and pure and healthy in body and mind. It is considered healthy, to have a half-moon mark at the base of the nails. When your digestion is fine and the blood is pure, then that mark appears at that place. When one is unwell, it gets covered with skin and white spots appear on the nails. If someone's nails are pale, then consider him to be fond of arguments. A person with rough nails is poor. Black or cracked nails reveal a person's inferiority. If someone's nails are dirty, then he will also be of dirty nature. If someone's nails are sinking, then he will be dim-witted. If someone's nails are flabby, then he will be very weak and timid. The strength of the fingers increases with the nails. Therefore, if the nails are strong, then the fingers will be especially active, and fingers strengthen the entire hand; and the hand is the main helper and friend of a person. Therefore, take special care of the nails.

Now look at the fingers. The thumb is the king of the fingers. The thumb holds all the keys to the hand. The other four fingers together cannot hold any object firmly. They become strong only when they get the support of the thumb, only then the fist of the hand closes and only then any object comes in your fist. If you punch someone by keeping the thumb aside and joining only the four fingers, then he will not get hurt at all, but if you hit with the support of the thumb, then your entire power will be concentrated and you can attack powerfully.

g...Thumb--- Thumb has great importance. It is with it that the coronation takes place, with it you write and with it you hold any object. If the thumb is not there, it will be difficult to write even a single letter. If it is not there, you cannot even lift a pot straight. When the thumb becomes conscious and stands up, at that time the four fingers cannot cover the palm even with all their strength. Such an influential organ will definitely be a symbol of a person's influence and effort.

An English scholar has given a good method of human testing. The person, whose thumb stays above the four fingers when the fist is clenched, **is self-confident, patient, conscious, powerful, self-respecting, determined, courageous and efficient.** Person who keeps his thumb between his fingers and makes his fist is timid, courage-less, weak, doubtful, lazy, inactive, dependent, unconscious and fickle-minded.

You can test it yourself. Keeping the thumb on top and making a fist not only strengthens the hand but also the mind, brings new energy and a kind of self-power. The fist cannot be made tightly by keeping the thumb inside. In this state the mind also remains loose and if the thumb is left out, the whole soul seems tied. Therefore, it is clear that the thumb is the gatekeeper of our power and the leader of its place. If children keep their thumb pressed between their fingers, then understand that they will be useless. If you want a very loyal servant for household work, then take such a person. He will never be of independent mind. If you are looking for a person for an important job, look for a person who knows how to clench his fist.

A person's thumb has special characteristics from birth. One of its special characteristics is that the lines on the thumb of every person are different. That is why thumb impressions are taken on government papers. Lines keep changing everywhere. But the lines on the thumb always remain the same, this is the proof that the thumb is the true symbol of our permanent personality. According to Vyas, the subtle body of a person or **"the soul is equal to the thumb"**.

Now know this much about the shape of the thumb in brief. It is considered good if the thumb is neither too big nor too small. A person with a very big thumb is arrogant, evil and intolerant. A person with a small thumb is cruel, slow, short-sighted and narrow-minded. If it is well separated, that is, it is far from the fingers and appears independent and influential, then the person's superiority is felt. Very close to the fingers and palm, it reveals the incompetence of a person. The thumb should be so big that on clenching the fist, it can go over the knuckle of the middle finger and hold it by pressing it properly. The thumb of a brave person is thick at the bottom, raised like the blade of a sword in the middle and slightly bent backwards but fleshy at the top. The thumb of a fool is like a Lota (Pot). The more sentience a person's thumb is, the more active and enthusiastic that person will be from within. The person who has a thumb with a thin base but thick upper part will be a weak person.

h...Fingers--- These are some things to know about fingers. People with loose and raised veins may be art lovers but they are not strong. If all the fingers are strong in their respective places, independent and do not look scattered when they are joined, then those fingers indicate the strength of the person. The one whose fingers do not show any hole between any two fingers when they are joined, is considered to be skilled and rich in wealth accumulation. Sparse fingers indicate poverty. The one whose palms are long, lives a long life. The one with crooked fingers are of curved nature.

i.... Palms--- If the palms are smooth, soft, lustrous and full, then a person is considered to be wealthy, of good nature and of good health. Those whose palms are dull, dry & sluggish are harsh, miserly and do hard work. A person with broad palms is generous, hardworking and efficient. One whose palms are red, look like lotus, raised at the base of fingers, and are divided by beautiful red lines, is considered to be powerful, skilled in governance, people-loving and intelligent. One whose Gowpen is narrow, inclined or appear completely empty, is filled with black or blurred lines or lacks in joining main lines, is deprived of ancestral wealth, is afraid of death, is lazy, careless, lacking efforts and is skilled only in physical labour. A benign man's palm is neither too hot nor too cold. The palm of a scared, unstable and deceitful person feels cold. The palm of a worthless person is soaked in sweat. The palm of a cruel, brave and arrogant person is hot and hard.

The raised places below the fingers and thumb indicate the strength of the person. You may or may not believe in Samudrika Shastra, but you will agree that the finger whose root is raised is livelier and more active. All the strength of the fingers come from their root-place. These raised places are called planet- site in Samudrika language.

Know It To Shine

There is a place of Venus below the thumb. The person whose Venus place is high is an idealist, lover of beauty-literature-music-art-dance, an artist and a lover of craftsmanship. The person whose this place is very high, is lustful, shameless and a great pleasure-seeker. If this place is low, then such a person is selfish, lazy, hateful and useless. The root-place of the index finger is called the place of Jupiter. If this place is very high, then the person is very arrogant and disorderly; if it is high, then the person is a lover of dominance, adept in ruling and brilliant. If it is low, then the person is deceitful and of mean nature. Place of Saturn is under the middle finger. If Saturn place is high, then the person is soft spoken, fond of fun and enjoyment and fond of solitude. If it is low, then the person is of low thoughts, arrogant and often has a tendency to commit suicide. Sun is at the base of the ring finger. A person with high Sun-place is restless, art-lover, inquisitive and a womanizer. Such persons usually like long hair. The person whose this place is low is lazy and confused. Mercury is under the little finger. If Mercury is high, then the person is scholar, orator, hardworking, courageous, wanderer and clever. If it is very high, then the person is dishonest, liar, treacherous and deprived of the happiness from women. If it is low, then the person is a traitor to education, lazy and foolish.

The part of the palm which we truss when writing, is the place of the Moon. The person whose place is high, is self-aware, music-lover, theist, thoughtful and serious. The person whose place of the Moon is low is devoid of the power of thinking. The places of Mars are between the Moon-place & Mercury-place and between the Venus-place & Jupiter-place. If the Mars-place above the thumb is high, then that person will be very courageous, valiant, fond of debate and instantly knowledgeable. If the Mars-place above the Moon is high, then the person will be patient, justice-loving, humble, determined, courageous and a lover of religion. The person whose both the Mars-places are high is ruthless, tyrant, fierce, ill-tempered, lustful and a lover of bloodshed. If both the places are low, instability and cowardice are expressed in the nature.

According to Samudrika opinion, if Jupiter and Sun are high then a person becomes wealthy. If Mercury is also high then he is proficient in science and jurisprudence; if Mars is also high then he is skilled in warfare. Those having high Saturn and Jupiter places are patient and suffer from gas and unconsciousness. If Saturn and Mercury are high then that person is a thief, short-tempered and disorderly by nature. If Saturn and Mars are high then the person becomes shameless and cruel. If the back of the palm is like the back of a turtle, then it is auspicious. A person whose palm back is elevated, shiny and soft will progress. A person whose veins are prominent in this part will be harsh and weak. A person whose this part is very swollen will be sick, useless and lethargic. A person whose entire hand looks like a lion's paw will be dangerous.

j... Lines on the hand--- Writing something on the lines of the hand will not be irrelevant. Ancient scholars have written a lot on palmistry. Among western scholars, 'Cheiro' was the great scholar on this subject. **He was a Pandit. He** had done scientific study of this Indian science and had predicted many such incidents in advance by himself, by finding out the date of death from palmistry, which turned out to be true. He had predicted the future of Lord Kitchener in his youth and had also said that he would die in water. In the end, Lord Kitchner really got Jal-Samadhi (water burial). This is the best proof of the truth of palmistry.

In reality, the lines on the palm are not useless or just for the beauty of the hand. If nature had made them for the purpose of beauty, then they would not have been in this form, but in the form of drawings of beautiful flowers. These lines are related to the personality of a person. The palm lines of one another do not match because everyone's personality is different. The truth is that the palm is the office of the whole personality where all the character related accounts are kept.

When an object rubs against another object for a long time, then a mark is left there. When our mind is rubbed with worry, then the forehead gets more stressed lines and when there is a lot of rubbing, then wrinkles appear on the cheeks. The lines on the palm are also formed as a result of the union or conflict of our natural forces. They develop and deteriorate along with the personality of the person; this is a good proof of the fact that they express our internal condition. If you have the willpower, then you can change the lines in some time.

Nine types of Buddha's handprints are found, which have nine types of line sequences. Hand-lines change keep happening according to the condition and with the increase or decrease in self-power. When one is healthy from within, the lines become red and when the health deteriorates or the mental attitude becomes distorted, they become black or yellow. This shows that the lines give information about internal activities.

The subject of palmistry is very vast. Very briefly we mention a few important points here. Apart from the main long lines in the hand, it is considered auspicious to have less long lines. The person whose hand is full of many lines is sad, harsh, poor, unfortunate and physically weak. The person whose hand lines are red in colour is eloquent, sensualist and furious. The person whose hand has a lot of deep-red lines is fierce, short-tempered, wicked and a traitor to others. The person with yellow lines is suffering from bile, has a fierce nature, is ambitious, hardworking and hateful. The person with black lines is guilty, hateful, and has a bad mind.

There are four main lines on the hand. The line that rises from the middle of the wrist and goes below the index finger encircling the thumb is called the life line or the father line or ancestral line. The line in the middle of the palm that goes to one side is called the mother line or Head Line. The main line above it, which is gently curved and end somewhere between the Index and middle Finger is called Heart Line. It may have a fork at the end. The vertical line that rises from the wrist and goes straight upwards is called the fate line.

Life-line (In the right hand). The person whose Life-Line is very broad and dull is anxious, unhealthy, crooked by nature and lacks self-confidence. It is being chained indicates weakness and physical ill health. If it is short and does not reach the lower border of the hand, the lifespan of the soul is reduced. The person whose line is broken at various places, suffers from various diseases from time to time. The person whose line goes towards the base of the thumb, his working-power is wasted. If its originating point is cut by various lines, then that person is snob and has unstable mind, but is prudent and trustworthy. The person whose paternal line has a line coming out of it and meeting the fate line, is famous, learned and a person who achieves success. The person whose maternal line does not meet this line, is stubborn, arrogant, proud and impatient. Such a person is skilled in showing off gestures, is adept at talking big and giving lectures, and is always at the forefront of self-promotion. At the same time, he is capable of doing something with full concentration and is daring. He may be an expert in some subject.

Head - line (also called mother line) The person whose head line is long and well-shaped is patient, business-minded and self-confident. The person whose line is broken is afraid of getting a head injury. If it has many branches at the end, then that person will be a big hypocrite and extravagant. If both this line and father line are short, then the person dies due to some accidental incident. If this line or father line (life line) is not present in someone's hand, then that person suffers a lot due to accidental incidents or injuries etc.

Heart-line being chained makes a person useless and lustful. If it is not cut, then the person lives a long life. The person in whose both hands this line is without branches has a short life. If this line breaks below the middle finger, then there is a fear of heart-attack and mental pain or injury. The person whose heart-line bends and meets the mother-line below the middle finger, dies suddenly. The person whose line is bent towards the mother-line and the mother-line is stretched towards this line, that is, if there is less difference between the Heart-line and the mother-line in the lower part of the middle finger, then that person will be of mysterious nature and will be a bribe-taker or will be desirous of accumulating wealth in an improper manner. If a branch of this line comes out and meets the mother-line and is also broken in the middle by some other line, then the marriage of that person will be deplorable and that person will suffer from mental pain. If there are no branches below the little finger, then the chances of having a son are less.

Luck Line or Bhagya-Rekha - We can call it a scale to measure the karma-power of a person. As soon as we meet someone you can see this line on his hand and can guess that whether the person is progressive or not. If you see that the line rises from the wrist to the root of the middle finger, then that person will always be very prosperous and progressive and happy. Whatever position he will be in, he will be the most successful in his class. Wherever this line is broken, the prosperity and wealth of the person will be broken. If another fate line is drawn near it after it is broken, then the personality of that person will again invigorate. If it rises from the middle of the wrist and goes towards Mercury, then that person will be skilled in business or science. Where it is curved, then trouble will be in front of the person. If some lines emerge from the place of Venus and cut this and the Life -line, then that person will be separated from his wife. The person in whose hand this line does not exist at all, then he is without enterprise, disappointed and suffers from financial difficulties. If this line rises from the ancestral line, then that person is intelligent and manly. If one of its branches goes towards Venus-place and the other towards Moon-place, then the person is imaginative and sensual. The progress should be considered to start from the stage where this line starts in the hand. Where this line crosses the mother line, the age of thirty-five years is considered to be there.

k... Wrists (Manibandh) shows the masculinity and strength of a man. Manibandh of a brave man is strong, elegant and joint-specific. One who has a strong wrist has a strong heart. A person with flexible wrists is also flexible i.e. fickle by nature. A man with bent or loose wrists is of feminine nature, is lazy and luxurious. Since ancient times sisters have been tying Rakhi on the wrists of brothers, during wars wives have been making them wear battle bracelets. Why? The reason is that they believe in the strength of Manibandh and want them not to bend. This shows the importance of the Manibandh, A healthy and prosperous man has three simple and beautiful lines on his wrist. The better his health becomes, the clearer these lines become. The wrist of a hardworking person remains straight, while that of an inactive and timid person is bent.

5.... From buttocks to the soles of the feet and some other things

a. **Buttocks** - A person with hard and very big buttocks is lazy, arrogant and self-centered. A person with fleshy and prominent buttocks is courageous, powerful and self-reliant. A person without buttocks is sincere, hardworking, but fearful.

b. **Thighs** -Those who are strong, healthy and capable of sensual pleasures have thighs like the trunk of an elephant or a banana plant. The thighs of an ordinary person are thin and fleshless like those of a dog or a jackal.

The legs are the pillars of the body. If they are strong, the body is also strong. If they are crooked or weak, the person is weak both from inside and outside. People with thin legs are not sensual pleasure-seekers.

c.   Soles - The soles of the feet of an excellent person are red, fleshy and juicy. When such a person walks, his entire foot falls on the ground. The impression of his entire foot is found on the road. The complete impression of the feet of a decadent person is not found.

These are the main hallmarks of human examination through each and every body part. These have been thoroughly researched in ancient Aryan texts. These have been scientifically considered in medical texts. Sushrut has even determined the measurement of each and every body part. He has also given the natural length of the whole body.

d.   Height - According to Sushrut, if a person stands on his feet and raises both hands, then from the toe to the tip of the hand, the height of the person is 120 Anguls as per the measurement of width of his fingers. According to Charak and Kautilya, if a person stands in a normal way, then from the feet to the head, the height of the person is 84 Anguls. The difference of 36 Anguls is due to raising the feet and hands. As per Vaidyas (Physicians) the person who is 120 Anguls tall (or 84 Anguls tall when standing in a balanced manner) is healthy, long-lived, happy and blessed with natural splendor. According to the **Brihat Samhita**, a person who is 108 Anguls tall when standing in a normal manner is a gentleman of the extraordinary category. A person with 96 Anguls tall is of the good category and a person with 84 Anguls tall is a man of the average category. A person who is less than this is **mean**. Generally, people are only 84 Anguls tall in height.

e. **Life-Span-** Sushruta has also explained the method of testing life span through body parts. For example, those whose joints, veins and nerves are deep, whose senses are stable, whose body is gradually more and more shapely from feet to head, they live long. Those whose feet are short, penis is long, chest ribs are narrow, back portion is narrow, ears are higher than their normal place, nose is raising upward and when he laughs the flesh of his gums is visible and who rolls his eyes a lot, he lives short.

Similarly, one who is healthy from birth, whose body, knowledge, wisdom grows slowly according to the age, he lives long. One whose body, wisdom etc. grow rapidly, he lives short. It is often seen that those who has a very beautiful physical development, whose future is considered very bright, death snatches them away at a young age. The secret of this can be understood from Sushruta's diagnosis.

f. **Voice and Gait-** A person is also tested by his voice. The voice of a good person is like that of an elephant, chariot, trumpet, drum, lion or cloud. The voice of a fool is like that of a donkey and the voice of a wicked person is harsh like that of a crow. The gait is also a good test. A person who walks without making any sound is powerful and gentle. A person who moves quickly and goes a long way is restless and impatient. A proud person walks jumping and stamping his feet. A man of good nature walks at the speed of a lion, elephant, bull or peacock. The feet of an honest man fall in the straight direction while walking; the paws of a wise and tactful man are outstretched to the left and right and the paws of a fool are bent towards each other.

g.   **Testing of Husband- wife relation-** One type of test is this - a husband and wife of 25 years of age should weigh themselves. If they are of almost equal weight, then they will be happy and loving each other. If the man is less heavy than the woman, then he is weak, unhappy and controlled by his wife. If the woman is less heavy, she will be well behaved and obedient to her husband.

h.   **Some other methods of Body Examination-** There are many other ways of body examination in medical texts. It is also described what kind of a person's nature is due to excess or deficiency of Vata, Pitta, Kapha etc. A skilled Vaidya can also tell the entire internal condition of the body from the external condition of the body. Without mentioning them in detail, we will now briefly describe some other methods here.

6.... Look at the whole body

When you examine someone by looking at his body parts, do not do it from a one-sided perspective. There can be a mistake in it. One side of someone may be wrong. A person's **One body part may be influential, but its opposite body part may be even more influential in the opposite direction and reduce the influence of the first.**

Identify a person from all the four body parts. For example, if someone's nose is round and flat from the sides, his eyes are not pointed, lips are thin and tongue is very loose, then consider him to be greedy. If someone's eyes are narrow, ears are taut, eyebrows are curved, forehead is narrow or flat, nose is curved, lower lip dominates the upper one, then consider him to be arrogant, grumpy or short-tempered. If someone's ears are erect, head is round, nose is long, lips are thin and chin is small and neck is long, then consider him to be home-loving and inordinately woman-loving. If someone's eyes are wide open, that is, it seems as if the viewer is staring with wide open eyes, forehead is sunken, hair is rough or erect, head is long, legs are thin and it seems as if all his body parts are shrinking inside the body, then consider him fearful.

If the cheeks are puffed, chest is bent towards the back, nose is triangular, head is particularly protruding towards the forehead, lips are pressed together, hair is scattered and erect, eyes are stretched upwards and outwards, forehead is either very small or very sunken, then consider him arrogant. If the mouth is protruding, lips are thick, cheeks are bulging and eyes are like a bull, then consider him foolish, lazy and dishonorable. If the whole mouth is hanging, voice is hoarse, hands are very thick or thin, then he will be unhappy and worried.

If the body parts seem to be stuck together with glue, nose is particularly flat, lower lip is protruding, mouth is wide, forehead is suppressed is miserly. The person whose head is raised, whose chest is broad and taut, whose eyes look straight wherever they look, whose every limb is measured and whose head is shaped like an umbrella, is considered to be intelligent, famous and brave. The person whose forehead is large, whose nose tip is sharp, whose Temple (Kanpati) is large and raised, all the organs are well-differentiated, he is a dedicated worker, enterprising, has strong judgmental power, is brilliant and is endowed with all the virtues (compare Gandhiji's shape). One whose face is dirty, eyes are covered or as if they are covered in mud, cheeks are pale, forehead is dull, all the limbs are lethargic, he can be considered to be suffering from a curse disease, mainly stomach ailments.

While examining the entire body, you should mainly look at these things: -Whether the teeth, skin, nails, and hair shine or not. The radiance in the body of a person is reflected from these appendages. All the places in the body which are dry, fleshless and have raised veins will be inauspicious and will not be very active. Another thing to be seen is what must have been the original form of the body part which is in a particular form at present. The structure of the body parts changes due to nature, specialty of food habits and the impact and reaction of circumstances.

If you worry for a long time, the shine of the hair will go away; they will become rough and they will lose their natural colour and turn white prematurely. No matter how prominent your eyes are, if you consume alcohol, they will droop. You may have a good waist by birth, but if you eat nonsense and lie down, a belly will appear in place of the waist. Therefore, while examining the original form of a person, his changing powers or circumstances should also be kept in mind - although the truth is that there cannot be much difference in the basic nature of the body.

Many of the children who are lean and thin, even if they are the sons of Kubera and eat gold and pearl ash every day, still remain lean. If a poor person is fat by nature, then he keeps on becoming fat even after eating only vegetables. Those who believe in rebirth and the fruits of karma will surely accept this mystery. A man gets a new body according to his previous deeds.

In the end, we would again like to say that the structure of body parts should not be considered as everything. It is fine if their form does not change, but every person can do their Sanskar. And the main thing is that by making his soul strong, man can make his personality great despite physical unevenness. Even a very ugly person can cover all his ugliness with virtues. Nature can give a person beautiful body parts, but if his mind is weak then those body parts will only be ornaments of the body. Therefore, while testing someone, test his mind especially. The mind is tested by behavior, movement of body parts and physical gestures.

Summary

The summary of all these things is this - a major part of a person's personality is revealed by the shape of his body parts. If a person has the will to do something, he can make his body parts shapely, sharp, i.e., well-characterized, as per his wish. He may not be able to make his body parts bigger or smaller, but he can compensate for the deficiency in one place from another. By knowing his natural nature from the structure of his body parts, he can suppress it with the power of his intellect by being more cautious and the deficiency also does get suppressed. For example, sometimes you will find a short man always trying, to be very alert, efficient and trying to dominate others. His actions are not natural, but intellectual. Therefore, to compensate for the deficiency of height, he wants to show himself superior by showing more agility and efficiency and also out of enmity, he has the attitude of ruling over those with better height. This feeling does not arise in a tall man.

Chapter-8

Neither Accept nor Reject Anything without Knowing

To understand how you appear in the eyes of others through your behaviour, conversation, body movements or change in appearance etc. and how others may appear in your eyes, i.e. to what extent and how their feelings or personality can be ascertained through the external activities of the body, keep these few things in mind:

1. **Mind is the cause of the functioning of all senses**: **'MANO HI HETUH: SARVESHA, MINDRI - YAANAAM PRAVARTTANE'**- (Valmiki) - This is the saying of the wise Hanuman. Every part of the human body is operated by the order of the mind. As thoughts arise in the mind, the body parts express themselves in accordance with them. The senses become conscious due to the consciousness of the mind, they become weak due to its slackness and they also commit mistakes due to its disorder. In short, the actions of each body part are the outcome of the actions or mental attitude of the mind.

2. **Symptoms of emotions are immediately visible on the body**- The mind cannot hide itself. It expresses its condition through its appearance, speech, behaviour or any gesture. Understand this from these examples. When the mind trembles, the speech trembles, the hands and legs also start trembling. When the mind is doubtful, the speech becomes unclear, the eyes become steady and the action power of the limbs slows down. When the mind trembles

due to some matter, the soft parts of the body also tremble. When the mind is afraid, the heart beats loudly, the hair stands up, all the parts of the body become restless. When the mind trembles, the eyelids blink repeatedly. When it is greedy, it starts drooling. When it is startled, the ears stand up.

When mind decides to kill, eyes turn bloodshot. When mind gets angry, breathing speed increases, face turns red, and limbs start trembling. If mind is suddenly hit, face turns white. When mind is in pain, voice becomes shaky and weak.

And the biggest proof is that when a mother is distraught with the love for her child or is overjoyed to hear his tales, her breasts start dripping milk. All this makes it clear that the shadow of your emotional world falls on your external world. Very few people are able to hide their emotions. Emotions can be hidden either by a yogi or by a completely bewildered person or by a shameless wanderer. When an ordinary person suppresses his emotions, he gets many disorders. Sometimes it has been seen that a woman becomes numb after the death of her child, neither a voice comes out of her mouth, nor a stream of tears comes out of her eyes. In that condition people try to make him cry otherwise there is a danger of her going mad or die. In normal condition emotions get expressed and every part of the body cannot hide them because they are not independent parts of the body. When the wind of the mind blows all the leaves of the body-tree move and their movement tells us the direction of the wind and its speed.

3. Disposition sits on the head: **'SVABHAVO MUDHNI VARTATE (Hitopdesh)**. Your nature is in the forefront in everything, is visible in every work and you behave accordingly or are influenced by the behavior of others. It is visible in your appearance; it is visible in your voice, in your eyes; in the subject of conversation and its manner and in your entire conduct. Also, the variety in your nature brings about a variety in all these. Therefore, before looking at someone's knowledge, test his humanity from his nature.

Many characteristics of disposition (Nature) are inborn. Everyone accepts that the true formation and development of a person's nature takes place according to his previous Sanskars and the environment of childhood. Later on, people refine their nature according to circumstances and also according to their knowledge and wisdom.

It would not be irrelevant to mention here that a person rules only 3/8th of his brain, the remaining 5/8th is automatically governed by his nature or his habits. It would also not be inconsistent to say that 50% of the intelligence in a person is inborn. Education, practice and experience add another 50% to it. From all this, the importance of the inner mind and its Sanskars can be understood. If the nature is not controlled from the beginning, then it will not improve with knowledge and power later on. It is clear from all aspects that it is easier to judge someone's personality by nature than by knowledge. If someone's nature is good, then his inspirational knowledge will only help him. If the nature is opposite then the conscious mind will also work in the opposite direction. Sometimes the nature can be hidden by the power of intellect and tongue, but not always.

4. Do not fall in the trap of beauty- Do not give importance to someone just by looking at his beauty. Test his conduct also. A prostitute is wicked even if she is beautiful. Do not try to throw away the musk thinking it to be black. You cannot estimate the depth of a pond by going onto its first step; go deeper. If someone meets you, do not assume him to be a lover of cleanliness just by looking at his white shirt. Look under that shirt also, there you will probably find a very dirty vest which will be hanging around his neck like a certificate of his dirty nature.

Don't consider someone a Mahatma just by hearing the tales of Sita and Savitri from his mouth. Also look at the walls of his room. It is possible that here you will find pictures of the world's chosen prostitutes that suit his nature. Look at his gramophone records or Desktop. It is possible that he sings Bhajans to you but listens to the Songs and Pop Music of: Boney M, Bryan Adams, Peter Andre, Bon Jovi or Justin Bieber on his Smart Phone, or on PC, or on Ipod, to satisfy his natural desires. Do not look at his table, but at his library. It is possible that he keeps religious texts on his table and you may find illustrated Kok Shastra hidden in his library. If you want to know how much cleanliness is liked by someone, you should look at his kitchen and not his drawing room. To what extent someone's life is happy, you should read it not from his appearance but from the appearance of his wife and children.

The happiness of a poet's personal life should not be known from his poetry but from his diary. In poetry, he may be giving away his golden treasure, but in his personal life he may be living by borrowing money from others. Do not see someone's courage and strength in his words or in his state of wealth. In adversity, see whether his tongue moves faster or his feet. Test a friend not in your happy days but in the days of crisis. Don't consider someone a Sardar by looking at his beard, rather see whether he has the heart of a Sardar or not. Don't consider a coin genuine by looking at its round shape and its shine, examine it and see if it is fake or not. Don't look at the general shape of every object, look at its special shape and then decide about it. You may not be able to read a person's ability or inability by his appearance, but you can definitely read it by his work, behavior and nature.

In this regard, remember the advice given by the fishes to Ram. When attracting the attention of the Lakshmana to Herons in Pampa Sur, Ram had said, "O Lakshmana! Look! What a saint this creature is; he slowly raises his feet; he is afraid that he might harm any living creature under his feet. On hearing this the fishes of the lake, immediately said to Ram, "What are you saying? This hypocrite has destroyed the lineage of our dynasty. Only the one who lives together can know the character of the companion: **"SAHAVAASI VIJANAATI CHARITAM SAHAVAASINAH:'**

5. <u>**Keep the country, time and situation in mind**</u>. While describing a person or a thing, think according to the country, time and situation. Not only think, make changes in your life according to the country, time and situation so that you can be contemporary. Do not forget the saying ***"JAISA DESH VAISA BHESH"*** 'As is the country, so is the dress'. If Pandit Jawaharlal Nehru opposed the

establishment of a Hindu state in India, then before calling him a Hindu traitor, think once about these things that we were in a country where people of other religions also lived and they had also right to live freely. Now we are in a period which is called the twenty-first century and in which democratic states are established everywhere, and we are in a situation in which religious fanaticism can harm the country and society and we can be deprived of international cooperation.

Time is changing and every part of civilization changes with time. Perhaps, if we were in that era when politics was just a branch of religion and luckily all the modern facilities were available, then it was possible that inspired by religious sentiments, the government would have made such rules that trains should run on Muhurat Time, not on Dishashul direction, the guards should blow conches instead of whistles; while the train is running, Havan and Mangal-Stotra should be recited in the guard's compartment so that the journey ends without any obstacles. But in the present times, even imagining such things is foolish.

This is in relation to public matters. In personal conduct also, we are tested by how far we are progressing with time. Whenever you meet someone, look at him with this perspective. Consider how far he is influenced by the external environment to behave the way he is behaving. Put yourself in his situation and then judge his personality.

Sometimes the same type of action changes under different circumstances; for example, in normal circumstances if a person kills someone, he is considered a murderer and is required to be hanged. But if he kills ten soldiers of enemy army in a war, the same person is considered a brave man and is worthy of Gallantry Award. Though the action is of the same type, the circumstances change the character of the doer. If you do not know the circumstances and know only that a certain person killed ten people, you will consider him a great violent person.

Take another example. There was a time when Hitler was a conqueror. His armies were shaking the whole world with their conquests. At that time people considered him all powerful, the best warrior of the historical era. With time, the situation changed. Now no one remembers Hitler's heroic form; everyone only tells and hears stories of his short-sightedness and inhumanity. No one even thinks about his special qualities.

Circumstances can have such an impact on someone's personality! The winner always becomes like a god in our eyes and the defeated becomes the incarnation of Ravana. When circumstances naturally have such an impact on our state of mind, how can we ignore them? Yes, we must keep in mind that we should not only look at the circumstances, not only the place and time, but also look at the personality of the human being by standing in the midst of them and think by placing ourselves in the midst of them.

6. **Think with a free mind** - While judging someone's personality, it is necessary to keep in mind his looks, his financial status and his activities etc. It is more important that you do not form an opinion about anyone on the basis of your own disposition and selfishness. It often happens that a person makes an opinion about others by placing them in his own position. It also happens, and often

happens, that we want to see others as we are. If they are not like that, we do not respect their personality. This is where the intellect becomes corrupt.

In fact, every intelligent person has the power to recognize others; he uses this power regularly. He makes mistakes only when he does not see the real face of someone in the heat of emotions or due to the compulsion of his nature or due to lack of experience or due to ignorance. Whatever he sees, he sees it from a one-sided point of view and according to the resolution of his mind.

Due to the presence of some pre-conceived desire in the mind, everything seen gets colored in that color. Suppose you are religious fanatic. In that condition, even a civilized person of some other religion will look like a Chandal to you. If you are an old-fashioned orthodox Sanatan Dharma Pandit, then you will consider a Shudra who is cleaner than you as extremely dirty and untouchable. If you are of liberal mind, then you will consider even a highly fallen person as your friend.

Understand this in another way like this. A healthy person is considered extremely innocent and weak by his mother. His wife considers him the king of lovers, her god. His children consider him their protector and ruler. His servants consider him as an incarnation of Dharma, his friends consider him as a capable friend and his enemies consider him as a demon. They see his personality in the same way in which they are related to him. But can you depict the entire personality of that person by taking everyone's views separately? Never.

A person in love never sees the faults of his beloved. A hateful person considers even the straightforward conduct of his enemy to be faulty. When we have a preconceived notion in our mind in favour or against a person or a thing, then our opinion cannot do justice to him. We do not care about his real character but we consider our preconceived notion as his true form and thus we fall in the trap of delusion and achieve nothing. Due to this most of the people may consider us worthless. On the other side, if some immoral person does something good for us with dishonesty, we may consider him a Gentleman.

Unless you think about someone, by keeping your personal pre-notions aside, you will surely make mistakes in understanding him. Therefore, it is necessary that you first set your testing instrument right. If one of your hands is lifeless due to paralysis, then even if the pulse of a living person is put in it to be felt, you will declare him lifeless. If there is a defect in the eyes, even a beautiful sight becomes painful. If you are greedy, then you will consider the person, who meets you with some gifts, to be a gentleman, and the one who meets you empty-handed will seem like a great selfish person. If you are weak at heart, then a strong person will appear like a Brahma Raksha to you and if you are a tyrant, then you will consider even the greatest of men to be a raw earthen pot. To a person who travels by train without a ticket, the ticket collector appears like a messenger of death.

Therefore, if you want to understand others, first remove false notions from your mind. If someone does not respect your good deeds, then you should understand that he also has some ill will towards you, due to which he is not able to see your true form. To get closer to each other, it is very important to clear such notions.

7. **There is natural affection or hatred between human beings** - This mean that if the nature of someone matches then they are affectionate towards each other, if it does not match then they become hostile. There is truth in this, thieves are also said to be cousins. "CHOR -CHOR MAUSERE BHAI. "A mad man is happy to see mad people, a gentleman is happy to see a gentleman and a truthful man is happy to see another truthful man.

There is a deep secret behind natural love and hatred: it should be known. The waves of thoughts that arise in a person's brain do not just dissolve in the body; they agitate the atmosphere around the body. This action of waves is natural. Those thought waves absorb the favourable thoughts nearby and clash with unfavourable thoughts. Their impact falls on the brain. This struggle continues in the atmosphere around the body. The brain silently experiences it.

One reason for the peace you get when you go to a holy temple is that the auspicious thoughts that float in the atmosphere there strengthen your favorable thoughts. Sometimes you must have experienced that when you go to a house or a particular place, a feeling of indifference or fear arises in your mind without any reason. You consider that place to be inauspicious. The reason for this is that it must have been a center of evil people at some point of time. The same thoughts remain spread there for a long time.

Similarly, you must have experienced that sometimes, as soon as you meet an unknown person, feelings of respect and affection for him arise in your mind. Sometimes, it happens that a person meets you again and again and expresses good feelings towards you every time, yet, in your mind, feelings of distrust and aversion towards him arise. The very face of such people creates irritation in your mind.

Why does this happen? The reason for this is also the same, which we have mentioned above. That person may be talking sweetly to you, but in his mind, there may be continuous ill-will towards you, whose electric waves may be silently clashing with your thought waves. If someone sympathizes with you from the heart, then his waves may mix with your waves and make your mind even more energized. This is a scientific mystery, which is accepted by modern western scientists.

Modern scientists have made another discovery in relation to smell. They say that when there is an intensity of any emotion in the heart, then different types of smells come out. We are not able to know them because the Smell Sense of a human being is limited. Such living animals whose power of smell perception is sharp, can perceive them quickly. When one is frightened, a foul smell comes out of the body. It is called Fear-Scent. It becomes unbearable to animals, there is truth in this.

Those who walk very cautiously at night, they do come across snakes and scorpions. Fearless people walk barefoot, but such living creatures do not attack them unnecessarily. If you go near a cow or a bull with fear, then they get furious and run to attack. If your servant goes fearlessly, then there is no such reaction in them. You can test it yourself. You will surely accept that in a state of fear, the contaminated substances of the body come out. Usually sweat comes out and sometimes urine and excreta also released. When a dirty thing comes out, the nearby creature will definitely find it unpleasant and will also resist it.

This is not a new discovery. The sages of Rigveda had already explored this secret. They say that when a feeling is strong in a person's mind, then a life-force inspired by that feeling comes out of his body, which pervades the nearby atmosphere. Dogs start barking as soon as they see a thief at night. Being quick conscious, they get influenced by that life-force. Similarly, when crows caw on the roof of the house or at the door, people say that a guest is about to come. Whether the guest comes or not, according to the above opinion of Rigveda, the secret behind this is that the mind of a loved one is focused on you; his feelings are focused towards you. Crows get influenced quickly by that type of air-pervaded life-force.

The Veda says that when a person walks, even the sound of his footsteps is inspired by the electricity of the Prana-Sutra for a considerable time. This is the reason that many dogs, without even seeing the thief or his footprints, go in the morning and start digging a distant bush or something with their nails and usually find the stolen thing there. The dogs reach the direction in which the thief had gone by smelling the soil there. This knowledge was discovered by Atharva Rishi to find lost cows. Hence, it is called Atharva Prana-Sutra after his name.

This life-sutra has special importance. The people around are influenced from within by good intentions and bad intentions. The attraction power of Life-Sutra depends on this. When a person who is well-liked by people comes in front, people bow down in reverence to him. The reason for this is that his life-sutra attracts the inner-self of everyone towards him. The life-sutras of each other get tied together.

The one who considers himself a friend of all, everyone becomes like his friend. This life-sutra is also related to blood. At the end of Mahabharata, Yudhishthira has accepted that when Karna was saying the harshest words to him during gambling, he looked up. Immediately his eyes bowed down in reverence towards Karna. He started looking towards his feet. At that time, he did not know that Karna was his brother. Some internal power awakened intimacy in his mind. That power was 'Atharva-Shakti'.

You will also see that sometimes people suddenly become anxious to return home, their minds get disturbed, on reaching home they see a loved one ill or in trouble. Blood calls out to blood. When a mother, sick or in trouble, thinks of her son, son's mind is immediately affected. The wife's thoughts do not rush that quickly. Blood relation strengthen and influence the life thread. You can understand from these evidences how strong the effect of the feelings of the mind can be on the external objects.

The tortoise does not nourish its own turtles. It buries them in the sand, and by staying in the water itself exerts its internal influence on them from a distance. They grow due to that influence. Remove the tortoise and the turtles will become lifeless. There are many types of snakes which do not go anywhere for hunting; they open their mouths at one place and intensify their hunger or willpower. Insects from far away are attracted towards them like iron towards a magnet. More examples of this kind can be given.

The summary is that attraction or repulsion happens naturally due to the favorable or unfavorable thoughts. If your thoughts are pure, then people with pure thoughts will be attracted towards you. If there is impurity in your heart, then you will find people with impure thoughts without searching. A thief recognizes another thief very quickly. An officer taking bribe usually does not make a mistake in recognizing the person who can give bribe.

Apart from this, it is also proved that man is constantly inspired by the inner feelings of each other. Therefore, whenever one is in a dilemma, one should consider one's soul as a witness. There is also a definite opinion of ancient scriptures that the natural attraction or aversion in man is based on the behavior of the previous birth. The Sanskar of the previous birth come with the soul.

As soon as a cow's innocent calf is born, it is attracted towards its mother. Even among thousands of cows, it will recognize its mother and run towards her; as soon as it is born, it runs towards the udder due to an unknown inspiration. Keeping all this in mind, the scripture writers believe in the previous Sanskar. Whether you believe this or not, you will definitely accept that many such inspirations arise in the mind whose cause is not known. Those inspirations also arise due to internal inspirations of some close person. One's soul quickly recognizes the soul of another. Do not ignore these inspirations without thinking. Examine the personality of others on the basis of these.

8. Do not test the personality of any great man immediately- Do not look for any great man in his body. See the reflection of his personality in his speech and his deeds. Do not see immediately in speech and deeds, but after some time in their results or effects. Great men are worldly like us in body but are supernatural. Their mind is deep, their speech is serious and their character seems unique.

Therefore, you cannot measure the depth of their mind quickly. Their mind is not agitated easily by happiness and sorrow; hence these feelings of the mind are also not visible in their appearance. Their mind-control is especially strong. There is depth in their speech; hence its meaning is revealed only with their deeds. The goal-path of their character is long. They move cautiously to achieve some distant object. The general public can doubt their method of action by not seeing that goal.
In this regard, keep these verses in mind:

VAJRADAPI KATHORANII MRIDUNI KUSUMADAPI, LOKOTTARAANA CHETANSI KO HI VIGYATUMARAHTI - (Bhavbhuti)
"The heart of a great man is harder than a thunderbolt and softer than a flower. Who is capable of knowing it?"

SAMPATAU CH VIPPATAU CH MAHATAME KROOPTA, UDAYE SAVITA RAKTO RAKTACHASTAMYE TATHA. - (Panchatantra) – "The great souls have the same form in prosperity and adversity. The sun remains red at sunrise as well as at sunset."

To understand the depth of character, you should study the life of Mahatma Gandhi. Many of his works were first considered as unpardonable political mistakes but seeing their positive results after some days, they used to praise Gandhiji's foresight.

Looking at these things, it seems that we should see the good men not in their appearance but in their deeds. Regarding God-visualization, Gandhiji used to say that God is not revealed through the body but through deeds. The same thing is true for those great men who are close to God.

It is the small things that test the greatness of a person. The way a person behaves in ordinary matters or with ordinary people reveals the strings of his nature which make up his personality. Everyone is cautious in front of big tasks or big people and advertises his artificial nature. In small tasks or in front of the general public, they do not make any special effort to pretend. Hence, they open up in their real form. If someone talks politely in front of elders, do not assume him to be polite or soft-spoken by nature. See whether he starts whining and doing throat exercises as soon as he goes in front of someone smaller than him. A man's personality is known not by the behavior displayed on special occasions, but by his daily behavior reveals, the course of his life.

While reading someone's body movements, one can gain more knowledge by observing their subtle parts. One can find pores standing up due to the attack of love, fear etc. The hair on the head will stand up only in their final state.

Similarly, the condition of society can be known by looking at the condition of the common people. There are many wealthy people in India, but we cannot call the whole country prosperous because of them. We will be called prosperous only when the economic condition of the common people is also satisfactory.

Never forget that the direction of the wind is determined by small straws, dust particles and leaves of trees. You cannot tell in which direction the wind is blowing from the **Wooden logs,** rocks of a mountain or the trunks of the trees. The natural direction of a person, a society or an object can be known only from its small and ordinary characteristics. First see it in its ordinary state and then see it in its extraordinary state and find out how many extraordinary qualities it possesses. Keeping all these in mind, try to understand the true nature of a man

The methods of human testing.

Many methods of testing human beings were prevalent earlier and are still prevalent. Apart from tests related to education and knowledge, tests of human qualities, nature, conduct and thinking have also been going on since ancient times. Not only this, earlier there used to be a difficult test like Agni Pariksha to test character. In this era, apart from school examinations, examinations are conducted in many other ways. Now scientific instruments have also been developed to test the thought direction of a person. In western countries, mainly in America, many systems of intelligence testing are popular these days by the names of Brain Test, Intelligence test and Thought Study etc. In India also, High-Ranking Officers are commissioned in Defense Forces after passing such tests. By answering many types of questions, examiner find out the talent, ability or ideology of a particular person. In the psychological world, by looking at the reaction of a person's behavior on a particular occasion, experts measure his mental state or his complete personality.

All these methods may be modern for westerners, but for Indians they are ancient. The questions asked by Yaksha to Yudhishthira in the Mahabharata were all intelligence testing questions. Ram asked Bharat many questions in Chitrakoot to understand his character and his working-methods. Some of them are translated as follows: -

1... Do you ever sleep at the time of approaching dusk?
2... Do you stay awake the whole night thinking of ways to accomplish your task?
3... Having decided that some important tasks can be accomplished at a low cost, do you start it immediately?
4... Do others understand your intentions without you saying anything?
5... Do you prefer to keep one learned man near you rather than thousands of fools?

6… Do you keep explaining things to your wife?
7… Do you not believe her words?
8… Do you not share the secrets of your mind with her?
9… Do all your employees come to you without any hesitation whenever they want or do they run away from you out of fear?
10… Are your expenses less than your income or not?
11… Are your studies of the Vedas and your actions successful?'

We have mentioned this questionnaire especially so that you may also think about what qualities wise men like Ram considered necessary for a person to be successful. There are many such incidents in Ramayana and Mahabharata. The only purpose of writing those texts seems to be that people should become familiar with the secrets of human life by seeing the conduct of people of different abilities and nature in different situations and by seeing the results of their conduct. In ancient scriptures, Indra and Dharma etc. used to roam around testing people. By considering them as pure metaphors, you can understand on what basis and at what places a person is tested. Our ethics have been written mainly to recognize a person. Therefore, to gain knowledge about a person, one should take recourse to those texts.

Nowadays, the art of recognizing a person even by his handwriting has started. Scientists say that when we sit down to write, five hundred small nerves of the body get connected. In such a situation, definitely, the formation and shape of letters must reflect our nature. One thing is clear that the letters of a person whose mind is stable are well-formed and measured. The letters of a nervous person are uneven and broken. Experts who detect paper fraud make their decision by looking at the formation of letters. The hand of a person who makes a fake paper or signs does not move as cleanly as that of a person who writes correctly. A wave of vibration is clearly visible in his letters. He writes in a scared and made-up manner, due to which the letters become artificial. This subject is very detailed and complex. Modern psychologists have developed another interesting system.

They ask you to draw your own sketch. Draw the image of yourself as you think you are. There is no need to show your painting skills. Keep creating your image, no matter how crooked it may be. Whatever you create, it will definitely have some imprint of your personality. On the basis of that, the scholars of anthropology read the hidden secrets of your nature. They say that your inner self moves your hands according to your nature. Those pictures reveal what thoughts you have about yourself, or what your structure is actually like from the inside.

On this subject, there was a useful article by a scholar in a famous American magazine. According to him, first you have to draw a picture of yourself as you currently think of yourself. After that, on another piece of paper, the psychologist asks you to draw a picture of yourself as you aspire to be. After this, the mind-swan discriminates between milk and water. It mainly does test on the basis of these things.

1..... Those who are simple and independent, whatever picture they draw, at least they make themselves look like humans and do not show their intelligence in it. Or they exaggerate the features which they consider beautiful, or they try to make the body parts which they consider weak, lively by using thick sketches etc. People who are very emotional and mentally disturbed make their figure look like an animal.

2..... People with weak minds, dull minds and childish intellects first make a circle, draw nose and mouth etc. in it, then draw lines here and there on the basis of the same circle and hang hands and legs. In hospitals, mentally challenged patients and immature children draw themselves in this manner.

3..... People who are shy, doubtful and cowardly draw light, broken or wavy lines after a lot of thinking. People who are excitable, egoistic and ambitious draw their pictures with very deep lines. A daring and fearless person draws the picture as quickly as possible. A person who is procrastinating, accomplish the task in its entirety, and overly cautious, takes a lot of time to complete his sketch.

4.... A person who considers himself to be the best, makes his portrait more beautiful than his actual form. Even if his neck is bent, it will be shown stretched in the portrait because due to his ego he will think it to be that way. Short men usually depict themselves as tall. This reveals their mentality. An unsatisfied man usually depicts himself as weak in his real portrait and fat in his imaginary portrait. This reveals that he has a strong desire for good food, sufficient wealth and happiness.

5.... People with a sporting mentality paint their hands or feet with special importance; those who consider themselves learned paint their forehead, those who are romantic paint their eyes, those with a suicidal attitude or those who are disinterested in life paint their faces actually like a Ghost.

Experts try to understand the inner state of a person through such symptoms. This system is used in every hospital in America and Canada these days. This system is also used in the jails there to understand the mental state of criminals. They use it in big companies; and even in the fights between husband and wife, they try to find out the feelings hidden in their inner minds with the help of this.

Test yourself with these things

The above-mentioned usage is impractical for the common man. Now think about the characteristics by which we judge someone in our daily life. Usually, people's personality is expressed through their speech, facial expressions, body gestures and behavior. Among all these, speech has a prominent place. It is rightly written in an ancient text called 'Narad Panchatantra' that "the mind is the root of all human actions; speech comes out according to the mind. The speech comes from mind and the secret of the mind is revealed through speech:"
MANASAM PRAANINAMEVA ARVAKARMEKAKARANAM.
MANONURUPAM VAKYAAM CHA VAKYAEN PRASPUTAM MANAH:

In fact, vocalization of words takes place with the help of the mind. Panini has written that "when the mind stimulates the body fire, it inspires the air; then the same air enters the throat and produces sounds:"
MANAH KAYAGNIMAAHANTI SA PRERAYATI MARUTAM, MARUTASTURASI CHARAN MANDAM JANAYATI SWARAM.

There is such a close relationship between speech and mind. According to modern science, when 78 small and big nerves of the body are connected to each other, then a word comes out of the mouth. In such a situation, speech definitely expresses the action power of a big part of the body, not just the throat. But it has to be accepted that speech is not the only way to reveal one's true status. Man can also be distracted. Apart from this, clever people also use pretense in their words and their sound. Therefore, Chesterfield, a great scholar of behavioral science, is of the opinion that when you meet someone, do not pay attention only to his words, but also try to understand his feelings from his appearance.

Even more intelligent advice is given by Ram. While returning from Lanka, Ram had already sent Hanuman to Bharat with the instruction to try to know the entire secret of Bharat's mind from the expression on his face, his look and his words: **GYEYAAH: SARVE CH VRATTANTA BHARATSYANGATAANI CH TATTVEN MUKHVARNEN DRISHTYA VYABHASHITEN CH.**- (Ramayana)

Now consider each of these and see how one Man expresses himself through these:

1. .... **Speech**----- A person's superiority, intelligence and gentlemanliness are revealed by the correct vocabulary, appropriate to the occasion, meaningful, clear, simple, beneficial, logical, subject-specific. Apart from these, who speaks on which subject with how much originality, in what tone he speaks and to what extent he can confirm his

feelings, this also reveals the depth of a person. What kind of ideology is expressed by words and to what extent the speaker's appearance is in accordance with it, this also reveals the inner truth and structure of a person.

A smart man speaks according to the situation and nature of the listener and puts forward the main topic. The main characteristic of a fool is that he forgets everything and speaks at the wrong time. He who speaks in meaningful, understandable and restrained language is considered intelligent. He who uses meaningless, vague and chaotic language is considered to be a babble-monger, cunning, fool and indiscreet. He who uses logical language is a gentleman, efficient, talented and courteous. He who speaks without logic is conceited, dull-witted, untruthful, deceitful and obstinate. One who talks with good intentions reaches a decision quickly. One with ill intentions keeps on making knots after knots in speech.

An intelligent person talks on serious topics in a serious tone and with a serious face. People with a gentle and pleasant nature talk on current topics in a sweet tone and with a simple face. An arrogant and a haughty person speaks about himself in an excited tone, about others in a harsh tone and then distorts his face. The subject of the tricksy is backbiting, the voice is very low and the face is extremely mysterious.

An intelligent person weighs each word before speaking. He talks on one topic at a time, speaks vigorously and uses soft words but presents irrefutable arguments. There is order in his thoughts, firmness in his voice and seriousness in his expressions. He usually does not get involved in discussions of unnecessary topics and talks about useful things. He expresses his original thoughts in an attractive manner and does not repeat the same thing again and again. By saying something himself, he gives others an opportunity to say something too. During a conversation, there are no signs of nervousness in his appearance because he is confident.

A gentleman speaks less and whatever he speaks, he speaks politely. In his conversation, he refrains from backbiting, talking about other women, self-praise and derisive topics. He has a gentle demeanor. His voice is serious but soft. The gentlemanliness of a gentleman is reflected in his saintly speech.

There is seriousness in the speech of a contemplative person, but it is not harsh. It comes out with a thumping sound. A man of strong will speaks on certain subjects with a decisive mind and in a powerful language. Usually, he talks about some important work related to the future. While speaking, all the brilliance of his mind is reflected in his expression. Self-respect oozes from both his speech and appearance.

A person with a simple nature usually discusses contemporary topics. He talks with humour and sarcasm and uses simple language. He likes flowery language less.

A person with a romantic nature often talks on interesting topics in a simple and poetic language, and when he talks, his inner fascination, excitement and sentimentality are reflected in his appearance. His words come out of his mouth in a gushing tone. He often talks while cracking jokes.

A smart man first talks in a favorable manner to the person he meets. He starts an interesting topic and gives him a chance to speak more and himself supports his words. After knowing his thoughts well, he then comments on them. In this way, after luring someone once or several times, he then talks about the purpose according to the occasion.

A Sly (Dhurt)--- is very talkative: **'BAHUVAKTA BHAVATI DHURTJANAH'** (Kautilya). By taking **'bricks from here and stones from there' he prepares Bhanumati's House.** His language is exaggerated. Filled with examples, loaded with promises and through provoking speech he talks in many ways on the same subject. He is afraid of arguments and starts speaking fluently by impressing the listener at some other point. If caught somewhere he digresses from the main topic and talks about irrelevant things. Such a person does not stay in the conversation for long. Usually he keeps on refuting his own words. In conversation he definitely mentions miraculous events, and especially discusses his experiences and openly describes his imagined favours to others. He talks in such a way that the listeners should consider him their well-wisher, the best of gentlemen and the destroyer the wicked by telling imaginary stories. He wants to take credit for all the big works.

Fools are immediately exposed by their words. That is why the writers of scriptures have advised fools to remain silent. First of all, a fool speaks in a foul language and whatever he speaks, he does so in a harsh tone. While speaking, he forgets the sequence of the talk and drifts in some other direction. If you provoke him to any topic, he either becomes silent or starts saying 'Yes' 'yes'. While listening to the talk, he only says 'you know' or 'then what happened' and does not understand anything. Often, he speaks two-four sentences himself and repeatedly asks the listener - 'what did you understand?' Do you understand...? Every now and then he remains stunned, starts stammering or becomes overjoyed with his own words without any reason or starts guffaw, convulsive laughter. Mostly, he always talks on one topic and makes fun of it by creating a mess of things.

Sick person Tulsi's this quote is enough for a suffering person: **"AURAN KE HIT RAHAT N CHETU, PUNI PUNI KAHAT AAPNI HETU."** "He is not aware of the welfare of others, but again and again he says his own purpose."

A flatterer speaks in a more polite and flowery tone than necessary. He usually talks by erasing his own identity, i.e., he praises others artificially ignoring his self-respect. He always agrees with everything; he uses many types of artificial words like 'very good', 'I am ready to sacrifice my life for you', 'Nothing will happen to you in my presence' etc. He usually speaks in a low voice and his appearance seems lost or impatient to serve you. He proves the saying **'small mouth big talk'** true at every step.

A traitor also uses flattery in the words, as well as self-advertisement. He repeatedly takes oath, invokes truth and God and shows excessive affection by saying cooked up mysterious and secret things without any reason. He tells mysterious things and keeps saying that don't tell anyone, I am telling you only. He talks in a roundabout way to know your secret. Usually, he talks slowly expressing surprise and sympathy. He probes the hearts of others by spreading his long arms of openness.

A Boaster (VACHANVEER) talks at length. Such a person may be called a Gappi. There seems to be no end to his talks. Apart from **'I did this, I did that', he knows very little.** When his stories are over, he tells cooked up stories of his forefathers. When those too are over, he tells jokes of Raja Birbal etc. He shows his bravery at every turn, roars and fumes. He is used to giving threats, but if you scold him a little, he backs off and makes up excuses and says that I did not mean this, but this. He cannot say even one useful thing, because the one who talks too much, his power of thinking is weakened and he never gets time to ponder over anything.

A weak person also chatters a lot. In old age, a man talks a lot because all his other senses become weak, so he advertises his previous strength with the help of his speech and naturally tries to prove his immediate usefulness. One who talks a lot is definitely timid, unstable, weak and inactive. Active people will always be taciturn.

The mouth of a "mean person" is full of words like a quiver. Learned people have compared him to the burrow of a snake. A mean person is foul-mouthed, speaks loudly, is intolerant and has a harsh tongue. His crow-like nature cannot be hidden. He makes backbiting the subject of his conversation. He becomes bewildered in other subjects. He talks in a confusing manner and raves for a long time. Abusive words stay in his mind. He is adept in mocking. Wherever his selfishness is involved, he becomes a very sweet-voiced person: **'VYADHA MRIGVADHAM**

KARTUM SADA GAYANTI SUSWARAM' (Vyas) – "While hunting a deer, the hunter sings in a very sweet voice."

2...... Behaviour----- A man expresses himself more through his behaviour than through his speech. A gentleman is seen to follow decorum in every situation, and a wicked man often violates decorum. A civilized man takes care of etiquette, courtesy and politeness even in the smallest matters. Understand about an uncivilized person by antonyms of these words.

3....... Facial expressions and body gestures----- As we have said, a person's emotions are immediately reflected in his face. Speech and behavior can be easily made up, but it is not easy to change the expressions in the face.

Let us briefly know about the natural tendencies of different types of people.

A person of stable nature remains stable in every situation. He is less swayed by the gusts of circumstances and conversation. He becomes even more stable in adverse circumstances. No kind of restlessness is seen in his senses and no discoloration is seen on his face. It is said in the Gita that "the one whose senses are under his control; his intellect is stable:" **'VASHE HI YASYENDRIYAANI TASYA PRAGYA PRATISHTITHA'.** A tolerant and intelligent person will always be found to be stable. Such a person is hardworking, protector of society, caretaker of gentlemen and extremely trustworthy.

A person with an unstable mind changes his colors many times, keeps struggling with every part of the body and shows various types of physical movements. If you look at his eyes, they will appear restless. Sometimes his face will glow with simple things, sometimes it will become dry, sometimes it will turn white. Often while talking, his feet start moving like the feet of a tailor working on a machine. His hands keep moving again and again towards his mouth. If there is a table in front of him, he starts turning the things kept on it or starts biting his nails with his teeth.

The criminal's eyes remain downcast. He lowers his eyes and looks here and there, but does not look ahead. He cannot talk with his eyes open. He usually hesitates at every word. He finds it difficult to sit anywhere. His complexion looks somewhat like a demon, his ears are red and his face is like that of a devil. There is a special filth in his appearance and his mind is tensed. He always has the fear of getting caught. That is why he listens intently to even the things happening at a distance and looks at each person with suspicious eyes. His hands and legs often tremble.

An arrogant person looks around a lot, less in front. His eyes are always bulging. His chest is overly tense and his eyebrows are furrowed. He often talks while flinging his hands. His limbs keep twitching at every little thing, his neck lifts and his forehead becomes outlined. One row of his teeth sits on the other and he takes deep breaths. After flinging his hands and legs, the arrogant and angry person appears to be very restless, as if he is jumping or when helpless, he starts banging his own head. If he goes to meet a civilized person, he will pull a chair and sit down with a noise and while leaving, while shaking hands with his friend, he will shake it so hard that every part of his body will shake.

A frightened man remains stunned and every hair on his body is seen trembling. It is written in the scriptures that "a person whose mind is terrified and fearful, his hands and legs become numb and he is unable to utter words and there is more tremor in the body":

BHAYASANTRUSTMANASAN HASTPADADY-AUKRIYAH: PRAVARTTATE NA VANI CHA VEPATHUSCHADHAIKO BHAVET.

He gets startled every now and then, and sweats profusely even without exertion. Often, he either falls silent in the middle of a conversation or starts stammering. The colour of his face fades completely, his body parts start shrinking, his eyes become dull, his hair either trembles or stands up. In appearance he looks like melting ice. He looks at everything with wide open eyes. His heart beat becomes faster, his eyes flutter and his gaze flares.

The person whose heart is in pain, his actions are sluggish; his face remains pale; his hands and legs also remain motionless and wherever he looks, he stares with lowered eyes. His voice is hoarse and his face is tense. There is anxiety in his every action.

Every part of a satisfied and healthy person smiles. Every part of his body is prominent and alert. There is enthusiasm in him, there is peace on his face. Usually, he shrinks his body parts less.

A nervous or confused person yawns or sneezes repeatedly, starts picking his nose while talking or scratches his head and scratches the ground with his toes. His ears rise up, his eyes start gazing in the sky and his limbs move sometimes forward and sometimes backward. His mouth remains open.

A maniac does jump around a lot, but he does special activities at night and especially on moonlit nights. It is a scientific fact that the moonlight increases the mania of a mentally ill person. It has been observed in mental asylums that by evening, the mad people do not move much, but with the moonrise their waves of passion surge like the sea. On the night of the full moon they jump and dance like a rough sea. Therefore, a psychopathic or psychotic or mad person may be tested at night. It is also that even the emotions of an ordinary person become intense at night. A scientist has written that stretching and yawning repeatedly is a symptom of madness.

A hardworking and self-confident person remains unperturbed and the expression on his face does not change from beginning to end. He gets influenced, agrees, but never shows any sense of self-surrender due to fear of anyone.

A useless person gives his body and mind to others. He laughs when others laugh, cries when others cry. Apart from excreting urine and stool, no other bodily activity of his is performed by his own will.

A narrow-minded person or a hypocrite is very dangerous. He does not listen to anyone. He shows the pride of his family and education through his speech, behaviour and appearance. Wherever his false pride is supported, he becomes mesmerized; wherever a social event comes, he frowns and behaves like a fool or a cruel person. Such a person can do any evil act on seeing his ego being hurt. He does not consider himself responsible towards the society, on the contrary, he considers the whole society responsible towards him, because according to him, whatever he understands, everyone should understand the same; whatever he does, everyone should do the same and whatever things he abandons, everyone should abandon them.

Such narrow-minded people appear to be extremely satisfied and conscious in their homes, but as soon as they come to the outside world, they look like lunatics and seem to be sinking and rising in appearance. They often misbehave with others as they are unaware of social etiquette and there is a natural aversion to public behavior. The author Allen Carpenter had written that **apart from the problems that naturally arise in the brain due to old age, narrow-mindedness is the most widespread of all brain diseases**. People suffering from this disease create their own small world and live in it. The external reactions that naturally occur in the general public do not occur in them. They are neither affected by the world's activities nor do they understand it.

{"Excluding mental diseases incidental to old age, Schizophrenia… (mental disease of total indifference to the world but total attachment to oneself) … is the most prevalent of all diseases of the mind. Sufferers from it exist in a small world of their own which they themselves have created. Influences to which normal people react, become deadened and meaningless to the Schizophrenia."}

Such a person appears to be limited in his thoughts, nature, appearance and everything else. He likes to live in a limited space and is always afraid that someone might attack his castle in the air. If someone attacks, he may get agitated and even kill the attacker because he does not care for others. He considers himself to be the descendant of the people of Satya Yuga and the rest of the people to be of Kali Yuga. The saying **"JYON TELI KE BELL KO GHAR HI KOS PACHAS"** "Just as for an oilman's bull, home is fifty Kos (100 miles) away" is completely true in his case. By looking at an oilman's bull, understand the appearance of such a person to be similar to that.

People who are industrious, ambitious, healthy and skilled in conversation and behaviour usually exchange views about the future. There is no sign of sadness, despair or any kind of worry on their faces. Usually, they use their right limbs more. There is a secret behind this. The left part of our brain controls the right side of the body and the right part of the brain controls the left side of the body. This is the reason that if someone suffers paralysis of the left side, the lower right side of the brain becomes weak or deformed.

The stimulating and controlling fibers of thought-filled speech are located in the left side of the brain, this is the opinion of anatomical doctors. When new thoughts are born in the brain and they want to appear, the right side becomes especially active. When an authoritative person decides on a thought and gives orders, the index finger of the right hand naturally rises. A thoughtful person indicates with the right index finger while explaining something.

Writers express their thoughts with the right hand; those who give lectures or those who speak well, indicate their thoughts by raising their right hand or balance the brain activity.

As soon as any stimulating thought comes, the right side automatically starts twitching. The left side of women twitches because they often have waves of emotions or apprehensions or worries. The left side of the body usually works according to the nature that resides in the right side of the brain. The left brain takes immediate decisions. Ancient psychiatrists knew this secret. They used to say that the twitching of the right side of the body was an omen of doing some good deed because it revealed that the person's mind had become firm for the said work.

In the Ramayan, when Shurpanakha provoked Ravana to attack Rama, he told her "to raise her right leg quickly after deciding to win:" **'SHEEGHRA MUDDHRIYATAM PADO JAY- ARTHAMIH DAKSHINAAH:'**. The one whose lower right side is motionless should be considered to be foolish or a follower of the line. In normal behavior also, the person whom you consider to be elder to you, you give him a seat on the right side. Due to the natural pride of being the master of your wife, you give her a seat on the left side. If a woman is not your wife or girlfriend, then out of respect for her, you will seat her on your right side.

With the thought of action, the right hand automatically starts moving. Understand this with another proof. People hang the sword on the left side and not on the right waist. Why is this so? The obvious reason is that they think that as soon as the thought of attack or self-defense comes, the right hand will move first and for that the weapon should be kept in a convenient place. There is not so much trust on the left hand. Otherwise, people would have hung a sword on the right side as well.

The personality of different types of people can be understood by many such characteristics. The simplest way is to study the appearance of some types of people and keep their appearance in mind. After this, compare the conduct, behaviour, body language etc. of the person you want to test with those characteristics. For example, keeping in mind the calm, serious, gentle and sharp facial expression of Buddha or Gandhi and finding the same facial expression in someone else, you can understand that he will be a person almost of the same conduct as Gandhi or Buddha. To know the characteristics by which someone's anguish is expressed, think of the appearance of a widow or a childless woman. By seeing those characteristics in anyone, you can guess the pain in his heart.

Although a lot of a person's inner secrets can be known from his speech, behaviour and appearance, but these can also deceive us. Movie characters or spies always assume many forms. Therefore, one should not form an opinion by looking at someone at one go or in one situation.

Along with the above, a person should be tested by some other means also as stated hereunder: -

These things should also be kept in mind

1...Home Conditions--- The position of the planet may or may not have an effect on man, but his House environment definitely has an impact. One who is of noble family follows the rules of the house to some extent. He is mindful of the honour of his ancestors. Apart from this, one whose house is in a good condition, i.e. one who is a happy householder, takes care of his responsibilities even outside and does not dare to do anything wrong. One whose house is in a bad state, behavioral disorder is bound to happen. One whose house is in a financial crisis; he also becomes helpless and small in social life or starts cheating or stealing. One who is not satisfied with his wife becomes a recluse or immoral, cruel or impotent.

To understand a person, it is necessary to have some knowledge about the lives of his ancestors, especially his parents. Children of disciplined parents are usually disciplined. It has also been observed that in a lineage in which more than one ancestor has lived a long life, people in that lineage also usually have a long life. Sushruta has also mentioned this in 'Sutra-Sthan Khand' (Sushruta-Samhita).

Whether anyone has an influence or not, the mother definitely has an influence on the child. Due to the immoral behaviour of the mother, the child inherits many diseases from birth. The mental state of the mother has a complete effect on the unborn child. A well-known doctor has proved this by researching on this. He has mentioned many incidents. One incident is this - a farmer had a pet pig. It fell ill. The farmer cut open its ear and took out some blood from it and it got cured. That cruel act remained in the mind of the farmer's pregnant wife for many days. When the child was born, his earlobe was broken. There are many such true stories which show that mental trauma causes abnormality in the womb. The desires of the pregnant woman have a complete effect on the unborn child.

The child of a wicked woman is rarely seen to be a gentleman. The reason is that the maternal element is present in every drop of the child's blood. Whatever thing is made from sugar, there will definitely be sugar elements in it. After birth, the child develops according to the mother's ability and intelligence. If the mother is timid, she always makes the child demotivated. If she is bright, she does the same thing that Anjana did for Hanuman and Vidula for Sanjay. Among the modern arrogant heroes, Napoleon, Hitler, Mussolini and Stalin etc. are indebted to their mothers only for their courageous nature.

It is certain that the child's nature is influenced by his mother and his intelligence by his father. During pregnancy and even after birth. Valmiki has also written that "a man does not imitate his father, that is, he imitates his mother:" **'NA PITRYAMANUVARTANTE MATRIKM DVIPADA ITI.'** It is not that the father does not have any influence. Due to the father's semen being contaminated, the child becomes physically defective. It is the father's vitality that goes into the womb: **'ATMA VAI JAYTE PUTRA:'** The son gets physical and mental strength from the father only. After birth, the behaviour of the father affects the character development of the child. If the father is very cruel and aggressive, then the child's enthusiasm will wane and cruelty and cowardice will become part of his nature.

Children who are troubled in childhood, later on, start stammering, their intellect gets frustrated and their self-confidence is destroyed. Try scolding any weak person, show him the fear of cruelty, these symptoms will appear in him. The person whose heart is repeatedly made to drub, will surely lose patience later on.

Domestic life has a similar effect. The outline of a person's nature is formed in childhood. The beliefs that are inculcated in the mind at that time develop in the future as well. The company of that time also has an impact in the future. After knowing all these things then see the current situation of a person. His inborn characteristics influence his future characteristics.

To know the Home Conditions, the relationship of a particular person with his wife and details of his married life should also be taken care of. If the wife is from a very rich family, has many hobbies or is very thrifty, then all these will have an effect on the husband's life. He will always appear troubled and worried. If there is mutual discord, then the man will also appear rude in his external behavior. Similarly, the success or failure of domestic life also affects the nature and behavior of a person. Modesty, etiquette etc. are considered to be a part of nobility and double-manneredness, arrogance, rudeness etc. are considered to be a part of ignobility. 80 percent of the criminals punished by the courts are those who become criminals due to the breakdown of domestic life.

2...Economic condition--- To understand someone, one should also look at his economic condition. Someone may be extremely generous by nature, but due to financial constraints, he cannot show it. If someone remains poor even after working very hard, then before considering him incapable, unfit, we should also see whether he is paying off the debt of his ancestors or whether the number of his dependents is too many. It is possible that someone is proud by nature, but due to poor economic condition, he has been forced to bow down before everyone. It is also possible that someone is very cruel by nature, but lack of money has suppressed his misdemeanor.

Economic condition makes or breaks a person's character in many ways. The self-respect of the person taking loan is lost; and the person giving loan often forgets good behavior. There is a small story in 'Gulistan' on how strange changes come in feelings due to transactions. A large number of devotees used to gather around a "Sadhu". People kept coming to him for darshan throughout the day, so he did not get time to worship. One day he asked a businessman for a solution to his problem. The businessman said- You should give some money as debt to those who come to meet you and ask for a loan from the one who seems to be rich. The Sadhu did the same and the result was that those who had taken the loan did not come with the thought that the Sadhu might ask for it back and the rest did not come with the thought that he might ask for something again.

3...Company, profession--- Company is a good test of a person. A European scholar has written that "if I come to know with whom you spend time, then I can tell who you are i.e. what type of person you are." **"Tell me with whom thou art found and I will tell thee who thou art"**. ---Goethe

Profession also reveals personality to some extent. If someone does independent and permanent business, he is more self-respecting, efficient in management and stable-minded. Those who do service business may be efficient in management but not that independent and self-confident. Those who drink water daily by digging wells cannot be calm and stable-minded. How can a person who does gambling business be trustworthy and truthful?

If someone is a servant of someone, then his master's personality will tell about him. How can a servant of Churchill be a follower of Mahatma Gandhi? The servant of an angry person cannot be self-respecting. The servant of a prostitute has to be a pimp. The servant of a coward may be a goon, but not a brave man. Similarly, the master is known from the servant. The master of a thief will either be a thief himself or a fool; the leader of a dacoit is a bigger dacoit. Hanuman's master was more powerful and influential than Hanuman.

4...Dress--- Look at the dress too. A simple man's dress is also simple. A well-dressed man shows off a lot. An entrepreneur's dress is tight and that of an intelligent businessman is loose. A person with a disorganized mind also dresses in a disorganized manner. The clothes of flexible people are very loose, full of decorations and made of very fine cloth. One who does not have artificiality in his nature wears thick clothes. People with flashy nature wear very colorful flashy clothes.

Dress has such a great impact on social life that most of the common people are influenced by it. The personality of a police constable is revealed by his uniform and not by his face. In the British rule, wearing trousers was the proof of being a big man. Now people consider, khadi dress, Nehru Jacket wearer as a sign of being a Leader and many people also take undue advantage of it. In villages, foolish Brahmins still get themselves worshipped by tying very high turbans and pretending to be pundits. In this way, people exaggerate their personality by wearing artificial dress. Seeing all this, there can be a big confusion in judging someone's appearance only by his clothes. Still, it has to be accepted that some reality is revealed by dress.

5…The power of knowledge--- Who will not accept that the good qualities of a person are also formed by the acquisition of knowledge! An educated person, whether he is of good nature or not, whether he is intelligent or active or not, will definitely be a learned person. His company will be more beneficial than that of fools. It will be difficult to rule over him. He will definitely have self-respect to some extent. Therefore, while considering the self-form of someone, it should also be seen how much and what kind of power of knowledge he has, how many subjects he has knowledge of and how much practice he has of those subjects. It should also be seen whether he has the power of intelligence in his mind or he has only acquired a degree by rote learning. It should also be seen whether he makes good use of that knowledge in worldly affairs or misuses it.

Mainly, it should be seen whether he has lientery of knowledge.

6...Etiquette--- Etiquette is also something that needs special attention. Politeness, affection, courtesy, hospitality etc. are not expressed only through speech – they become attractive through eyes, appearance and behavior. By following etiquette, one manifests the nobility of a person. Foolish people are caught only by the advertisement of their rudeness. Being unaware of how one should behave on which occasion, they often become rude. There is a Russian proverb, which means that "if you make a donkey sit on a chair near a table, it will jump and sit on the table and will think that human beings are fools who have left such a big flat ground and are sitting in narrow chairs".

7... Food and drink--- who eats what kind of food and how does one eat it, this also test a person. We have already written about the effect of food on the brain and character of a person. It has also been written about how a person, who eats too much inappropriate food, becomes. A person who eats too much is a fool. The way a person eats his food also determines his state of mind. A person of stable nature chews his food well with his mouth closed and there is no sound of chewing from his mouth while eating. Even his fingers do not get dirty. A person of restless nature eats very fast, swallows food with a slurping sound by opening his mouth and not only dirtying his hands but also the clothes in front of him.

8...Laughing--- The simplicity or ugliness of a person is definitely evident while laughing. A calm person often smiles; a simple person laughs out loud or laughs heartily when he is very happy; a hardworking person often laughs heartily; a worthless or cunning person neighs like a horse; a civilized person laughs at the right time, an uncivilized person at the wrong time.

In the laughter of a civilized person, the back part of his teeth is less visible. While laughing, the entire throat of an uncivilized person opens up like the throat of a demon. A cheerful person is happy, a person who never laughs has a very dry attitude and the person who always makes fun of others has a wicked mind. Good person laughs out of humor. A wicked person laughs when he sees others in trouble or makes a fool of them. A person with a bad nature often makes lewd jokes.

Know something more

Keeping in mind the above-mentioned things, recognize the personality of a person with the help of some other below-mentioned things:

1. **An arrogant person's gaze is above everyone's head**; people of heroic nature, truthful and pure nature look into eyes. The gentleman and affectionate look at the other's face; the shy and well-mannered look at the chest; the mean person looks below the waist; the very lowly at the shoes and the ashamed person looks at his own body parts. A completely worthless person looks only at the back of others because he is used to following others. A buffoon-natured person rolls his eyes. He does not look at anyone; others look at him.

2. **A gentleman praises someone's qualities openly**, a bad person does it in a low voice, a flatterer does it by beating the drum and a conceited person does it adding 'but' and 'however'.

3. **A person who wastes words is also a waste of time.**

4. **A civilized person shows simplicity by showing respect and affection on his face.** He greets someone with a polite hand. A pompous person either says something in a disdainful manner or drops his hand flashing like lightning. A cunning person bows down heavily and folds his hands repeatedly.

5. **A good man never says that this is his principle.** His principle is revealed by his actions. The one who has no principle shouts that he believes in a certain principle. Cunning and selfish people give even small things the form of their principles.

6. **When two people have mutual trust**, then only they behave in a trustworthy manner. When there is distrust, even a good person often hides his personality from a bad person.

7. **By knowing what is someone's favorite subject**, one can know his mental inclination. Gentlemen like public subjects. Brave men like subjects related to governance, ordinary people like subjects related to entertainment,

lowly people like subjects that displease others and fools find the whole world worthless.

8. Do not get confused... while forming an opinion about someone. Someone may have ten or five bad qualities, but at the same time he may have fifty good qualities. Those bad qualities will be hidden in those qualities – just like the blemish in the moon and the seed in the mango. In normal circumstances, one's good and bad qualities do not appear well. Consider him victorious whose personality appears to be above the circumstances. Wherever you have doubts about someone, test him. Stare at someone for a while and see whether he remains stable or becomes unstable or runs to poke your eyes. Tease someone and see whether he has patience or the nature of getting angry quickly. Try praising someone and then try criticizing him a little. It is possible that he may prove this saying: -

NEECH CHANG-SUM JANIYE, SUNI LAKHI TULSIDAS; DHEEL DET BHUIN GIRI PARAT, KHINCHAT CHADHAT AAKAS---- Tulsi:
"Tulsidasji says that wicked persons and kites are same. If slacked, they fall down onto earth and if pulled, climb up to the sky."

See his opinion on a subject, whether he is helpful or a hindrance in solving it. Assign a responsible task to someone, see whether he stands there or makes a way for his escape. If someone tells you the secrets of others, try telling him your code secrets too and tell him not to tell anyone. It is possible that he keeps telling each other's secrets. Do a favour to someone and see whether he remains grateful or becomes ungrateful. If you catch someone's mistakes, see whether he accepts his mistakes like a truthful person, or show his displeasure like a demure, or tries to cover them up with words like a Sly, or starts behaving with you like an enemy. Such experiments can reveal you the real character of a person.

There can be many other types of misconceptions. Seeing someone with a saintly demeanor, calm mind and aloof from women, people consider him to be a Noble person. He can also be a self-restrained person. Old-fashioned people see some independence in a fourteen-fifteen-year-old boy and think that the boy has gone astray. Seeing pimples on his face, they think that his celibacy is being broken. There is a grave misconception here. At the age of fourteen-fifteen, youth begins, and the glands of the body start making some changes in the body, due to which the nature of the child also changes a bit and due to the changes in some glands and special heat in the blood, pimples appear. In a way, the spring season arrives in the body. The wind of autumn blows in the thoughts and the buds of the season appear on the face. In such a situation, while examining someone, it is necessary to keep in mind the natural characteristics of his condition.

9.   Look at your faults too- If you find any fault in someone's behaviour, then before blaming him for everything, you should also check whether you yourself have pushed him away from his path. If someone gets agitated, then think about the root cause and then blame his nature. It is possible that you might have laughed at him or at something he said, or you might have unjustly criticized him in front of others with a truthful but very harsh tone. In such a situation, even a calm person can get agitated. Every person likes flattery and wants that people should not make fun of him in front of others at least. If you do not take care of this, then the victim will definitely lose his temper.

The second mistake of cursing is when you resort to logic in an emotional matter. If someone does not accept your logic, you will consider him unworthy, useless or foolish. But you should keep in mind that man cannot always be controlled by logic, he is easily bound by emotions. You cannot pacify a separated wife by logic. An angry son is not pacified by logic, but by affection. If he ignores your logic, then do not consider him evil, but consider yourself inexperienced.

The third major mistake you can make is that instead of being worthy of special respect, you expect others to respect you and if they do not respect you, you consider them arrogant or rude. Your place in the eyes of others will be according to your ability-inability, greatness-smallness and usefulness. No matter how much you stare, a lotus cannot bloom on seeing that.

The fourth grave mistake can be that you do nothing yourself and expect others to do all your work and if they do not do it, you consider them bad people. It should be remembered that no person can do the work of another person completely. The other person can only be a helper. Even a servant works only when the master also does something. The master who sleeps, his servants also sleep. Before considering others careless or lazy, see whether they have not become like that because of your carelessness.

The fifth mistake can be of your memory. If you forget something, you will make the other person a liar on the next occasion. You can verify someone's statements only if you remember them correctly.

Another mistake can be that you yourself are not of a sociable nature and blame others for being too uncultured and boastful. First test yourself and see to what extent you have the virtues of being social.

Summary

By using all these methods together, you can become especially knowledgeable about the personality of others. Keep in mind the things mentioned in the previous chapters. If you cannot recognize someone in normal state, then see him in a mad state. Whatever be the type of madness, man reveals his true form in it because then the cleverness of the intellect does not work. Mainly in the intoxication of alcohol, tobacco, etc., the naked form of the personality is visible.

Sushruta has thought about this in a scientific way. According to him, the intoxication generated in a person of **"Satvik"** nature stimulates purity, generosity, happiness, desire to adorn the body, singing, studying, desire to do famous work, feeling of enjoyment and enthusiasm. In a person of **"Rajas"** nature, excessive intoxication leads to sadness, self-destructive actions, courage and tendency of quarrel. In a person of **"Tamasic"** nature, impurity, jealousy, lying and various kinds of bad habits arise after drinking alcohol. That is why you find people of **"low"** nature wallowing in the drains. The reason for this, according to Sushrut, is that almost everyone restrains their basic instincts to some extent and behaves according to tradition and customs. Due to the effect of alcohol, nature gets excited and breaks that artificial bond and becomes free. At that time, all those deep things of the mind, which keep influencing our behavior and thoughts from within, become strong and appear.

That is why Charak has called alcohol **'PRAKRITI-DARSHAK'.** Modern scientists also believe that the effect of intoxication varies according to human nature. Not only under the influence of alcohol, but also under the influence of cigarette and tobacco, a person acts according to his inner instincts. Therefore, on such occasions, his facial expressions, behavior, conversation should be studied. If you do not understand anyone's figure, then examine the figure of the elderly. An Englishman has written absolutely true that **"in old age a person acquires the face he deserves"**. The face of a brilliant person becomes sharper in old age, the face of a man with low thoughts turns into ashes or coal. Gandhiji's face looked alive even after his death.

We believe that you have found out sufficient material on this subject in this chapter. Observe others with keen observation and also keep in mind that others too must be observing you with similar keen observation. Therefore, in order to come in close contact with others, make necessary refinements in your own appearance, conduct and gestures etc.

Now, we give some questions below, by answering which you can find out to what extent you are capable of entering a civil society. By asking these questions to others also you can know a lot about them, therefore we have considered it appropriate to mention them in this context.

Some personal questions

1. Do you interact with people, young or old, in any dress with self-respect and confidence?

2. Is your pronunciation correct?

3. When you meet a friend, do you start the conversation with a question?

4. Do you often say, 'I am sorry, I could not do that', 'I am sorry, I will not be able to do that' or 'Please don't mind', 'This is what I meant'?

5. Do you meet your friend at his office in the morning?

6. Do you meet even big people with self-respect?

7. Don't you feel upset when you hear your own criticism?

8. Is your voice clear and deep?

9. Are you considered sociable because of your conversation ability?

10. Do you find yourself obedient to some people and officer to some others, and thus can get the work done efficiently and smoothly.?

11. Do you bend or not...? In any of these three Positions - while walking or standing or sitting?

12. While talking to someone, do you know how much the listener is interested in your conversation?

13. Do you ever remember the old comic strips?

14. Are you often able to free yourself from the demands of your friends?

15. Do you maintain your truthfulness even when joking?

16. Do you pay attention to the weaknesses of your acquaintances?

17. Do you consider your married life successful?

18. Do you sometimes laugh at your mistakes?

19. Do you keep taking advantage of your friend's friendship?

20. Tell the truth, do you ever feel this that you would have been happier if your wife were as beautiful as the wife of one of your fortunate friends?

21. Do you feel any hesitation in standing in front of women?

22. Do you often discuss Sexology, Geology, Ideology, Vedanta and Philosophy with your acquaintances or not?

23. Do you often go out with your friends?

24. When your friends take you to watch movies, would he buy the tickets himself and take you inside respectfully or not?

25. What about your frequent visits to a friend's house? Did his family not show any dislike towards you?

26. Do you remember some proverbs, idioms and beautiful sayings of poets?

27. When there is a discussion in a group of friends on some serious but important topic, do you think of returning home soon?

28. Do you interact more only with your colleagues or friends?

29. Do you reveal all your sorrows to your friends?

30. Where people tell stories of the twists and turns of fate, is your name mentioned as a hero or character in them?

31. When you finish your speech, do people feel

pity for your situation?

32. Do you immediately point out the grammatical mistakes of others or not?

33. Do you get mesmerized on hearing Filmy songs?

34. Do you sometimes sing a song for yourself?

35. Do you usually prefer to go out somewhere in the evening rather than watching TV.?

36. Do you take class of your family members in your house every morning and evening?

37. Don't you like boys' clothes out of your own interest?

38. Do you feel that your life was happier before than it is now?

39. Do you have to think long and hard before writing personal letters or communicating to the people you know?

40. Do domestic worries sometimes bother you?

41. Does your evening program remain fixed?

42. Do you sometimes feel that you have become old now?

43. Do you sometimes feel jealous of your elder son

and do you secretly plot or humiliate him with the fear that he might snatch away the laurel of the house from you? Or do you ever think that it would have been better if your son had become a full-grown adult after your death? Do you ever think that if he stays away from you, your wealth will be more secure?

44. In your house, is the blame for any sudden domestic trouble put on a newly married housewife or a new-born baby?

45. If your servant gets separated or falls sick, are you forced to eat in the market?

46. If you make arrangements for the treatment of your servant when he falls ill, do you deduct the cost of the medicine etc. from his salary or not?

47. Do you often show hypocrisy so that people serve you more out of fear? And sometimes show artificial indifference in household chores? Do you perform all kinds of dramas by showing them?

48. When someone is upset, are you able to persuade him without threatening him?

49. Do you get more happiness when you are a guest at others' places than at your own home?

50. Do your servants keep you happy and insult your family members whenever they want?

51. Can you remain absolutely independent at home and not take anyone's advice even in matters like marriage etc.?

52. Do you beat or hit someone or the other to establish your dominance at home?

53. Are you addicted to finding faults after the work is done and cutting the wages of servants and laborers?

54. Are you very learned and popular but still very rude to your family members? Are you unable to show feelings of intimacy?

55. Do you speak in two different ways at home also, that is, you keep one thing in your mind and say something else and after saying something, you change your mind later?

56. Do you like to make new laws for your family members and impose section 144 IPC (189/4 BNS) every day?

57. Do your relatives like to visit your house again and again?

58. Are festivals or auspicious occasions celebrated in your house or not?

59. Do your boys and servants look like your disciples?

60. Are you such a terror that your children keep

their eyes glued to the book's day and night?

61. Are you the husband of many living women?

62. Does everyone in your house feel that you love them the most?

63. Do all people willingly participate in your joys and sorrows?

64. When you bring something from outside, do you first set aside your share of it or not?

65. Do you usually sit at home?

66. Do you regret getting angry?

67. Do you ever get bored when you are alone?

68. Can you keep company of children, old people and young people happily at any time?

69. When someone shows affection, respect or gratitude towards you, do you fall under their control?

70. Do you often fail to congratulate or thank someone?

71. When you are talking engrossedly and someone else talks and diverts the attention of the people from you, then do you get upset?

72. Do you have some knowledge of various

subjects?

73. Do you remember the names of your acquaintances easily or not?

74. Do you go to many places just to mark your attendance?

75. Do you get along with everyone?

76. Do you respect other people's time?

77. Can you talk to someone for ten-fifteen minutes on your first meeting? And you mainly focus on discussing your work?

78. Do you sometimes help out in someone's household chores or not?

79. Do you go to others just to gossip?

80. Do you listen to others carefully or not?

81. Do you often create doubt in the mind of others then assure them that you will tell them later.?

82. Do you become a joker when other people make fun of you?

83. Are you cheerful and quick-witted?

84. Do you always keep talking when others are quiet?

85. Are you able to change the topic of conversation

easily or not?

86. Have you practiced talking to servants in an abusive manner or not?

87. So that your servants or children remain cautious, do you scold them severely and rebuke them even for small mistakes or not?

88. While correcting your mistake, do you stoop too low?

89. Do you always remain in fear of miscreants due to not having a pistol with you?

90. If these secrets of yours, which have been revealed in the form of answers to these questions, are told to your friends, will you not feel some uneasiness in your mind?

91. Do you behave equally with all your friends while getting up, sitting, eating & drinking?

92. Do you reply promptly to ordinary letters Messages on social media from acquaintances?

Know It To Shine

Weigh your answers

You must have answered 'yes' or 'no'. We also answer in the same way. Compare the two. If the number of matching answers is 75% or more, then consider yourself passed in the first division, if 50% is in the second division, if 35% is in the general division. If the number is less than this, then you will remain in the same category and those behind you will soon become your equals and move ahead.

1. Yes. 2. Yes. 3. Yes. 4. No. 5. No. 6. Yes. 7. No. 8. Yes. 9. Yes. 10. Yes. 11. No. 12. Yes. 13. Yes. 14. No. 15. No. 16. Yes. 17. Yes. 18. Yes. 19. No. 20. No. 21. No. 22. No. 23. Yes. 24. No. 25. No. 26. Yes. 27. No. 28. No. 29. No. 30. No. 31. No. 32. No. 33. No. 34. Yes. 35. Yes. 36. No. 37. No. 38. No. 39. No. 40. No. 41. No. 42. No. 43. No. 44. No. 45. No. 46. No. 47. No. 48. Yes. 49. No. 50. No. 51. No. 52. No. 53. No. 54. No. 55. No. 56. No. 57. Yes. 58. Yes. 59. No. 60. No. 61. No. 62. Yes. 63. Yes. 64. Yes. 65. No. 66. No. 67. No. 68. Yes. 69. No. 70. No. 71. No. 72. Yes. 73. Yes. 74. No. 75. No. 76. Yes. 77. Yes. 78. Yes. 79. No. 80. Yes. 81. No. 82. No. 83. Yes. 84. No. 85. Yes. 86. No. 87. No. **88. No. 89. No. 90. No. 91. Yes. 92. Yes.**

Chapter-9
Some Relevant Excerpts, Quotes and Self - Evaluation

Denouement: In this final phase, we additionally present a curated selection of verses, hymns, Quotes and relevant excerpts to enrich the Reader's journey and deepen their immersion. Readers are invited to contemplate these different Era -specific citations, scholarly references and quotes for edification and intellectual replenishment in the field of Human Behavior. Thereafter, we shall present a series of questions for the readers to answer, enabling them to examine their own Virtues, traits and Persona and evaluate themselves in the light of their now enhanced understanding of Human Behaviour and overall conduct.

1. Few Verses, Hymns etc. written in our scriptures in Ancient Era: are given hereunder. This Hymn is mentioned in "**Brihadaranayaka Upanishad**", points the ethical way, on which we must walk on in the life.

ASATO MA SAD GAMAY,
TAMASO MA JYOTIRGAMAYA,
MRITYORMA AMRITAM GAMAY
"Take us from Lies to the Truth
Take us from darkness to the enlightenment.

Take us from death to immortality".

UDDHAREDATMANA ATMANAM NATMANAM VASADAYET ATMAIVA HAYATMANO BANDHURAT MAIVA RIPURATMANAH----- GITA.
"It is proper for a human being to self-liberate and not self-degenerate. A man, himself, is a friend or enemy to him."

One such sacred hymn written in **"Aitareya Brahamana"** (Rigveda) encompasses all the four Yuga:

KALIH: SHAYANO BHAVATI, SANJIHANASTU DWAPARA: UTTISHTHANSTRETA BHAVATI KRITAM SAMPADYATE CHARAN. CHARAIVETI, CHARAIVETI.
"Lying down and sleeping is "Kaliyug", dozing is "Dwapar", sitting up is "Treta" and walking is "Satyug". So, keep going, keep going".

Ashtadashpurananam saram smuddhrutam Paropkarah: Punay Papay Parpidanam
"The essence of all the Ashta Purans is that doing good to others is **Virtu**e (Punya) and harming others is **Sin** (Paap)"

2. Few Wisdom-words, written by Sages, Literary Giants in **Medieval Era**, who considered all the sides of Human Behaviour for years together and poured down their well-earned wisdom in their literary work. Many of such Pearls of wisdom have found their appropriate places, earlier in this Book. In addition to them few of such instructive, guiding and informative citations are given hereunder to top-up:

YAH: SATATAM PARIPRACHHATI SHRINOTI SANDHARYATYHARNISHAM. TASYA DIVAKARA KIRANAIRNKAMALINIV VIVARDDHVATE BUDDHI: ... (Panchatantra)
He who always asks, listens, and follows it day and night, his intelligence increases like Kamalini (Candock) grows by the rays of the sun.

UDYAMEN HI SIDDHYANTI KARAYANI NA MANORATHAIH: NA HI SUPTASYA SIMHASYA PRAVISHANTI MUKHE MRIGAH). (Panchatantra)
Work is done not by wish, but by efforts. The deer does not move itself in the mouth of a sleeping lion.

VIPADI DHAIRYAMATHABHUDAYE KSHAMA, SADASI VAKPATUTAYUDHI VIKRAMAH: YASHASI CHABHIRUCHIVRVYASANAM SHRUTAU, PRAKRITISIDDHAMIDAM HI MAHATMANAM. (Bhartrihari)
To have courage in adversity, to be forgiving despite being rich, to show eloquence in assembly, to show prowess in war, to have passion in learning, to be addicted to learning - these qualities are inherent in Mahatmas.

The one who has conquered himself is a far greater Hero than he who has defeated a thousand time a thousand men----------------Budhha

Live and allow others to live, hurt no one, life is dear to all living beings. ---------------Mahavir, Jain Tithankar

DHEERE-DHEERE RE MANA, DHEERE SAB KUCH HOY, ... MALI SEENCHE SAU GHADA, RITHU AAYE PHAL HOYE ---------(Kabir)

Hey Man! Slowly – Slowly, everything happens: Slowly Even if a Gardener irrigates a tree with hundreds of pitchers of water, the Fruits would come only in its right season)

**KAHU NA KOU SUKH-DUKH: KAR DATA
NIJ KRUT KARAM, BHOG SAB BHRATA------(Tulsi)**
No one can give you Happiness or Sorrow, Brother! You have to endure your own deeds.

**A bad man is worse when he pretends to be a Saint
--------Francis Bacon, (Father of Empiricism)**

**Even the Best things are not equal to their Fame
---------Goethe**

3. Few quotes, Citations etc. from the World Leaders, Saviors, Legends of **Recent Era,** who have also expressed their thoughts on Human Behavior and Psychology through their speeches, Dissertations, Autobiographies, etc.:
**"Live as if you were to die tomorrow
Learn as if you were to live forever".
--------Mahatma Gandhi**

**"The Policy of being too cautious is the Risk of All"
-------Jawahar Lal Nehru**

The Crowd loves the Strong Man, the crowd is like a woman------Mussolini

For me and for us all, reverses are nothing but strokes of the whip, and it is practically these which we need to drive us forward-------Hitler

"Arise, Awake and stop not until the goal is reached"
------------Swami Vivekananda

"Old Age is often a return to Childhood"
----------. Munshi Prem Chand (Famous Story Writer)

"You can't cross the Sea merely by standing and staring at the water" ------------Rabindranath Tagore

"Like timidity, Bravery is also contagious"
------ Munshi Premchand

"Nobody is Superior, nobody is inferior, but nobody is equal either" ------------Osho

The future belongs to those who embrace Knowledge, Technology and innovation
----------Man Mohan Singh

I have always been convinced that the only way to get the things done is to do them yourself
----------Ratan Tata

Self-Evaluation

Having read the entire book, we hope readers have gained a clearer understanding of human virtues, traits, persona and overall conduct. we present, hereunder, a series of questions to evaluate their own improved comprehension of human comportment and deportment.

Further, understand your mistakes yourself by answering the following questions, because usually other people remain silent even after seeing your mistakes due to politeness or shyness. We have deliberately not arranged these questions in a sequence:

Questions

1. There are many situations when the decision has to be taken to do or not to do a task. You struggle within you and in your soul regarding it. In that case, do you ultimately become victorious over the soul? Or does your own soul defeat you?

2. Sometimes waves of joy or sorrow suddenly arise in your mind. Do you immediately get swept away by them or do you float in them for some time?

3. Is there any explosive substance in your mind due to which you get burnt by a simple spark of Conversation?

4. On seeing you coming, do people start reciting Sankat Mochan in their minds out of fear?
   In other words, do people fear you thinking that knowingly you say something contrary,

or I do not know the customs and rituals of love'?

5. When you start speaking, does a beautiful string of words come out of your throat or does an air gun start firing?

6. Is it true that while praising others you feel poverty of words and while criticizing them
you get the tongues of Sahasranaga?

7. When you meet others, do you appear like a spy? Or do people think you are someone's spy?

8. If there is any fight around you, is your name included in it like NARAD ...?

9. Have you become accustomed to getting into arguments with someone or the other?

10. Is it true that you cannot express a subject without exaggerating it?

11. Blaming Kali Yuga, making the laws of the creator inverted, criticizing Him, putting or
blaming the entire responsibility for your plight onto the government, God or some other person, reciting a long list of the glory and joys of the past. Are the main topics of your conversation?

12. Do you immediately start telling your autobiography upon meeting someone?

13. Do you memorize the faults of others by finding faults in them or not?

14. Anyone whom do you meet, is always cunning, untrustworthy, or dishonest?

15. Do you alone praise others or is there someone who praises you too?

16. Who praises you the most? Yourself or your friends or your enemies?

17. Do you have more friends or enemies?

18. Does even a simple gust of wind make you sneeze? In other words, do even simple things cause big blisters in your heart?

19. Do you do the act of misleading others? In other words, by wearing a khaki shirt and pant and hanging a fake pistol, or, on joining at the lower cadre of the Police Force, do you go around advertising that you have become the Head of all the police officers, or though you are a Yes- Man of your Boss but after meeting him, do you advertise that Sahib has taken Your valuable advices in matters related to administration, or after studying till sixth or seventh standard, do you try to tell others that you are so capable that you can cut off the ears of even the bigwigs; or after getting an imaginary job, do you advertise that you have become or are going to become a high ranking official?

20. Do you enhance your glory by narrating the glory of your ancestors?

21. Do you threaten others at every opportunity, shock them, and try to get your work done in this way?

22. Are you afraid of every type of competition and are you doubtful that others might surpass you?

23. Is God's name also included in the list of your servants? That is, do you think that a certain work will happen only if God wants, or does it?

24. The scorching sun in summer, torrential rains in monsoon, cough-fever and cold in winter - these three must be hindrances in your work. While leaving home, apart from the happiness of home and the attachment to family members, the problems of direction, inauspicious time, bad omens must often catch your feet. You have to go far away - **'PARDESKALES NARESUHU KO'**, everyone is a stranger there, work cannot be done alone - these worries must often keep you sitting idle. Is it correct?

25. Do you find yourself incapable and frustrated in most tasks?

26. Is it true that your house has become your prison, where your wife is the jail superintendent and your children are the guards at the prison gate?

27. To what extent is it true that if you had not had the troubles of your house, you could have lived more happily and made great progress in this world?

28. Do people interpret your words in one meaning or in many different ways?

29. Do you meet others to exchange ideas or to confirm your opinions?

30. Usually when you meet someone, does your listener doze off while listening to you? Or, does he keep doing something else while talking?

31. In a conversation, do you like to refute or argue more, or to agree with everything, or to split hairs, or to answer a brick with a stone?

32. When you go among people, do you get the feeling that everybody is staring at you and your attire, and wants to pounce on you and your mistakes are being discussed all around?

33. When you go to a gathering, you usually look for a corner to sit. Your mind remains calm when you sit. And if you have to sit in the middle of everyone, your heart will start pounding, your eyes will flutter and you will get angry every now and then. Is this assumption of ours about you or someone else?

34. Does your cap or turban jump and fall at the feet of others many times a day? That is,
are you the beneficiary or indebted to many?

35. Do you often bow your head or walk with your back bent?

36. Do you find it particularly difficult to maintain friendships and do you change friends as often as a cunning person takes a U-turn or changes his words?

37. Do you have any secret friends whom you meet secretly?

38. Do you have a natural affection for Poetry, art, literature, music, dance or any recreational activity...?

39. Do you read a daily newspaper? Do you watch News Channels on TV every evening? If you do, what kind of news are you interested in? Do you particularly read/watch thrilling accounts of thefts and robberies, news of immorality, incidents of lightning or a buffalo getting hit by a train, or a husband cutting off his wife's nose or do you read / watch advertisements of medicines?

40. Is it true that you become the unpaid slave of the one who frightens you, and you climb on the neck of the one who humbly bows before you?

41. Do you laugh more or less? Do you like to laugh or smile? Do you laugh only from the throat or from the heart? Do you ridicule others or do you enjoy humor? Do you laugh and joke with your elders or with people of the same class and even with servants?

42. Are you respectfully invited to the functions of the city, locality or neighborhood? After being invited, does the host feel happy at your arrival or do you consider yourself blessed?

43. Do You suffer from some diseases which cannot be diagnosed and cured?

44. Is it true that as soon as any talk, thing reaches your stomach it becomes a laxative Tablet.?

45. Are you a father or a teacher or both to your children?

46. Are you the master of your wife or her friend or her slave?

47. Are you the husband of some fickle woman or a witch?

48. As soon as you enter your house, does there remain silence or starts a storm?

49. Do you pray to God daily to strike lightning on your enemies or not?

50. Are you yourself your own ideals?

51. Have you suddenly lost your temper after getting a high position?

52. Do you want to take credit for the success of every task?

53. Are you the one who gets happy easily?

54. In your dreams, do you see scary scenes or beautiful women or food items?

55. Do you walk with stamping of feet?

56. If you sit in your shop, do you remain serious or not?

57. Do you regularly give some pocket money to your wife and children every month?

58. Which powders or medicines do you use?

59. When you fail in any work, do you become unconscious or alert?

60. Do you sometimes have suicidal thoughts?

61. Does it sometimes happen that you get success after success without any reason?

62. Are you overly optimistic or pessimistic?

63. Are you ancient or modern more than necessary?

64. Your personal character has no bearing on your business- would you agree?

Explanatory Answers

1.   If there is a conflict between you and your soul, i.e. between good wishes and conscience, then the only way to win is by accepting defeat from the soul. God's indication comes in the form of self-motivation. Kalidasa has written that in doubtful matters, gentlemen consider the testimony of their soul as proof: **SANTA: HI SANDEHPADESHU VASTUSHU PRAMANMANTAH: KARAN-PRAVRATAYAH: -** (Kalidas)

2.   Some famous American psychologists have studied and observed that every thirty-third day a natural wave of

joy or sorrow comes in the mind of every human being. When a wave of joy arises, the mind becomes joyful without any reason, generosity, simplicity and humility appear in the intellect. When a wave of grief arises, the desires of anxiety, remorse, anger or detachment become intense without any reason. The day such a change is suddenly felt in the mind, one should understand that a natural wave of sentimentality has arisen. In that condition, the mind will be inclined towards joy or sorrow. On the thirty-third day, a similar change in the state of mind will occur again. This sequence continues, but it is not certain that once the wave of joy arises, it will arise again. Grief can also arise after joy. In some people, these waves arise on the thirty-fourth or thirty-fifth day and keep rising in the same order. This is definitely experienced in the fifth week. One should be careful during emotional outburst and should not do any emotional action suddenly.

3. If you are tolerant, then only the name of some shameless or unfortunate person will be missing in your friends list. The one who gets agitated at every small thing, travels on the road of madness riding on the motor of despair.

4. If people are terrified due to your bad behaviour then you are no less dangerous than an infectious disease. It is human nature that the person who is afraid or suspicious of someone does not love him. If you are so bad-natured that people are afraid to talk to you then you cannot get true sympathy from the society. Tulsi has considered people of such nature to be in the evil class:
VACHAN – VAJRA JEHIN SADA PIYARA SAHAS NAYAN PAR-DOSH NIHARA 'He who lovingly uses

his words like thunderbolts, always looks at the faults on others with many angles'

5.　　If you speak harshly, your words will not have any effect on anyone. Harsh arguments in beautiful words are as effective as sarcasm in beautiful eyes. Firing air guns of words does not bring victory in the battle of life.

6.　　If you are unable to praise others but are capable of criticizing them, then your heart must be filled with ill-will. People must be afraid to sit near you and must have less trust in you. A critic roams around with the blackness of others on his mouth, believe this to be true.

7.　　In a civilized society, if you try to find out the secrets of others, try to listen to two people's conversation discreetly without any reason, try to see other people's mobile phone messages and chats, try to whisper into someone's ears, then people will definitely look at you with suspicion. It is possible that you may be stunned due to nervousness and stare at others with wide eyes, due to which people may think you are a spy. Whatever it may be, being looked at with suspicion is humiliating.

8.　　If your name is attached to disputes like Narada, then there must be some reason for it; you have not become the incarnation of Devarshi in vain. You may be addicted to getting involved in most disputes, or famous for twisting things, or by nature quarrelsome or biased. It is possible that you may not have a hand in any particular dispute, but earlier you must have earned enough fame for starting a fire, due to which whenever there is a fire anywhere, people remember your name. Fame runs before a man. It is wise not to get involved in others' disputes; even if you do, do it impartially.

9. Many people develop such a nature that they move ahead like a conqueror, they get into a fight with someone without any reason. If they do not find anyone to fight with, they start blaming someone based on their imagination. And force him to come to the arena for fight. They get addicted to daily atrocities on family members, relatives, friends, servants etc. If you are like this, then make a friend or servant who is habitually shameless. Make him a punching Bag and punch your Tongue-Mitts on it every day. If you do not do this, you will suffer from insomnia or indigestion or fever or diabetes. Sheikh-Saadi also met such a person whose description he has given in Gulistan. There was a king who used to harass someone or the other every day. One day a saint came to meet him. The king asked him which worship would be best for me? The saint said- Sleeping during the day, because till you sleep, at least till then the lives of the poor will be saved from trouble and you will get "Punya"

10. If you are used to heaping mountains of imagination on the truth, then the truth will surely die. Those who add wings of imagination to their talks to make them entertaining, lose the talks out of their hands. Adding spice or exaggerating things or making a mountain out of a molehill is self-respect destroying. When this is practiced, the speaker himself starts believing his imaginary stories to be true and the listeners start thinking his true stories to be imaginary.

11. Blaming time or someone else for your failure advertises your inefficiency. If you are strong, you will find everyone helping you, and you will look to the future instead of the past. 'All help the strong, but no one helps the weak'. **SABAI SAHAYAK SABAL KE, KOU N NIBAL SAHAY'**

12. If you talk about yourself everywhere, people will get bored of you. When a person gets addicted to telling his own story, he seems like a crow who keeps repeating his own name.

13. If you are a fault-finder, then the society will consider you like a fly. Seeing the bad qualities of others and talking about them is like carrying garbage from the streets in a cart. It is an advertisement of one's nature. Keeping the good qualities of others on one's tongue is like applying perfume on clothes. On the contrary, keeping faults of others on the tongue is like a foul-smelling substance keeping in one's pocket. Before criticizing someone, the critic himself becomes the object of criticism.

14. If you consider everyone except yourself to be dishonest or untrustworthy, then you yourself are immature and suspicious by nature. The one who considers or makes everyone dishonest is himself dishonest. Trust is built only by trust. The one who is trustworthy himself, finds others trustworthy too. The one who is suspicious, doubts his wife and children too.

15. If you sing the praises of others and are not renowned yourself, then your importance will be no more than that of a Darbari- bard. If you are talented then there

Know It To Shine

will be people who sing your praises. There is no dearth of spectators for a scene.

16. A self-Praiser is a low-grade person. A mediocre person is praised even by his friends. A good man is praised even by his enemies. Even Krishna used to praise Karna:
**SWATAH: TATHA MITRA-SAMAJ SE SADA
KAHAN NAHIN KAUN PRASHANSANIYA HAI
GUNI VAI HAI JISKE PRABHAV KI
KAREN VIRODHIJAN BHI SARAHANA**

17. If the number of your friends is more, then it is a sign of your brilliance, sociability and trustworthiness. Gentlemen and brave people always have no enemies. If the number of your enemies is more, then your nature, behaviour and efforts will be devious, rude or incapable. You may be a conspirator, harsh-spoken or hateful. It is more likely that you are weak, fearful and very short-tempered. Due to this snake-like nature, people may be after you with sticks. A snake is physically weak, timid by nature but when provoked, it becomes very short-tempered and daring. All three things usually go together: **'KSHEENA NARAH NISHKARUNA BHAVANTI.'** A weak person is pitiless. While comparing the number of friends and enemies, keep in mind that twenty friends are equal to one enemy.

18. Just as a weak person catches cold due to change in the normal climate, similarly people with weak heart and false Ego get upset on ordinary things. False ego creates aversion in other people. People with False Ego always face problems in finding friends.

19. The first sign of a fool, a person of low morals and a person with limited knowledge is that he keeps on falsely advertising himself. 'A learned person of high morals does not show pride, a person without qualities is always proud' – **"VIDWAN KULINO N KAROTI GARVAH: GUNAIRVIHINA BAHU JALPAYANTI"**. In this regard, we should accept the opinion of the great Socrates that the simplest and surest way to live a respectable life in this world is that a person should express himself as he really is. **"The shortest and surest way to live with honour in the world is to be in reality what we would appear to be"**. We should also keep in mind George Bernard Shaw's observation that **"A good way of keeping poor is pretending to be rich"**. A good way to remain poor is to show Rich or pretend to be rich."

People of petty nature have a tendency to falsely advertise their influence and try to make themselves look superior in the eyes of others. They want to take undue advantage of casual acquaintance with a big man and they do take it, but a time comes when their remaining reputation also turns to dust along with their false reputation.

20. If you want to get yourself worshipped only on the basis of the fame of your ancestors and not on your own merit, then this is your delusion. Chanakya has written that virtuous people are illuminated by their own qualities, who looks at their birth (i.e. caste, lineage etc.): **"PRAKASHYAM SWAGUNODYEN GUNINO GACHCHANTI KIM JANMANA"**. We consider a person who lives on the fame of his ancestors to be a potato-class creature. Like a Potato, his entire identity remains buried in the soil of his ancestors. If one is famous

himself, the fame of his ancestors helps him, if it is not, his glory diminishes even more, because people say how did this insignificant person took birth into such a high family. Shaw has even said that **"It is maddening to be related to a celebrated person and never be valued for own sake".** Being a relative of a big person is very painful, because we are introduced by his name, and our independent personality is not considered at all.

21. The one who threatens is always a coward. **Bullies are always cowards-** G.B. Shaw. A powerful man does not threaten. He just shows what he wants by doing it. The one who attracts people with shocking talk is considered a liar and often gets cheated like the shepherd described in Aesop's fables. That shepherd used to shout everyday saying **'The wolf has come; the wolf has come'**. When people ran to help, they saw that nothing was there. One day the wolf really came. The shepherd shouted a lot, but people did not come for help, thinking that it was just his habit to shock. The wolf ate him.

22. Due to natural cowardice, people are often afraid of competition and take up such tasks in which there is no fear of competition. They are afraid that if they fail, people might laugh at them. This shows lack of enthusiasm, courage and self-confidence. A strong person always welcomes competition because it helps him prove his Self-worthiness and in achieving success. One also gets to know one's strength. America's former President Roosevelt once said that "A **little rivalry is stimulating, you know. It keeps everybody going to prove that he is a better fellow than the next man. It keeps them honest too**". A little competition is encouraging because it awakens the feeling

in every person to prove himself more capable than his colleague; because of this they also remain truthful.

23. If you think that God will do your work, then you make that Supreme Lord your porter. No one with authority accepts to be someone's servant. He may even punish you for this audacity. **"HO HI SOHI JO RAM RACHI RAKHA"** 'Whatever happens is what Ram has written' - this is the mantra of the Shirkers and the Unfortunates. In the words of Shukra, only impotent people rely on God for the accomplishment of their work: **'KLIBO DAIVAMUPASATE.'** The respectable intelligent people give importance to hard-work only: **'DHIMANTO VANDYCHARITA MANYANTE PAURUSHAM MAHAT'**

Calling God for help is a sign of weakness. Its strong proof is that when a person is weak due to illness, the name of Ram naturally comes out of his mouth. Ethicists say that a person who makes efforts gets Lakshmi through hard work. Cowardly people say that 'God gives'. Forget God and make efforts and if you do not get success even after trying, then see where the mistake is:

UDYOGINAM PURUSHASINGAHMUPAITI LAKSMIH: DEVAM HI DAIVMITI KAHPURUSHA-VADANTI, DAIVAM NIHATYA KURU PAURUSH-MATMSHAKTYA, YATNE KRITE YADI N SIDHHAYATE KOUTRA DOSHAH:

Tulsi has also written that: Respect the mind fully and Do work. The lazy person calls
'God …God. **"KADAR MUN KAR EIK ADHARA, DEV DEV AALSI PUKARA"**

Without self-reliance, one cannot get the blessings even of the gods. There is a force of God, but this does not come from outside; it is generated only by self-sadhana and the use of intellect. One who sits in the guise of being loved by the gods is a goat, an animal, a fool or a mad person. These are the literal meanings of being loved by the gods.

The best thing is to keep your efforts motivated. In this regard, Mahaveer Karna should be considered an ideal. Abandoned by the mother Kunti, he raised himself with his own efforts; established a kingdom, conquered the world and fearlessly showed his efforts and sacrificed his life in the field of action. With his efforts, he fascinated and even let down Lord Krishna. In this context, we remember this praise of Karna written by the Kuru King in front of Krishna in the royal court:

The glory of the kingdom is conquered by his own arms, and the fortune is accumulated by his own work. Karna is a stubborn, truthful and generous King. If the Creator himself tries to erase the invisible writings on his forehead, he will never be disheartened in his heart. He who is capable with the power of effortful-courage.

24. The one whose work is not hindered by cold, heat, fear, love, wealth or poverty is called a Pandit, this is the opinion of Vidur:

YASYA KRITYAM NA VIGHNANTI SHEETMUSHNAM BHAYAM RATIH: SAMRIDDHIRASAMRIDDHIRVA SA VAI PANDIT UCHYATE - (Mahabharata)

An industrious man does not depend on season, means or non-means. Only the lazy is affected by sunshine, cold, rain and economic condition. Every moment of an industrious man is an auspicious moment. Nothing is a burden for him because he is capable.

For a businessman, there is no place too far; no place is alien to a learned person, because wherever he goes, he makes everyone his own with his knowledge. No one is alien to a sweet speaker, because his speech is mesmerizing:

KOTIBHARAH: SAMARTHANAM KIM DOORAM VYAVSYAINAAM. KO VIDHESH: SAVIDYANAM, KAH: PARH: PRIYAVADINAM. ----- (Panchatantra)

If you are not like this then you will be non-industrious, sad and frustrated.

25. If you find yourself incapable of doing work, then it is not an advertisement of the difficulty of the work, but of your incompetence, weakness and inferiority. Difficulty is experienced due to lack of strength, enthusiasm and laziness. According to Carlyle, **"In idleness there is perpetual despair."** 'There is eternal disappointment in inaction.' The question of the impossible does not arise before an industrious person; everything is achievable for him. **'UDYUKTAANAAM MANUSHYAANAAM GAMYA- AGAMYAM NA VIDYATE.'** (Markandeya Purana). If you are strong-willed, you will first see the importance of the task and will be ready to make it successful without worrying about difficulties. Strong-willed Hard-workers do not care about happiness and sorrow: **"MANASVI KARYARTHI NA GANAYATI DUKHM: N CH SUKHAM"**- Bhartarhari

26. If you make your home your prison, then you will be unsuitable for the outside world. A person who is attached to his home never progresses. Being like a bull, he gets bound in the illusion of his home and dances in the courtyard of his home and the proverb **'Just as an oilman's bull has to go to his home for Hundred miles'** is applicable to him. He lies down looking at the faces of his wife and children and in a few days, his face becomes gloomy. When he becomes poor, his wife and children also become detached from him. Without going out, a man remains indolent, as idle as he was born.

In this regard, we should have the Marwaris our ideals. The dictum **"JAHAN NA JAYE RAVI, TAHAN JAYE KAVI"**- 'Wherever the sun does not go, the poet goes there', can be rephrased "Jahan Na Jaye Gadi, Vahan Jaye Marwadi"- 'Wherever the car (Gadi) does not go, the Marwari goes there'. The Marwari is also a great lover of his country, his own race, his own family, but he does not sit idle. When he goes out for business, he is not bothered by home attachment. Going to foreign countries, he collects wealth and increases the prosperity of his home with it. He is farsighted in all matters; he sees the distant places suitable for business, he sees the coming opportunity in advance; he recognizes which work will be profitable in the future and by understanding how far away Lakshmi is standing, he walks on the that path.

27. If you think of home as a mess, then you are mistaken. It is because of its control that your natural arrogance and animality remain suppressed. Had it not been there, you would have been born or brought up in an orphanage. No matter how bad the home is, it is a place

where a man takes his last refuge. Dr. Johnson has rightly written that **"To be happy at home is the ultimate result of all ambition"**. Being happy at home is the ultimate aim of our every aspiration. If someone holds your string properly at home, you can fly anywhere you want like a kite. If the string breaks, you will fall or get stuck somewhere.

28. If people interpret your words in many ways, it does not mean that you are an extraordinary speaker. Certainly, your words will be confusing, you will not be a clear speaker, your thoughts will be uncertain or you will speak with 'but' and 'yet' out of deceit. It is also possible that you do not know the art of expressing your feelings.

29. An English scholar says that most people, when they come to you for advice, are actually doing so to get your support for their own preconceived ideas. They come to seek your consent in a matter related to them. This does not benefit them in any way. Support them and they will consider your opinion to be great; If you criticize their opinion truthfully then they will consider your words to be useless. A smart person always welcomes new ideas and completes his incompleteness by taking clear consent of people.

30. If the listeners start dozing off or become distracted while listening to you, it means that you are talking nonsense, you are a polymath, you repeat the same thing or your style of talking is not impressive or you are not self-impressive in the eyes of the listeners. It may also be that you are praising yourself or criticizing others, which may not be liked by listeners.

31. One who refutes or defends others is not an interesting speaker. One who always agrees with everything is thoughtless. One who splits hairs is considered to be narrow-minded and the one who answers a brick with a stone is arrogant.

32. If you feel shy in public, then you are probably a very solitary person, bashful, lacking in self-confidence, mentally isolated or very suppressed. Even pompous people get shy or angry because even after dressing up and going out, they still have the illusion that their makeup is incomplete.

33. If you cannot sit fearlessly in front of everyone in a gathering, then there is some natural, character or social weakness in you. It is possible that your financial condition is such that you consider yourself inferior to others. It is possible that you are by nature lazy, dirty or fond of solitude. It is possible that you are a conspirator. It is also possible that your education has been such that you remain a follower of others. It may also be there you suffer some physical ailment like hearing problem or fatigue.

Whatever, if you do not make an effort to claim the rightful position, it reveals your cowardice and incompetence. A progressive person tries to make himself the center of attraction and a regressive person tries to hide himself. President Roosevelt's son, looking at his father's attitude, used to say about him that when he used to go to someone's wedding, he used to wish that it would be so nice if he were the groom; how happy he would be if he were the dead body when he attended someone's funeral, because then everyone's eyes would be on him. The desire to open himself up in front of society in this way will arise only in a person who is progressive and whose social ideals are high. Such a person believes that even if a thousand eyes look at him, his appearance will appear blemish-free. The one who has evil thoughts and fear in his heart, he sits in a corner like a criminal.

34. The one who does not have self-respect, stands with folded hands in front of everyone. A self-reliant man is proud of himself. Only the lazy, cowardly and criminal people get moved by small things. If you cannot save the dignity of your cap or turban by your self-influence, then it would be better to wear someone's shoes instead.

35. Bowing down or walking with bent back is certainly a sign of weakness. The proof is evident- as a man becomes weak in old age, his back and neck also bend. Keeping the spine erect and the brow high shows manliness. Only a self-controlled, strong-willed and powerful man keeps his body standing in an upright position; a criminal, a fearful and a coward becomes accustomed to bowing down or touching feet without any reason. It should be remembered that whether the body is small or big, only when it stands straight, the personality of the man becomes impressive. At that time, it is known that the Measuring Tape of his humanity or self-power is in front of us in the form of the erect body of that man. In our own poetic words, we can express this **in a more attractive way**: Raised like the horn of a golden rock, the body of this man looks ornamental. It is the proof that he **"knows how to shine"**; a yardstick to measure standard humanity.

36. If you always find it difficult to maintain friendship then first blame your nature. Perhaps you make friendship

with someone out of selfishness and your friendship also breaks when you become selfish. It is possible that ego, ingratitude, dishonesty and arrogance are present in your nature due to which you have to face friendship problems very often. It is also possible that you make anyone your friend without thinking and later become aware after getting cheated. Whatever it may be, one should accept that friendship is not something that can be changed again and again. By maintaining it, one's pride increases, one's power and prestige become stable. If your nature is blameless, then 'make such a person your friend who not only enjoys your happiness but also supports you completely in adversity and sorrow'. In this regard remember this saying **MITRA AISA RAKHIYE DHAL SARIKHA HOYE, SUKH MEIN TAU PEECHHE RAHE, DUKH MEIN AAGE HOYE** Follow this dictum for yourself and protect your friendship with all out efforts.

37. If you have some friends whom you meet secretly, then your life will be full of secrets. You may be cunning; your activities may be strange. There is an English saying that **"A man is known by the company he thinks nobody knows he is keeping"**

38. If you do not have a natural liking for any entertaining art, then you will be extremely dry and also worthy of distrust. You will have harshness, inertia, despair, impurity in nature and narrowness in thoughts. Bhartrihari had said after deliberation that 'a man devoid of literature, music and art is an animal without horns and tail':
SAHITYA- SANGEET-KALA- VIHINAH: SAKSHAT PASHU: PUCHH-VISHANAHEENH:

39. After praying to God, reading newspapers, watching TV, social media on Mobile Phones & Computers are the most important work these days. If you do not read/Watch them, you will remain behind the times. If you see only meaningless things in them, you are killing your knowledge. One should learn about the progress of the country, society, human thoughts and current affairs from the print as well as electronic media.

40. If you bow down before the oppressor, you will be a coward, impotent. If you become a lion before someone who bows down before you, you will be a jackal at heart. A cat does not become a lion by posing a lion in a raspberry forest. Courtesy and greatness lie in respecting the one who respects you. Sheikh Saadi's advice is that you should also bow down before the one who bows down before you. By being cruel to the weak, you will make him despair of life at some point of time and remember that the attack of a person who despairs of life is very terrible. Remember these lines of Tulsidas in this regard: **ATISHAYA RAGAD KARAIEN JO KOI, ANAL PRAKAT CHANDAN TE HOI** -(Manas) Anyone who rubs it excessively, Fire appears from sandalwood.

41. The famous scholar Goethe has written that man does not advertise his nature or character so clearly by any other action as by laughing after looking at any particular object. **"By nothing do men show their character more than by the things they laugh at."** On what occasions a man laughs and how he laughs - this is how one's nature can be known. A civilized person is civilized even in humor. A shameless person ridicules others, laughs cruelly

at the mistakes of others. Serious, unhealthy, worried or dirty people laugh less. Uncivilized, lazy, carefree, playful and humorous people guffaw. People with a well-mannered and gentle nature love smile and occasionally laugh loud. A sycophant and a flatterer laugh only from the throat and a kind and fearless person laughs even below the heart, from the navel. Giggling with elders is an unauthorized gesture. Dominance decreases in joking and laughing with servants or inferior people. When Lakshman had mocked Shurpanakha, Ram had given him this advice that one should not joke with evil-minded and low-class people. **CRUAIRANAYEN: SOUMITRE PARIHASAH: NA KATHANCHAN.** - (Ramayana)

42. If you are invited to local functions without any reason, then we will accept that you have a place in society. If you are not properly welcomed after being invited, we will understand that you were invited only as a neighbor or to increase the number of people in the function. If you consider yourself blessed after going somewhere, then understand that you are not worthy of respect yet. If other people consider it their good fortune to meet you, then first give credit to their politeness and then be satisfied that you are not insignificant.

43. Experienced doctors say that for every three sick people, there is one sick person who actually has no illness. Therefore, do not become discouraged by suffering from an imaginary illness. Check carefully whether your mind wants to relax by making excuses.

44. If something which reaches to your ears and then spreads all over the city, you would be a very dangerous

person. No one would believe you. Keeping the mantra secret reveals the greatness of a person. People who can digest big things are really great. Small people are like Petrol which start burning even with a spark.

45. If you want to remain a father to your children, then become their father. As soon as you become a teacher, you will be deprived of their love and your position will be taken away from you.

46. If you are the master of your wife, you will be happy. If you are a friend, you would live like a friend, if you are an extraordinary obedient to your wife, you are a henpecked Husband, if you are slave to your wife, you would be a Shrimpy Man.

47. If you are the so-called husband of a fickle woman, then your heart- sky must be filled with the clouds of sorrow day and night. If you are like Chandesh (Shiva), you must be swallowing Halahal (poison) several times a day. May God give you peace. Before praying for peace, take a fair look at one thing, whether you, yourself, have made your wife self-willed and arrogant by worshipping her. Also see whether your manhood is intact. Also find out whether your wife, who was well behaved & of high Character earlier, has become bad-natured after marrying you. If you are innocent, then do not ruin your life because of some wicked woman.

48. If terror prevails as soon as you enter your house, then who will be more unfortunate than you? You must be a coward and you must be venting your outside anger on your dependents at home. The saying **'a stumbler over a**

hilly rock, break the Sill of his house' must have been written by one of your ancestors.

49. Worshipping Gods for the destruction of enemies is futile. Like saints and sages, Vishwatma also does not help in any evil deed. It would be better if you do Sit ups and again Sit ups during that time, so that seeing your strong body, the enemies get scared of you. Prayer has a great force but only when it is done in good faith and with good wishes.

50. If you are the ideal of yourself, then it will not be possible to make much progress. How a person, who is a keen observer of his own feet, will look at the path ahead?

51. Despite being an unqualified person, if a person gets a high post, and becomes proud of his position, then his condition will be like that dwarf who, standing on the top of a mountain, thinks that the people below must be considering him huge. If a skinny man is made to sit on an elephant, will he become fat? If, despite being ineligible, you have become high-ranking official by some trick, then you should not overestimate yourself. Even after sitting on the pinnacle of a palace, a Crow cannot attain the position of an eagle: **'PRASADSHIKHARSTHOPI KAKO NA GARUDAAYATE.**

52. There is an English proverb that if a person does not worry about who will get the credit for a particular task, then he can complete every task successfully. Many tasks go wrong because everyone wants that all the credit should go to him, that is why everyone does not cooperate with each other fully. If you want success, then share the credit with others so that they also share in that work.

53. If you are easily impressed, you will have to make many promises and you will not be able to fulfil all of them. Remember one more thing-the one who gives quick blessings gets some quick retribution just like Shiva got Bhasma Sur.

54. If you see horrific scenes even in your dreams, then guess your mental cowardice from that. If you see beautiful women, then pay attention to your unsatisfied love-lust. If you see feasts in your dreams, then understand that you are not getting satisfying food. If you see senseless dreams, then improve your digestive power and the disorder of your mind. In this condition, relieve the burden of the mind. Dreams during deep sleep are dangerous. Western psychologists earlier did not believe in dream science. Now they claim, by writing big books, that by studying the Dreams of a person, his internal mood can be understood. Because the conscious mind remains dormant during the Dreaming, and, therefore, the inner thoughts cannot be hidden with great intellect skill. On the dream stage, the instincts grasped by dreams start to play openly.

55. Arrogant and foolish people stamp their feet while walking. A troubled person walks slowly. According to Samudrika, stamping one's feet is considered unfortunate. This does not mean that you will be considered lucky if you walk stealthily like thieves. The meaning is that you should neither walk like a demon nor like a thief, but walk with a balanced pace like a human being.

56. If you are a businessman and deal with many customers, then it is important for you to be polite, well

behaved and soft spoken. If you become serious or arrogant, you will lose customers. An experienced person has said that **one who is not cheerful should not do the work of a shopkeeper.** Customers are as much impressed by your goods as they are by your polite behavior. They want to value not only your goods but also your simplicity and gentlemanliness. Nowadays women are appointed as salesgirls in the sales department of big companies. The secret behind this is that they attract customers with their natural softness.

57.   A foreign sociologist has published some rules for preventing domestic discord. One of them is that every month you should give your wife and children some money as pocket money, which they should consider as their own and be free to spend or save. This will not let them think that they are dependent on you for every penny. Not doing so can give rise to feelings of jealousy and hatred towards you in their minds.

58.   If you consume any medicine or powder regularly, you will be either physically unhealthy or addicted to them. When Aushdhiyan (Medicines, Powders) become the regular daily diet, the natural functioning of the body slows down. Natural diet is food only.

59.   Getting disappointed after failing in any work is cowardice. There is no harm in falling, but the harm is in lying down after falling. An idle person falls once and lies there groaning, while even the torso of brave men stands up and fight.

60.   If sometimes thoughts of suicide arise in your mind, then believe it, your soul is guilty; you are lazy,

selfish, cowardly and cruel. If you get a chance, you will kill someone and fulfill your selfish desires. You do not get such a chance, so you want to calm your murderous instincts by thinking to kill yourself. Sometimes in case of suffering from incurable disease, thought of committing suicide comes into the mind and your domestic life fails. No matter how terrible the physical pain is, it should not cause the thought of suicide. Suicidal thoughts arise in mental pain, guilt, shame, cowardice, intolerance, inability, and excessive anger. Therefore, treat your mental diseases. The treatment is to make hope strong and engage yourself in some work.

61.   Sometimes it happens that we keep getting success in small tasks and even where there is no hope of success, we get success there. At that time, we should believe that the time is in our favor, our fortune is rising. At that time there will be more hope of success by doing any important work. That is why philosophers have said that **when time is smiling on us, we should take maximum advantage of it.** Whether one believes in destiny and pre-determined karma or not, one has to accept that favorable and unfavorable circumstances come silently and affect our life-condition. There are innumerable waves in the atmosphere which not only affect our body but also touch our life and become support or hindrance in its progress.

62.   If you are too optimistic, then you would live in imagination and as a result will have to bear many gusts of disappointment continuously, because the created and exaggerated happiness of the world of imagination cannot be found in the real world. Only those with the attitude of **'MATI ATI RANK MANORATH RAAU'** are extreme

optimists. They eat Manmodak, (mun ke Laddoo) bathe in the Milky Way, drink the water of mirage and worship the Sun God in the west with a flower from the sky. The feet of such people often fall on the wrong path, because their vision remains floating somewhere else. Whereas a pessimist considers "Inaction" to be his dharma. He is troubled by imaginary fear and is doubtful. He is completely faithless, indifferent, insensitive and apathetic.

63. While living in the present time, one should neither be too ancient nor too modern. One should move with time. Time and space are all changeable and "Change" is the fixed religion of the world. Therefore, one should follow the contemporary customs and traditions. Sheikh Saadi's statement is valid to some extent that when you reach the land of blinds, you should also close one eye. This does not mean that you should abandon your ethnicity and civilization on going to Foreign Land. This means that in the practical world, one must take care to **'be consistent with time'. T**here must not be hotchpotch of antiquity and modernity. If you perform Havan, do it with ghee, not vegetable ghee; if you go to the temple, blow the Conch, not the motor's horn; if you go to the office, wear shoes, not Khadaoo (wooden sandals).

64. Personal character has an impact on every task of life. Character remains with the person. According to an English thinker**, "He who acts wickedly in private life can never be expected to show himself noble in public conduct, for it is not the man, but only the place that is changed"**. 'A person who is bad in his personal life cannot be a gentleman in social life, because even after changing the place, he is still an evil person.

Summary

Measure your own qualities and demerits with these answers and see where you fall short. Based on these, you should also judge others. But first of all, define yourself. Self-deception will keep you in trouble. If you want the society to accept your artificial form as real without improving yourself, then this is your self-delusion. In front of the microscope of society, even the smallest things of human character are clearly visible.

Kartuti Kahi Det, Aap Kahiye Nahin, ... O Lord!!!!

Even if you sit with your mouth shut, your behavior and deeds start telling your self-story to everyone.

EPILOGUE

This tome attempts to provide a panoramic view of Human Behavior throughout life, encompassing all the facets of human character and conduct. The term Human Behavior covers wide range of actions and reactions demonstrated by individuals in various situations throughout their life. Human Behavior is a daedalian web of thoughts, emotions, and actions, which are influenced and formed by several factors embracing genetics, circumstances, culture, social environment, political conditions etc. Only on understanding this web, one can improve his Virtues, Traits, Persona and overall behavior.

Mother Nature unstintingly instills Ego, Ambition, Aspirations, Determinations, Motivations etc.in the mind of every sensible and realistic Human Being, since the origin of mankind. These virtues constantly encourage every realistic person to achieve something in the life and prove himself better than others. This is happening from time immemorial. Therefore, our scriptures, Religious Books Like Ramayan, Mahabharat, Gita, Vedas, Purana, Upanishads etc. are full of texts, hymns, verses, sermons which guide us how to improve and invigorate our abilities to achieve our goals. Scriptures are like Occean, out of which only few Pearls could be churned out and are inserted in this book at proper places, for compassionate understanding of the human nature.

The intrinsic Human Behavior is almost the same since the entire history of humanity. Upon careful reading and reflection, the Readers might have noticed that the Sagacity and Sapience imparted in the Verses, Hymns from the Scriptures, and in the words of hard-won Wisdom of the Seers, Sages, Enlighted Souls and the prominent quotes of Legends of the recent history, as cited throughout in this work, encompass the full spectrum of human behavior and conduct.

All-out efforts were made to discover the full Insight of Human Behavior, Virtues, Traits and Persona through the remarkable citations, quotes, directions, Instructions, Guidelines laid scattered in our ancient scriptures, Mythical Literature, Fantasy Literature, Folklore, Religious Books, Hard-won Wisdom of Legends in their literary work, in this tome on human behavior. This tome carefully outlines Human Behaviors essential for individuals **to Shine** their Persona in order to live respectfully, satisfactorily and comfortably in a Civilized Society.

Therefore, these Wisdom -Words can guide us to vivify our lives for a purpose. Wisdom in the form of Verses, Hymns, Proverbs, Quotes from various sources can offer valuable insights and perspectives. These wisdom words can help us to understand our values, passions, and what truly matters to us. This can lead to a clearer sense of purpose and direction in life. They can provide encouragement, resilience and the strength to persevere through difficult time. By applying these wisdom words to our daily life we can cultivate virtues, like compassion, gratitude, and self- awareness, leading to more meaningful and **Shinning** existence.

Afterword

Readers might have noticed numerous Citations of Mahatma Gandhi, among other Legends' quotes, along with verses, Hymns etc. from scriptures, in this book. **This is for a reason**. In the last few years, younger generations have started critiquing certain aspects of our Rashtrapita Mahatma Gandhi's legacy. They question some of his actions and make him responsible for India's partition. It can be said that they have not understood Mahatma. Therefore, as per the general acceptance of his Authenticate Persona viz. is Genuine Personality, Idealized Persona viz. Aspirational Personality, and Socialistic Persona viz. Public Personality, many of his citations have been quoted in this book, to counter the misconceptions and misinterpretations surrounding his life and work, to explain his philosophy in a more accessible way, to provide direct evidence of his thoughts, beliefs and also to inspire readers to delve deeper into his life and teachings and thus make their own persona **Shine**.

Further, in this era of rapid change, resulting due to the unprecedented advancements in Information Technology, people have shifted from reading Books, to social media, like Instagram, Facebook, X (Twitter), WhatsApp, TV Channels, 4DX Movies, searching on Google, Meta AI etc. to satiate their hunger of getting knowledge and information. Hence, the Number of Book Readers are diminishing day by day. Even though, it is hoped that the subject matter which is articulated in this book: duly supported by the citations, including thousand years old Hymns, Verses etc., may make it attractive to the classical readers and bibliophiles.

Know It To Shine

www.ingramcontent.com/pod-product-compliance
Lightning Source LLC
LaVergne TN
LVHW091616070526
838199LV00044B/812